Signs of the Times

Signs of the Times
Theological Reflections

JUAN LUIS SEGUNDO

Edited by
Alfred T. Hennelly, S.J.

Translated by
Robert R. Barr

ORBIS BOOKS

Maryknoll, New York 10545

The Catholic Foreign Mission Society of America (Maryknoll) recruits and trains people for overseas missionary service. Through Orbis Books, Maryknoll aims to foster the international dialogue that is essential to mission. The books published, however, reflect the opinions of their authors and are not meant to represent the official position of the society.

Library of Congress Cataloging-in-Publication Data

Segundo, Juan Luis.
    Signs of the times : theological reflections / Juan Luis Segundo ; edited by Alfred T. Hennelly ; translated by Robert R. Barr.
      p.   cm.
    Includes bibliographical references.
    Contents: Theology and the social sciences — Capitalism-socialism —Conversion and reconciliation from the perspective of modern liberation theology — Human rights, evangelization, and ideology — The shift within Latin American theology — A note on irony and sorrow — On absolute mystery — The option for the poor — Revelation, faith, signs of the times — Ignatius of Loyola — The legacy of Columbus and the hierarchy of Christian truths.
    ISBN 0-88344-791-6 (paper)
    1. Liberation theology.   2. Catholic Church—Latin America. 3. Catholic Church—Doctrines.   4. Sociology, Christian (Catholic) 5. Latin America—Church history—20th century.   I. Hennelly, Alfred T.   II. Title.
BT83.57.S443   1993
230'.046—dc20   93-941
                                                                          CIP

Contents

Introduction

As the twenty-first century and the third millennium of the Christian era begins to dawn on the world's horizon, it is more and more apparent to theologians throughout the planet that the most enduring and widespread theological movements at least since the Second Vatican Council have emerged as the various theologies of liberation. One of the earliest to erupt and flourish has been the Latin American liberation theology, but other dynamic approaches have also arisen, such as women's, black, and Asian liberation theologies, among others. The articles in this volume, however, are all products of the Latin American movement, and are selected from the work of one of its earliest and most prolific authors, Juan Luis Segundo. For readers who are not familiar with the background of this writer, it may be helpful here to provide a sketch of his career. It will be brief, for Segundo has always been much more interested in communicating his theological insights than in the details of his biography.

The author was born on March 31, 1925, in Montevideo, Uruguay. Most of his life has been spent in Montevideo, working as a chaplain with various lay discussion groups on contemporary issues in theology, as well as in the social and cultural sciences. The interaction and dialogue with these groups, moreover, have widened out to a much broader world audience: he has produced a stream of articles and books that have been translated into the major languages of the world. It is quite appropriate that the Spanish title of his first five-volume series was "An Open Theology for an Adult Laity."

It is surprising and somewhat ironic to note that Segundo has never taught in a university in Uruguay, although he has been assiduously wooed by and has taught in such prestigious universities as Harvard, Chicago, Toronto, Montreal, Birmingham, São Paulo, and many others in Latin America. His articles and books have been used as texts and resources in countless other universities throughout the world, especially in the United States and Canada. Truly, "No prophet is acceptable in his own country" (Lk 4:24).

Another important factor in the author's life was his decision in 1941 to enter a religious order, the Society of Jesus or Jesuits. Jesuit spirituality and traditions have deeply influenced his work. In the course of his philosophical studies in the Jesuit seminary of San Miguel in Argentina, he also initiated a lifelong dialogue with the philosophies of existentialism (especially that of the Russian Nicolai Berdyaev) and phenomenology.

1

These studies have stamped an indelible imprint on all his later writings, as is readily apparent in his first published work, *Existentialism, Philosophy, and Poetry: An Attempt at Synthesis* (1948).

Like many of his compatriots, Segundo journeyed in 1951 to Europe for his theological studies in the theological faculty of St. Albert. Europe was universally acknowledged at that time as the world center of Christian thought. Later he became much more critical of European theology, sifting out its weaknesses as well as its accomplishments. Above all, he was indebted to two great scholars: Leopold Malevez, for his systematic studies on the universality of grace, and Gustav Lambert, for his understanding of the gradual development of revelation in the Bible. Another extremely important influence outside the university was his contact with the writings of the Jesuit priest-scientist, Pierre Teilhard de Chardin. Teilhard's evolutionary ideas reecho as a leitmotif throughout the entire corpus of Segundo's work. At the same time, Segundo had no hesitation in updating and criticizing the French priest's philosophical, theological, and even scientific ideas: *amicus Pierre, sed major amica veritas*.

In 1963 Segundo defended two theses before a jury of the Sorbonne of Paris. These were *Berdyaev: A Christian Reflection on the Person* and *Christendom: A Utopia?* For this, he was awarded the highest classification for the Doctorat ès Lettres in theology.

In 1959 Segundo returned to Montevideo for good, with later trips to Europe only to defend his theses. In 1965 he founded and became director of the Peter Faber theological and social center in Montevideo, as well as editor and chief contributor to the center's monthly periodical, *Perspectives on Dialogue*. In 1971 both were abruptly shut down by the Uruguayan government, apparently because of its anger at his critical reflections on the volatile Uruguayan politics at that time.

Since then, aside from relatively brief intervals at the universities already mentioned, Segundo has devoted his time to working with lay communities and continuing his stream of articles and books. Among his principal works in English are included: five volumes in the series *Theology for Artisans of a New Humanity* (1973–74), *The Liberation of Theology* (1976), *The Hidden Motives of Pastoral Action* (1978), another five-volume series on *Jesus of Nazareth Yesterday and Today* (1984–88), *Theology and the Church* (1985), and *Liberating Dogma: Revelation, Faith, and the Signs of the Times* (1992).

On the basis of these works and a number of others still untranslated, Segundo can be considered the most original and the most profound of the Latin American liberation theologians. His books are sometimes considered complex and difficult reading by English-speaking readers, but the only solution to such objections is to plunge reflectively into his works; exponents of speed-reading may well be disappointed. A book that touches on most of the important themes of his theology is *The Liberation of Theology*, which may be the best place for interested readers to begin.

Since his thought is complex and long-range in its implications, and firmly opposed to all efforts at oversimplification, any summary may lead to distortion. It may be helpful, however, to emphasize the importance that Segundo places on theological method. As he has expressed it, "the one thing that can maintain the liberating character of a theology is not its content but its method. In this lies the best hope of theology for the future."

To understand his method, it will be helpful to look briefly at one of the major currents of theology in the past century. This was the demythologization pursued by the Lutheran theologian, Rudolf Bultmann, in which he employed the existentialist philosophical categories of Martin Heidegger. For Bultmann, these concepts were considered necessary for a modern hermeneutic or interpretation of the "mythical" concepts found throughout the Bible and especially in the New Testament. This entailed a hermeneutic circle, involving a continuous circulation between the meanings of the original texts and those of their modern interpretations. In recent times, Bultmann's method has been widely criticized, but an especially severe critique was leveled at the individualistic nature of Bultmann's solitary figure responding to the Word of God, which was seen as a reflection of the individualistic Western society and culture in general.

In a sense, then, Segundo's method moves from the individual to the social aspects of the interpretation of the text, as befits the sufferings of the majority of the poor of Latin America. His basic method, then, is considered to be a project of *deideologizing*—that is, unearthing and exposing the ideologies that are employed both by modern Western societies and by the Christian churches to hide, disguise, or legitimate oppression or social injustice. The most important aspect of this deideologizing is its positive impact, for its ultimate goal is to arrive at an authentic Christian theology and an image of the true God of Jesus of Nazareth. Thus, theology should liberate the Christian churches from the ideologies of church and state, and thus provide the vision, motivation, and courage to work for a just society or, as the gospel calls it, the kingdom of God. Segundo's hermeneutic circle, then, is far more comprehensive and profound in its implications for all of humanity than the demythologizing project of Bultmann and the theologians who have followed him in this century.

Segundo's approach, consequently, is a kind of social phenomenology in conscious opposition to the individualistic one of Martin Heidegger and Bultmann. It is also eclectic, since he draws material for his theology from scripture, tradition, various philosophers, social and physical sciences, literature, drama, anecdotes, and so forth. This eclecticism may be seen as a weakness by the system-builders, but I think it is a valid approach if it illuminates, as Segundo does, our present reality and Christian responsibility, and at the same time animates the churches to transforming and liberating action in the world, above all in an option or commitment to the poor and afflicted. Finally, Segundo is one of the few Catholic systematic theologians (along with Edward Schillebeeckx) who consistently and painstakingly outline the scriptural warrants for their theology. He is also one of the few who have successfully integrated the teachings of the Second Vatican Council in all their work.

For all the above reasons, I believe the publication of his essays can be of great value to Christians and to all persons of good will. Because of restrictions of space, I have had to select what appeared to be the most significant of a far larger number of articles that Segundo has published during his career. Whether this task was worth the effort, I now leave to the judgment of the reader. My deepest hope is that the dialogue with the reader will lead not only to new and liberating ways of thinking but also to new and liberating ways of acting in order to bring about partial but real steps toward the kingdom of God preached by Jesus of Nazareth.

ALFRED T. HENNELLY, S.J.

PART I

BUILDING THE KINGDOM OF GOD

CHAPTER 1

Theology and the Social Sciences

This article is concerned with the science of sociology, but its implications could be extended to the rest of the social sciences. In it Segundo clearly points out the present shortcomings of both Western and Marxist sociology that forestall a fruitful dialogue with theology. The talk was delivered at one of the first meetings between Latin American and European theologians in El Escorial, Spain, in 1972.

Source: "Teología y ciencias sociales," in *Fe cristiana y cambio social en América Latina: Encuentro de El Escorial, 1972* (Salamanca: Sígueme, 1973), pp. 285–95.

There belongs to the primordial reality of authentic Christianity a deep suspicion of any collective praxis that conceals its real motives, ignores its own mechanisms, and takes refuge in ideal conceptualizations of its most concrete and keenest reality. From the gospel itself we know that collective human praxis disguises itself, shuns the light, prefers darkness, and does not want to stir up crisis.

The notion of ideology, even in the strict sense (the sense in which I use it here) of a system of ideas employed to conceal and justify a given relation of production, is profoundly rooted in the Christian message, and is not the monopoly of Marxism, except perhaps on the merely verbal level.

After all, the New Testament itself contains repeated reference to the *material* needs of the human being as the criterion for unmasking the ideologization with which religion, love for God, and the human being's "vertical" dimension are conceptualized.

But this criterion is still too general. It only indicates the existence of an ideologization operating within the complex edifice of a theology or a religious practice. We know that there is ideology, because, as St. James says, we speak of religion *and* our brothers and sisters are hungry; because we say we love God, as John says, *and* we do not love—in works—our visible sibling. This is fine, as far as it goes. Nevertheless, especially in more

7

complex situations, we should like to have a better understanding of the concrete mechanisms by which ideology has de facto infiltrated the edifice of our faith. And it is not out of any theoretical considerations that we should like to have this appreciation; we need it in order to understand— once more, operatively—a possible reverse route: a way of deideologization.

Obviously the Christian message impels us to take this reverse path; but it does not offer us the concrete scientific instruments we need for accomplishing the task. In all logic, we may suppose that, if these instruments must come from somewhere, it will be sociology—the science of collective behaviors—that will provide for our needs here.

Perhaps the most important—and painful—observation to be made by liberation theology in this matter is that, apart from rare exceptions, it cannot rely on the cooperation of sociology in this crucial area, the theme of ideology.

We find help in our search for the cause of this unexpected failure by the contribution of Elíseo Verón to the collective work, *Lenguaje y comunicación social*,[1] especially in the introduction, which deals with the evolution of sociology from Marx's *The German Ideology* to our own day.

The interest of Verón's observations is all the greater in that, first, while they are those of a professional sociologist, they trace the origins of sociology back beyond its official beginning, so to speak, and situate us in one of the most fertile and transformational views of society ever conceived, which is, precisely, that of a nonsociologist. In the second place, Verón's point of departure, the need for an "ideological sociology"—a sociology of ideology, a sociology whose object would be the ideology prevailing in social behaviors—is precisely the one starting point that could constitute an *intrinsic* element of the theological task.

Let me begin, then, by presenting Verón's characterization of this evolution on the part of sociology—or rather, of this progressive ideological evacuation of sociology—and connect it with some of the more important Latin American sociological problems so that we may have some examples of how the latter cannot find their full theological solution without a sociology to rescue theology from its impotence here.

FROM A BROAD FIELD OF FACTS TO THE FRAGMENTATION OF THAT FIELD

Verón indicates that, in the definition implied in the "sociology" of *The German Ideology*, the ideological element, as contradistinguished from the reality of life, embraces the totality of cultural content, or more precisely, the whole of culture. The later development of sociology, on the other hand, issues in a fragmentation of fields—law, art, religion, politics, and so on— with the resulting loss not only of the interrelationship among the cultural phenomena thus divided, but also, and especially, of their comprehensively ideological character: that is, their character as a superstructure confronted with an infrastructure. The sociology of law confronts one right with another, rather than rights as such with the social whole. The sociology of religion produces religious typologies, and so on:

> The sociology of law, of art, of religion are specialized disciplines, in which the notion of ideology, bound up with a comprehensive model of culture, is not utilized systematically.[2]

One of the most important problems in the Latin American theology of liberation, in its pastoral perspective, is that of providing the church with goals, and with sociologically consistent mediations to those goals. It is a fact that integral pastoral approaches with comprehensive goals are making their appearance in many places on the continent. But it is also a fact that the mediations conceived with a view to these goals are conceived from a starting point in a markedly ideological fragmentation (a religious fragmentation) of total reality. Hence the fact that they immediately, but systematically, encounter unexpected obstacles.

For example, the functioning of base communities is supposed to bridge the gap between intensive and extensive pastoral approaches, between the maturation of faith and popular Christianity. In neglecting to search out the ideology present in whatever is social, we ignore the fundamental mechanism of the base communities: their rapid radicalization in opposition to the lie of an extensive pastoral ministry that constitutes one of the indirect but powerful bases of the status quo. Innocent of the suspicion of any such phenomenon, the attempts of an integral pastoral ministry either simply founder (for example, in the marginalization of the base communities), or else regress to simple incidental reforms (presacramental conversations) having no operative relationship with the initial goal, or even contrary to it. An analysis of the ideological component of any social whole, then, is indispensable if Latin American theology is to address the problem of the authentic goals of pastoral work. Indeed, pastoral "idealism" is simply an outgrowth of the aseptic, conservative compartmentalization of the human being's "religious" dimension and its mechanisms.

FROM THEORETICAL ABSTRACTION TO DAILY LIFE

Scholars of ideology seem to have come down from the heights of metaphysics and philosophical abstractions to the familiar ground of daily life. They shift their attention from works that are significant from the viewpoint of the ideas or culture of a historical era to the opinions of ordinary human beings on the aspects of society that these latter perceive in their immediate context.

When Max Weber analyzed the spirit of capitalism, he appealed, for purposes of his research and as a decisive factor in that research, to abstract notions like predestination, grace, salvation, merit, and faith—the most intricate terms of a Calvinist theology. And as he was able to show that such notions—not because they are abstract—ceased to exert a decisive influence on a given economico-social system, we are led to wonder what abstract categories of this kind would exert an influence in the opposite direction, toward socialism.

Obviously it was not abstract ideas as such that, hypothetically, played such a role, but the symbolical system they originated. Just as obviously, the theologian attentive to the role of ideologies must look in the opposite direction, and wonder, for example, what the symbolical impact of abstract Catholic ideas concerning grace and justification will have been on the mental universe of Latin American peoples. But for this a sociological method is required. And it is even more required for the verification of the suspicion of ideology, since ideology does not stop with the symbolical universe, but moves on to the concealment and justification of real relations of production. If these relations are oppressive, we must suppose the existence of some connection between the abstract idea and the oppression. Now, this second step, from symbols to behaviors, pertains almost in its entirety to the domain of sociology. And in practice, no current sociologist dares address this problematic. What is interesting is religion as it is lived "in its immediate context." What keeps the sociologists on the sidelines is precisely the "rich abstraction" of the theological notions and symbology in confrontation with daily concretion, which is poor in references, but available to quantitative, exact observations.

Thus, while theological criteria do not arise *solely* from the social impact of the notions with which theology deals, one of them—the most radical because it issues from the comprehensive liberative plan of God (which can neither found nor conceal any slavery)—will perhaps be absent from its development. One of the basic requirements for the authentic development of dogma will be missing in Latin America.

FROM OVERALL IDEOLOGIES TO SPECIFIC OPINIONS

The third step, while intimately connected with the first and second, differs from the first in that the fragmentation of which we are here speaking is the one that takes place not among areas of culture (art, religion, philosophy, politics), but within any of the areas, keeping in account facts without "great referential scope." It differs from the second in that the ideologies with which the first "sociologists" were concerned, whether or not these ideologies were constructed of abstract elements, were "*systems embracing a general interpretation of social reality.*"

For example, one of the core elements of today's social systems is the place they "systematically" reserve for freedom. But current sociology, while concerned with freedom, works with "opinion content," whose reference is to very limited, ambiguous aspects of freedom.

When a liberative theology gains an awareness of the mediations it requires for its conception of freedom to be realized within a social system, and becomes conscious of its obligation to judge that system in terms of the concrete opportunities of freedom and grace that it comports, it likewise becomes aware that by bringing to this practical judgment preestablished notions of, for example, freedom and grace, it can actually be supplying this social system with the most powerful of ideological weapons for holding Christians aloof from social change.

Every comprehensive society is constructed on the basis of a balanced exchange of energies. Antecedent eccentric demands on this exchange would be tantamount either to social suicide or (in order to avoid suicide) social paralysis. Accordingly, an analysis of the concrete opportunities of freedom *in a given society* will more properly determine when and to what extent notions like grace and freedom have been impregnated with the ideology of the dominant system. But once again, sociology must gauge comprehensive systems, and not content itself with specific opinions on freedom.

FROM COGNITIVE CATEGORIES TO EVOLUTIVE DIMENSIONS

The German Ideology was what we might call a "sociology of knowledge"—a study of the mechanisms by which, in relationship with social processes, the ideas and systems of ideas had been formed that expressed (concealing their negative phase) and justified those processes:

> In modern empirical sociology, on the other hand, a refinement of techniques has been accompanied by a change in the focus of interest: most applied instruments measure adherence—degree of acceptance or rejection.

One of the deepest problems of Latin American theology is what we might call the *theological qualification* of opinions encountered regarding the operative interpretation of essential points of Christian teaching. The problem occurs less on the terrain of *orthodoxy* than on that of *orthopraxis*. But it is praxis, today, that constitutes the criterion of truth of the *doxa* that underlies it, rather than the other way around. It is a fact, as we have seen, that there is a far more profound affinity (in terms of overall systems of operative thought) among atheists, Protestants, and Catholics than among "Catholics and Catholics."

When the claim is made, then, that these internal oppositions do not affect orthodoxy today as they did in times past, we are dealing with a judgment—and verdict—of sociology rather than with a properly theological assertion. After all, the only possible foundation for such an optimistic judgment would be a statistical demonstration of explicit adherence to the dogmatic formulas themselves. The tools commonly employed by sociology go no further. When we move from this formal adherence to the comprehensive cognitive system, we doubtless suspect far more substantial differences today between "Catholics and Catholics" than, for example, between Arians and Athanasians, or between the Reformation and the Counter-Reformation.

But we only "suspect" such a thing. This judgment, crucial as it surely is (for theology itself, as well as for the future of Latin American liberation), can be pronounced only by a sociology of knowledge. And that sociology does not exist. The theologian, who can expect no cooperation from such a sociology, will be limited to *suspecting* that the celebrated "unity of Christians," the most threadbare subterfuge in the pastoral closet, performs a powerful ideological function. By sacralizing a phenomenon of division, it serves to tranquilize the conflict that lies at the basis of liberation.

FROM "IDEA SYSTEMS" TO ISOLATED OPINIONS

It is not easy to see the difference Verón attempts to indicate between this step and that "from overall ideologies to specific opinions." It would seem that this new step refers to the dynamic character of primitive sociology, which "made it possible to analyze internal properties of idea systems: their coherence, the procedures of derivation of some ideas from others, and so on." There are "many efforts" in this direction in modern sociology, but "the laws of organization" arising from such attempts, as we shall see in the subsequent steps, are incompatible with an ideological investigation properly so-called.

In this order of things, it is of the highest interest, indeed it is of the essence, to attend to the mental contradictions that mark the pastoral activity of the church, springing from an equally contradictory conception of the ecclesial function. The church lays claim to a liberative function independently, in the name of the gospel. But to liberate means to make an option for the oppressed against the oppressor. For a church whose members are the actual oppressors and their (voluntary or involuntary) accomplices, to liberate will mean to make its option in the name of the demands of a more mature, demanding, heroic faith. Meanwhile, the liberative radicality of the gospel will collide with the conduct of masses passively integrated into the status quo. In the presence of this huge passivity, a church "committed to liberation" opts for no one, and will brand as "elitist" any tendency to insist on an evangelical breach with the system of oppression.

To put it another way, the church is dealing with two dimensions of the gospel: the radical demands of liberation, and the principle of universal salvation, the latter being supposedly realizable only if that evangelical radicality is reduced to the minimum of demands that most persons can accept. Theologians attempt to clarify this basic problem by going to the sociologists and asking them to explain the dialectical relationship obtaining between the masses and the minorities in the social process, and the potential function of evangelical radicality in this dialectic. But they find that the sociologists speak of statistical masses and minorities — that is, they compute isolated opinions, or (what amounts to the same thing) lifestyles and competence. On the other hand, they ignore and claim to be unable to explain the concept of masses or minorities in terms of the "idea systems" that characterize both. In such terms, the relationship between the gospel and the masses is delivered over to a voluntaristic idealism in the pastoral activity of the church, an attitude that, once more, constitutes support for the status quo.

FROM THE UNCONSCIOUS TO CONSCIOUSNESS

This is perhaps the most significant step in the gradual separation between operative sociology and ideological field:

> The ideological system determines the representations of the social entertained by the actors, but its laws of organization do not appear as such to the consciousness of these actors.

They do not even appear, as Althusser shows, to the consciousness of the dominant classes themselves. Before employing such instruments of domination, they must first *believe* in them, to the point that this tranquil belief itself, without any awareness of its being used as a tool, endows these classes with the ability to dominate.

Currently, however, "a great deal of research is reduced to the pure and simple recording of opinions, in polls that reflect the manner in which various aspects of society are consciously perceived."

Theology's "great unknowns," which rear their heads in each and all the problems to which I have alluded, and which theology cannot handle with methods of its own, precisely constitute the unconscious element that has infiltrated these same methods, imperceptibly placing the interpretation of revelation by and large at the service of domination.

It is understandable, then, that Latin American "professional" theology should continue peacefully flowing along its alienating channels, so long as sociology, despite its excellent intentions, fails to offer it a convincing demonstration of the impact of the role played by the concepts it wields and the system of symbols arising from the concepts. This is precisely the admirable achievement of Medellín.

FROM SOCIOLOGY TO PSYCHOLOGY

For a precise understanding of the meaning of the seventh step, and its consequences in terms of my considerations, I must relate it to the preceding. In the first and richest sociology, "the foundation of the difference between conscious representation and its unconscious laws of organization can be explained only by way of reference to objective characteristics of the social system." In current sociology, "the most important efforts to go beyond conscious content . . . have had recourse to psychological laws." And, I should have to add, the psychological laws to which they have recourse are the ones that measure the degree of *subjective* adaptation to the system or to any one of its parts—without discussion, and without even taking account of the objective, *utterly* social reality of this adaptation.

For example, we find an abundance of studies on sacramental problems, religious vocations, or problems of the priestly life, based on psychological references to problems of adaptation or inadaptation, problems addressed in total neglect of the hypothesis that inadaptation within a dominating system can be an eloquent index of a capacity for adaptation to another, distinct social whole. Here as elsewhere, theologians must limit themselves to suspicion, since sociologists refuse to follow them in their questioning of the social whole. Their sociology is functional, or, in Verón's terms, more psychology than sociology properly so-called.

It is urgent that we take note of the fact that this conjures away one of the thorniest and most serious questions in Latin American pastoral theory and practice: To what extent, because of ideological infiltration suffered, might the church on our continent actually constitute an immense danger for Christian salvation—that is, the danger of replacing, for reasons of psychological security, the sole criterion of salvation, which consists in effective love.

In this negative—as Verón regards it—development of sociology, we have at one end of the chain Marx, and at the other, the functionalist or positivistic sociology of an American type. We must ask ourselves, then, whether a more adequate instrument for the theological task that we propose might be at hand in Marxist sociology. Logical as this hope may be, however, it is dashed by the facts.

1 Marxist sociology is not consistent in its application of the concept of ideology to religious phenomena.

At once we encounter a difficulty, and in Marx's own thought. It is difficult to decide whether religion is a superstructure of the same kind as the others he cites—art, politics, philosophy. On the one hand, its superstructural character seems beyond doubt. But unlike other superstructures, religion is destined to disappear rather than to be ideologized. Marx does not conceive communist society without art, and it would be in order to inquire whether the disappearance of the state in that society would entail the disappearance of all political superstructure. And as for philosophy, to what extent is Marxism not philosophy?

Where religion is concerned, Marx's principal texts swing to and fro, now requiring its antecedent suppression in order that the revolution may occur, now postulating its suppression precisely by the establishment of socialist society, inasmuch as, in banishing exploitation, that society will likewise make away with the anguish of the exploited and their ineffective, evasive religious lament.

Later Marxism, with some exceptions, seems to continue to assign the religious superstructure a role illogically distinct from that of other ideological superstructures. Only, it has impoverished the mechanism of suppression still further (thereby moving the Marxist position closer to that of American positivism): the element charged with doing away with religion is science, rather than the implantation of socialism. Although both elements are linked, the experience of the relative ineffectiveness of the latter has shifted the emphasis to the former.

At all events, if sociology, following Marx, already found it difficult to take an interest in the nuances and the liberative potential of a superstructure destined to disappear sooner rather than later, it finds it even more difficult in the concrete situation of the Latin American struggle for liberation. In that struggle, Christians are courted as tactical allies: they are promised "freedom of worship" in the future society. That is, they will have the right to continue to be Christians in the internal, private forum, provided they make no attempt to influence society. The current Marxist task is to recruit as allies all Christians who have made a radical political commitment such that they are willing to wage the struggle for liberation alongside non-Christians and atheists.

It is understandable that, in such a situation, Marxist sociology, even to the meager extent that it is authentically Marxist and not wedded to techniques ideologically akin to those of American sociology, should have little interest in the religious phenomenon, or offer the theologian any assistance in its deideologization.

2. Marxist sociological methodology has not accepted the relative autonomy of the superstructural levels.

As we know, Marx made it a law that the infrastructure determines the superstructure. In other words, the economy of relations of production determines the ideological forms of thought. He called this dependency materialism.

Were we to take terms like determination and materialism literally, independently of any context, sociology could never move beyond a mere statistical verification of the concrete state adopted at a given moment by the determination of the superstructure by the relations of production.

But apart from the fact that any texts of Marx to this apparent effect are few and ambiguous, Engels himself, reacting against certain "economicists"—mechanistic economists—expressly insisted that neither Marx nor he had ever spoken of economic determinism, but only of a determination "in the last instance" of the superstructure by economic factors.

Concretely, this would be tantamount to saying that superstructures move within a field of possibilities framed by the existing relations of production; that in one manner or another these superstructures adopt a position — authentic or camouflaged — with respect to such relations of production; but that they enjoy a relative autonomy, in mechanisms of their own, such that only in the last instance does the economy emerge as the determining factor.

There is nothing in this that would be unacceptable from the viewpoint of the ideological criticism upon which we are here engaged. Indeed, if sociology accepts this proposition, it will then have to accept the further proposition that *all* superstructures — including the religious — may play a determining role in impeding or promoting social change in the precise measure that they are or are not left to the mercy of the ideology infiltrating them. And it is inevitable that a sociology undertaking the task of determining such roles will have to refine its methods a great deal.

But it is here that we encounter the paradox. Official Marxist sociology, born in a country where the economy was determinative only "in the last instance" indeed, grinds out and changelessly promotes sociological analyses in which the economic and what is immediately connected with it play the role of a *sole* instance. Hence the extreme poverty of these analyses when it comes to acknowledging the least degree of liberative capacity on the part of superstructures. Current Marxist analyses of society or its cultural structures insist, with evident "idealistic voluntarism," on the ever-increasing internal contradictions of the capitalist economy, and on a similarly swelling awareness on the part of the exploited masses with regard to these contradictions. And if the latter are ever referred to the superstructure, it is only to assign one or other segment of art, philosophy, law, or religion to a determinate sector of the class struggle.

This inadequacy in official Marxist sociology (with little counterpoise on the part of nonorthodox Marxists), which is the product of an ideological concern with the feasibility of revolution, has been pointed out and established from positions both orthodox (those of Althusser) and heterodox (those of Sartre).

As theologians, then, we feel the lack of a needed support from social science. We find, in principle, a greater comprehension in modern anthropology, which is far more attentive to a nonsimplistic relationship among all super- and infrastructural elements. But here again, anthropologists prefer to study primitive societies (where their tools acquire remarkable precision), and abandon us before the looming shadow of the great urban agglomerations that comprise more than half the population of the Latin American continent.

Is what we ask of sociology genuinely impossible? The burden of proof rests with the affirmative. Perhaps it is typical of the nonsociologist to venture these sorts of conjectures and suspicions. And perhaps theology must rest content with treating them as meaningful, in its own ambit, without any hope of ever verifying them scientifically.

At all events, the problem is there, and acutely there, now that Latin American theology has accepted the challenge of being efficaciously liberative.

CHAPTER 2

Capitalism-Socialism: A Theological Crux

Segundo presents here his theological and scriptural reasons for a socialist option as a means of achieving a more just society. He also presents a probing critique of recent European theology, which denies human causality in the (partial) construction of the kingdom of God, and thus functions as an ideology that absolves human beings from adult responsibility in history. This article was part of the first issue of Concilium *that was completely devoted to the new liberation theology in Latin America.*

Source: "Capitalism-Socialism: A Theological Crux," in Claude Geffré and Gustavo Gutiérrez, eds., *Concilium 96: The Mystical and Political Dimension of the Christian Faith* (New York: Herder and Herder, 1974), pp. 105–23. The translation used here is taken from *Frontiers of Theology in Latin America*, ed. Rosino Gibellini, trans. John Drury (Maryknoll, N.Y.; 1979), pp. 240-59.

Latin American theology, particularly that strain which deals with such themes as liberation, is taken to be somewhat of a passing fad in more advanced circles of European theology. Seen as a burst of momentary enthusiasm, it does not deserve to be taken too seriously in their eyes.

Needless to say, that view disturbs us. For one thing it calls us and our work into question. For another, with very few exceptions we find that Latin American seminarians are still being educated in and by a theology that at best is merely a copy of the best and most up-to-date European theology. Thus in the academic education of our future priests and pastors of souls the whole theme of liberation comes across as political and kerygmatic rather than theological in the strict sense. Added to this is the fact that the whole focus on liberation and related themes was introduced primarily by pastoral praxis. So we find that the "theology of liberation," however good or bad that designation may be, is more the subject of talk and conversation than of serious writing in Latin America.

The reader of this volume will by now have noted one point repeatedly stressed by the contributors. What is designated as "liberation theology" does not purport to be merely one sector of theology, like the "theology of work" or the "theology of death." Liberation is meant to designate and cover theology as a whole. What is more, it does not purport to view theology from *one* of many possible standpoints. Instead it claims to view theology from *the* standpoint which the Christian fonts point up as the only authentic and privileged standpoint for arriving at a full and complete understanding of God's revelation in Jesus Christ.[1]

For all the reasons just noted, I am of the opinion that the whole debate about the seriousness of liberation theology cannot really get anywhere now unless we take some concrete problem as a *test case.* I therefore invite the reader to join me in a concrete theological experiment. Let us confront theology with one of the most urgent human problems facing the Latin American continent: i.e., making a choice between a capitalist society on the one hand or a socialist society on the other.

Before we begin, however, I would ask the reader to keep one decisive fact in mind. The choice in our case is not between the possibilities of an already well developed capitalism on the one hand or of an equally developed socialism on the other. For us in Latin America it is not a matter of choosing between the society existing in the United States and that existing in the Soviet Union. Our option must be made from the oppressed periphery of the great economic empires. We must choose some socio-political scheme from our own context as an underdeveloped continent. Which choice, then, will be both effective and consistent with the kind of society we desire for the Latin American people we know?

That is the question, a vital one for us today, that I pose to theology here. Unfortunately it immediately gives rise to another question: Does it really make any sense to pose that kind of question to theology specifically? It is not easy to answer this. Here I am not going to linger over one classic theological opinion which answers in the affirmative, and which is much heard in Catholic circles. It answers "yes" to the question; but it does so on the basis of theological presuppositions that are very debatable and, in my opinion, ultimately unacceptable.

This classic opinion begins by saying that the question is very much in line because the choice in question falls in the area of *moral* theology, which operates on its own particular track. It then usually goes on to say that the option for socialism is morally inadmissible because socialism fails to recognize the natural right of human beings to private ownership, even of the means of production. In my opinion, however, the principles underlying this position are not solid enough to merit any special attention at all. Those principles are: that an unbridgeable gap is to separate dogmatic theology from moral theology; that there is a "natural right" involved here; and, most importantly, that this natural right can be invoked to defend the proposition that the means of production might be owned privately by *only a few people.*[2]

The two negative replies to the same question seem to me to be much more subtle, profound, and worthy of attention. They deny the right or the suitability of posing the option between capitalism and socialism *to theology* at all. One of these negative replies, the more influential in Latin America, is pragmatic in origin. The other, more influential in European theological circles, is theoretical in origin.

I

As one might readily imagine, the pragmatic refusal to deal with our question is based on the task that the Christian churches see as their own proper one. And since it is a pragmatic refusal, it is particularly interesting for *what it does not say,* for its hidden reasons or motives: i.e., for the theory that underlies it.

This negative answer to our question above is perfectly exemplified in the answer of Chile's Catholic bishops to the vital question under consideration. Here is what they said: "The church opts for the risen Jesus. . . . Politically the church does not opt at all; it belongs to all the people of Chile."

Now what is the logical presupposition underlying that practical response? The presupposition is that it would be senseless to make an *absolute* value (a religious value having to do with salvation) dependent on a relative value (preference for one particular system of political coexistence, all of them being imperfect always).

Among intellectuals we find a strong reaction against this sort of pastoral practice and its theological implications; it can go so far as outright contempt. Nevertheless it is quite certain that the vast majority of Christian churches continue to be structured officially as autonomous centers of salvation. They sincerely believe in that. If they do in fact adopt progressivist positions on historical issues, they do so only to add attractiveness to the absolute value of salvation that they claim to communicate to their faithful members.

But would it not be possible, and quite evangelical, to invert that hierarchy of values; to declare, as the gospel does, that the Sabbath is made for man, not man for the Sabbath? Couldn't we then translate that declaration into concrete terms, there really being only one possible interpretation: i.e., that a human societal life liberated as much as possible from all alienation constitutes the *absolute* value, whereas all religious institutions, dogmas, sacraments, and ecclesiastical authorities have only a *relative* (i.e., functional) value?

In Christian circles capable of *theoretical* reflection, this inversion of values in line with the gospel message is relatively easy and is going on in Latin America. But what is the result? The result is that there is ever increasing disagreement and antipathy, and an ever widening gap, between those Christians and the official churches. For the churches continue to be structured around the very opposite principles.

Now we could drop the issue at this point and summarize the situation as follows: So long as the church goes on attributing absolute value to those words, objects, gestures, and authorities that seem to link up the faithful vertically with God, and only relative value to the historical functionalism of all that, then one cannot seriously ask ecclesiastical theology to tell the faithful how they should view the option between capitalism and socialism. We could drop the issue there, leaving it up to pastoral activity to convince the hierarchy of the Christian churches of the authentic scale of values, and hence of the necessity of involving their pastoral activity in a human problem as basic as the one under consideration here. More and more, however, we are pushing the matter a bit further in Latin America. While still remaining within the framework of this pragmatic refusal, we are more and more interested in launching a theoretical attack on such mistaken pastoral motivations to the fullest extent possible.

Now to do that we could follow the approach of European theology. We could make full use of the arsenal of tradition to show from *past* history that the authentic attitude of the church toward such issues was completely different. We could point out when the whole process of deviation began and how the church slowly forgot that the ecclesiastical realm was supposed to maintain a functional relationship with human history. That approach is what is known as the "return to the sources." It is exemplified by Hans Küng, for example, in his work on papal infallibility and the structures of the church.

As I see it, however, there is now a marked tendency in Latin America to tackle pragmatic church problems of that sort with a different approach. Instead of resorting to the past, we are offering *here-and-now* explanations based on the psycho-social sciences. We might ask this kind of question, for example: What might be the underlying psycho-social motivations that would explain the pragmatic attitudes we find generalized in ecclesiastical circles today? Here Latin American theology moves towards an interdisciplinary effort involving the aid of what are called the human sciences. With that aid I think that theology is able to posit and verify the following hypothesis about ecclesiastical attitudes: When gestures, formulas, rites, and authority centers are related directly to salvation and the absolute, when they are situated or located outside and beyond the finalistic system in which everything else operates, it is a clear indication that those who employ them know very well those things would lose not only their absolute but also their relative value if they were introduced into the finalistic system.

That is the danger facing the absolute. Either it is absolute or it is nothing. So when the churches make absolutes out of things that are not absolute, they are really trying to preserve some relative value for them by linking them up with human insecurity. Thorstein Veblen put it this way:

"Only individuals with an aberrant temperament can in the long run retain their self-esteem in the face of the disesteem of their fellows. Apparent exceptions to the rule are met with, especially among people with strong religious convictions. But these apparent exceptions are scarcely real exceptions, since such persons commonly fall back on the putative approbation of some supernatural witness of their deeds."[3]

Many people in scientific and scholarly disciplines would of course be inclined to draw up arguments against Christianity in general from such a statement. But when we Latin Americans propose to work with the human sciences for the sake of an interdisciplinary approach, we are proposing to theologize in the strict sense. We are trying to get back to the inner and often unconscious mechanisms that are operative when we think about God, his message, and his church. Our feeling is that it is there, in the realm of those motivating mechanisms which are not just theological, that we will find the roots of the passionate differences now evident on the interconfessional Christian level. In an earlier day, when other mental factors were operative, those passionate differences were framed in terms of christological and trinitarian controversies.

If we turn the proper evangelical hierarchy of values upside down, as in fact the official churches are now doing, is that not heterodoxy? If interdisciplinary study does verify our aforementioned hypothesis, will it not also prove that the heteropraxis of the absolutized churches is grounded on a radical heterodoxy: i.e., a steady, ongoing loss of faith in the gospel message of Jesus Christ? To put it another way, will it not verify a steady, ongoing loss of faith in the gospel's functional use for human beings?[4]

Here theology faces an enormous task. It must pinpoint the frustrated evangelical experiences that lie at the roots of this ecclesiastical insecurity. It must try to discover the criteria governing the authentic historical functionality of the gospel message. It must also try to determine the limits of any such functionality, since every incarnation has limits. We are led once again to the same conclusion. If people decide that the gospel message has nothing to say about such a critical human issue as the choice between capitalism and socialism, then it is obvious that the gospel message can only have an absolute value, a non-functional value. In other words, its value is nil.

II

Aside from the pragmatic objection that we just considered for the sake of example, I said there was a theoretical objection to the view that theology could or should get involved in the political option under examination here.

After all, what currents among the many to be found in theology would seem to be the most likely ones to offer us guidance on this issue? Would it not be that of "political theology" and that of the "theology of revolution," two currents of thought that arose in German-speaking circles of

Protestant and Catholic theology? I think so, and yet here we run into something very curious. We find that both political theology and the theology of revolution leave us disoriented when we are confronted with the political and revolutionary option par excellence.

I said above that Latin America is anxious to plan out and construct its own future. Hence it is confronted with an emotion-laden choice between two different systems and their respective logics regarding the person and society. But what does political theology have to tell us? Metz makes this observation: "What differentiates 'Christian eschatology' from Western and Eastern ideologies about the future is not that it knows *more* but that it knows *less* about that future ... and that it persists in that poverty of knowledge."[5] According to Metz, then, an eschatological theology should know less about capitalism and socialism than the theoreticians of the two systems.

What this means, then, is that the church is much more reticent than any political program. According to Metz, the church "should institutionalize this eschatological reserve by setting itself up as a court or instance of critical liberty vis-à-vis social development, so that it can stand up against the tendency of the latter to present itself as *absolute.*"[6]

Once again, then, we run into the distinction between *relative* and *absolute*. And once again the political option is ranged on the *relative* side. Only this time the absolute factor is not the church, but something which the church itself must serve: i.e., the eschatological kingdom of God, the ultimate future, the future that comes down from God himself to humanity.

Here the church does fully recognize its functional nature with respect to the eschatological kingdom. It is the triumph of the kingdom, not its own success, that is the important thing. Moltmann, for example, puts it this way: "Only through the dialectics of taking sides is the universalism of the crucified one realized in the world. By contrast the false universalism of the church [the first pragmatic objection discussed above] is a premature and untimely anticipation of the kingdom of God."[7]

According to Moltmann, then, the real and proper function of the church is to preclude "premature and untimely" anticipations of the kingdom of God. In this passage he refers explicitly to one of them: the false universalism of the church, the church turned into an absolute. But when we examine this position in the broader context of his work as a whole, we find that *every historical project* tends toward the very same universalism and absolutization. The critical space created by political theology will attack absolutism from whatever direction it comes—from the past or the future, from East or West. It will deabsolutize both the existing order and any projected order.

It is for this very reason that one gets a very definite impression when one reads discussions centered around the "theology of revolution." The revolution envisioned by that theology seems much more akin to the Cartesian theoretical revolution based on methodic doubt than to a real practical revolution. If you like the term, it does revolutionize our way of focusing on socio-political systems from our secure installment within them; but it does not choose between one system and another. If there is any tendency to take sides in the theology of revolution, it is a tendency to opt against whatever system is existing today. That is to say, one rejects the capitalist system where it now prevails, and the socialist system where it now prevails. But since both systems now coexist in today's world, all forms of "eschatological" criticism tend to relativize all that exists. The relativization is revolutionary in name only.

Exploring a more profoundly theological track, we arrive at the same conclusion discussed earlier. The conclusion is that it is not proper to question theology about the relationship between God's revealed message and the political choice between capitalism and socialism. As we noted above, the point seems to be that it is not right to encumber the absolute (here the kingdom of God) with the weight of the relative (here perishable political systems). And the underlying reason is that relative values are not even fragments of the absolute value; they remain completely and definitively in their sphere of relativity.

German political theology is meticulously cautious in choosing the words it uses to describe the relationship between any relative political order and the absolute eschatological order. The former order is an anticipation (Moltmann), an analogy or analogical image (Weth), an outline (Metz). All of their terms expressly and systematically reject any idea of *causality* in the relationship.

But who dedicates their life to an "analogy"? Who dies for an "outline"? Who motivates a human mass or a people in the name of an "anticipation"?

Now we know that in Latin America there is a theological tendency that has come to call itself the "theology of liberation." For the moment we can prescind from the question as to how apt that designation is. We can also disregard the differences between various theologians who are included under that head. The point here is that there is something basic shared by all of them. They all maintain that human beings, both as individuals and as political beings, are already building up the kingdom of God here and now in history.[8] Obviously we cannot minimize the basic and radical difference between this position and one which in principle denies any *causality* to political options insofar as the definitive kingdom of God is concerned.

What argument is used by German political theology to deny such causality? Interestingly enough the argument used is the one which lay at the very roots of Reformation theology: i.e., *Paul's doctrine concerning justification by faith alone, and not by works.* Here is how Rudolf Weth succinctly puts it: "God *himself* performs the revolutionary action that is decisive for the coming of his kingdom. His action cannot be carried out or replaced by any human action."[9] Weth goes on to support his argument by citing a crucial passage from Luther's writings in which he applies the principle of justification by faith alone to the matter of the universal kingdom. Here

Luther is commenting on a passage in Matthew's Gospel (25:34) where the world's judge invites the good people to take possession of the kingdom prepared for them from the beginning: "How could they possibly merit what already belongs to them and what was prepared for them long before they were created? Indeed it would be more accurate to say that it is the kingdom of God which merits us as its possessors. . . . The kingdom of God has already been prepared. But the children of God must be prepared in view of the kingdom. So it is the kingdom that merits the children of God, not they that merit the kingdom."[10]

Obviously that exegesis completely rules out any choosing between socio-political systems that would purport to pave the way for the kingdom of God in "causal" terms. Here the reader might be inclined to say that this view represents only that branch of political theology that stems from the Protestant Reformation. But another fact is of great relevance here. The fact is that Roman Catholic theology in Europe, especially since Vatican II, has been drawing closer and closer to Luther's position on justification. In the point at issue here, then, one cannot detect any noticeable difference between the two camps.

In current Latin American usage, the terms "right" and "left" are *broadly* identified with the capitalist option and the socialist option respectively. Accepting that broad equation for the moment, I think it would be interesting to offer a bit of proof for what I have just been saying. Let us take as our example here a comment made by a French Catholic theologian, Henri de Lavalette. He is talking about the "ambiguity" of German political theology:

What possibilities does it open up? Does it tend to divide the church more and more into leftist Christians and rightist Christians? Does it permit a leftist current to exist in a church that is centrist for the most part? Or is it capable of getting Christians to confront their political divisiveness and to see it in terms of reconciliation in Christ? When Paul affirms that in Christ Jesus there is no longer male nor female, the point is that being male or female *is* no longer an *absolute* that divides people, that means only one or the other can be Christian. In like manner, the division between left and right, which is a political division and a political judgment, is not privileged to provide any exclusivist claim to the label "Christian"; it cannot be presented as the judgment of God. The church is open to males and females, *to the right and the left.*[11]

As this passage clearly indicates, the whole weight of theology as a science comes down on one side. Whether it is speaking in terms of ecclesiastical functioning or in terms of the eschatological kingdom, it tends to rule out the possibility that it might enlighten us on the practical political option which, on our continent, is the focal point for the most profound and total commitments.

And so we are left with a negative conclusion which to me seems unacceptable. There is only one thing left for me to do in the final section of this article. I will try to spell out the conditions that would make possible a theology capable of saying something decisive about the equally decisive options facing society. In the process I will offer a critical reconsideration of the negative arguments that were presented above.

III

If we are going to explore the possible relationship between theology on the one hand and a political choice between capitalism and socialism on the other, we must first be clear on two preliminary points.

The *first* point has to do with what I mean by "socialism" and "capitalism" here. By "socialism" I do not mean a complete, long term social project—hence one that is endowed with a particular ideology or philosophy. I simply mean a political regime in which the ownership of the means of production is taken away from individuals and handed over to higher institutions whose main concern is the common good. By "capitalism" I mean a political regime in which the ownership of the goods of production is left open to economic competition.

Some might ask here: Why not spell out the socialist model more fully? Or why not talk about the possibility of a moderated, renovated capitalism? For a very simple reason, I would reply. We are not seers, nor are we capable of controlling the world of the future. The only real and possible option open to us lies within our own countries. Right now today the only thing we can do is to decide whether or not we are going to give individuals or private groups the right to own the means of production that exist in our countries. And that decision is what I call the option between capitalism and socialism.

The *second* point has to do with what we mean by theology here. By "theology" here I do not mean simply the scientific investigation of dogmas: how they came to be formulated and how, in the light of changes in language and mentality, they are to be formulated today in order to maintain authentic continuity with the past. I indicated earlier my own opinion about that scientific discipline that is the relatively autonomous sphere of professionals. For some centuries now, in my opinion, it has been emptying out much of its own content to serve the needs of a conservative ideology. It is not so much that it always proposes "conservative" dogmas. It is rather that its own vaunted autonomy vis-à-vis concrete Christian praxis leaves the latter on a secondary plane where it is open and subject to criteria that are independent of the faith. This has given rise to a moral theology behind dogma's back, as it were; and it is a nontemporal moral theology remarkably similar to the civic morality required by the established society. The dogmatic theologian, in turn, has been turned into one of the many purveyors of abstract culture which the consumer society accepts and even protects.

By "theology," then, I mean here *fides quaerens intellectum* in a much more direct sense. I mean "faith seeking understanding" in order to give guidance and direction to historical praxis.[12] I maintain that not one single dogma can be studied with any other final criterion than its impact on praxis.[13]

Having set up those basic definitions of socialism and capitalism on the one hand, and of theology on the other, we can now consider the whole matter of the relationship between the two. Right at the start we reject the notion that the task of resolving the question is to be handed over to some "moral theology." What we are looking for here is a positive or negative relationship between *dogma* and socialism.

When, therefore, was dogma applied to political events? To begin with, there is no doubt that it was so applied in the preaching of the great prophets of Israel. And if I am not mistaken, we will find that prophetic proclamation—or the theology of the prophets, if you will—has precious little to do with the ecclesiological presuppositions prevailing today or with the criteria set forth by current European political theology.[14]

The *prophets,* of course, are not the seers of the future whom we envision today when we use that word. First and foremost they are simply seers, ones who look below the surface of events and discover a will, a plan, an evaluation—God's. But if that were all, then the seers would become legislators rather than prophets. They are prophets because in some way or other they project into the future the historical consequences of God's design or evaluation of events. With their vision of the divine present, they construct a project of the historical future.

Such was the project of Jeremiah, for example, when he gave advice to those remaining in Jerusalem after the exile had begun. He told them it was Yahweh's will that they remain there rather than emigrate to Egypt. He linked that proposal or project so closely to God's will that he made a prediction about all those who would choose to emigrate to Egypt instead: Not one of them would survive.

How exactly did his theological thinking operate? First of all, a more penetrating vision than the normal one showed him God operating in concrete happenings and judging them in terms of their authentic value. Being who he was (theo-logy), the God of Israel could not see what was happening any other way. He could not evaluate the historical data in any other terms. Convinced of that, the prophet imagines a future that is in line with that divine evaluation and endows it with the same degree of certainty. This projected view was a "political" one, and yet the prophet did not submit it to any "eschatologization." He did not try to make his listeners equally critical about the relativity of that historical alternative as compared with the absoluteness of God's kingdom.

What is more, later events gave the lie to his prophecy insofar as it purported to be a vision of the future. Henri Cazelles has this to say about this political fallibility of the prophets: "One extraordinary fact about the political activity of the prophets must be pointed out. As a rule it ended in political failure. Yet, despite that failure, the disciples of the prophets would collect their oracles and recognize their validity as the *word of God.*"[15] To this we might add: that has always been the case where a prophetic theology is being exercised, and it always will be.

What are we to say, then, about any theology that refuses to pass theological judgment, to invoke the word of God, on a political reality, on the pretext that a scholarly science cannot *demonstrate* that the future will be undoubtedly better? Any such theology is clearly moving far away from its prophetic function.

There is no doubt that one could claim that the classic stage of prophecy in the Old Testament had, at best, a very rudimentary eschatological vision of God's kingdom — if it had any eschatological view of it at all. For this reason I think we would do well to jump ahead somewhat and focus on the debate between Jesus and the theology of his time as it is recorded in the Synoptic Gospels. It is very important, I think, and too little attention has been paid to the major feature of that whole debate. The radical difference between the two contending parties is not to be found in the theological content under dispute. Far more important is the way each party does theology or "theologizes," and the tools that each side uses in that effort.

It is this difference that will occupy us here. I am going to leave aside the whole issue of Jesus' involvement or noninvolvement in the politics of his day, which is such a controversial issue right now. But I would like to digress for a moment and make one point about that particular issue. My feeling is that there is something very anachronistic about the way some people try to prove that Jesus had some interest in politics and political liberation. To do this, they resort to the meager data provided by the Synoptic Gospels on Jesus' relations with the Roman Empire. Many exegetes see the Empire as the political structure of that era. To determine Jesus' attitude, therefore, they point out that his followers included Zealots: political rebels against Rome who were condemned to death as political subversives. That is the sort of argument they use.

Such an approach is anachronistic, in my opinion, because they equate the "political" sphere of Jesus' day with the "political" sphere in our own day. And since the structures of the Roman Empire are the closest thing to a modern political empire or regime, they focus on Jesus' relationship to those structures. What they seem to forget is that the "political" life of Jesus' day in Israel depended much more on the "theology" prevalent among such groups as the scribes and Pharisees than it did on the Roman Empire and its structures. It was primarily that "theology" that organized the life of the Jewish citizenry, determined their place and position, fixed their obligations, and subjected them to oppression. It was the scribes and Pharisees, not the Roman Empire, which imposed "intolerable burdens" on the little people or dispensed people from them. It was they who were responsible for the real socio-political structure of Israel. For that very reason Jesus' counter-theology was much more political than any statements or actions directly against Rome would have been at that time.

But let us get back to our point and consider the confrontation between Jesus' theology and that of his Jewish opponents. Right at the start we note that the two theologies share one thing in common: Both attempt to find the presence and guidance of God in the historical events that are taking place. The theology opposed to that of Jesus is one which, according to the Synoptic Gospels, looks for "heavenly signs," or better, "signs from heaven." Relying on the immediate context (and recalling the "sign from heaven" which Satan proposes to Jesus when he tempts him in the desert), we are perfectly justified in describing these "signs from heaven" as anticipations, outlines, and analogies of some properly divine action, of something which by its very nature cannot be attributed to human beings, much less the devil. How else could one possibly look at a historical happening and discern a "sign from heaven" in it?

What sort of "signs" does Jesus set over against those "signs from heaven"? He points to "signs of the times," to concrete transformations effected by himself in the historical present and then entrusted to his disciples both for the present and the future. Remember what Jesus says when the disciples of John the Baptist ask him that "eschatological" question about "he who is to come." Jesus responds to their question by pointing to signs in history that are relative, terribly ambiguous, and a far cry from anything definitive or absolute. The deaf hear, but why? The lame walk, but where to? The sick are cured, but won't they fall prey later to new and even more critical illnesses? The dead are raised to life, but is it worth the trouble if they must succumb to further troubles and eventually death once again? The poor have the good news preached to them, but who is going to change their plight and when?

It is here that we begin to glimpse the different understanding of signs that underlies the two different theologies. The theology that requires "signs from heaven" is interested in knowing whether the concrete happenings in question, the very same ones to which Jesus alludes, proceed from God without any doubt at all or could possibly proceed from the devil. Jesus' theology of signs replies with a boldness that scientific Christian theology has lost completely. For all practical purposes it says that the sign in itself is so clear-cut that even if it is the devil who is liberating these people from their afflictions, it is because the kingdom of heaven has already arrived and is in your midst. Thus Jesus' theology completely rules out applying any theological criterion to history *except the direct and present evaluation of happenings here and now.*

Now in trying to judge historical happenings in themselves, from the standpoint of their human value, theology obviously needs a cognitive instrument that is being equally minimized or disregarded by scientific theology. To use a modern term, we might call it *historical sensitivity.* In the Synoptic Gospels the critical term, used constantly, is the "heart." They contrast the hard and closed heart to the open, sensitive heart.

This is evident when Jesus is engaging in a theological debate over what is a commandment of God and what is merely human tradition. Paradoxically enough, Jesus associates real commandments of God with a heart that is spontaneous and open to other people whereas he associates purely human traditions with calculated reasoning that stems from a closed heart. The fact he points out to his listeners is that an event cannot be judged in itself if it does not correspond with the expectations of a sensitive heart. Reason will remain paralyzed by the ambiguity surrounding the event, and the arguments derived from that event will merely serve people's egotism.

We can thus understand what Jesus has to say about the unpardonable sin after he has cured a mute and provoked a serious debate. Jesus points out that the unpardonable sin is not the theological judgment one may form about the divine or satanic origin of his work. The blasphemy resulting from bad apologetics will always be pardonable. What is not pardonable is one's refusal to recognize something as real liberation when in fact it is real liberation. What is not pardonable is using theology to turn real human liberation into something odious. The real sin against the Holy Spirit is refusing to recognize, with "theological" joy, some concrete liberation that is taking place before one's very eyes.

I say "liberation" quite deliberately because of Luke's Gospel. It is the only Gospel that indicates the broader context of that cure, and it is also the only one that adds a decisive trait to the picture. It presents a parable wherein Jesus describes the cosmic dimension of his work, and one feature of that parable serves as the only theological sign that can precede recognition and acknowledgment of Jesus' person. With the coming of Jesus, the "strong one" who had been dominating humanity and keeping it enslaved up to now is finally disarmed and overcome. But according to Luke's Gospel, the spoils of victory do not go to a new master; instead they are restored to their natural recipients. Speech is restored to the mute.

To complete this brief characterization of Jesus' theology, I must call the reader's attention to the name that Jesus gives to the concrete acts of liberation that he performs. As we have already seen, human reason is here faced with ambiguous events, particularly insofar as the future is concerned. Despite this fact, Jesus gives them the most absolute name in the theology of his own time. He calls them "salvation." Instead of de-absolutizing them, we would be inclined to say that he imprudently absolutizes them. Cures with an uncertain future are called the "coming of the kingdom." Zaccheus's ambiguous decision, made on the spur of the moment and not yet carried out, is considered to be "salvation coming to this house." Time and again he tells people who have obtained favors or cures from him that "your faith has saved you," though it is apparent that the favors and cures ever remain uncertain and fleeting.

Why, then, do we find this seemingly invincible repugnance of modern scientific theology, of European theology in particular to do the same thing? Why is it unwilling to make pronouncements on political alternatives which are exactly parallel to the alternatives that were the object of Jesus' theology throughout his preaching career?

The European advocates of political theology demand that we Latin Americans present them with a proposal for a socialist society that is guaranteed in advance to avoid the defects evident in existing brands of socialism. Why do they not demand the same thing of Jesus? Why do they not demand that Jesus, before telling someone that his faith has saved him and curing him, provide some guarantee that the cure will definitely not be followed by worse illnesses?

To give an example here, historical sensitivity in the face of starvation and illiteracy would seem to demand a society that was not ruled by competition and the quest for profit. Such sensitivity would regard the fact that an underdeveloped nation got basic sustenance and education as a form of liberation. Viewed in the light of potential problems in the future, this particular matter might not seem to be of overriding importance in affluent countries. But in our countries we cannot avoid facing the issue because we live with it twenty-four hours every day. When and if those ills are eliminated in our nations, what scientific exigencies or strictures would prevent theology from saying: "Your faith has saved you"? It is simply a matter of giving theological status to a historical happening in all its absolute and elemental simplicity: "Is it permitted to do good or to do evil on the Sabbath, to save life or to kill?" (Mark 3:1–5).

My remarks in the last section might seem to be some sort of gospel proclamation rather than a serious study of theological methodology. It is certainly true, moreover, that for some time now theological methodology has been looking to other scientific disciplines rather than to gospel proclamation to find analogies for its own underlying criteria. It prefers the categories and certitudes of the other human sciences to the seeming simplicity of the thinking of Jesus and the primitive church. For that reason I think a bit of translation is in order. The original requirements involved in a theological effort to really comprehend the faith in terms of ongoing history must be translated into modern methodological terms. I propose the following points:

1. Far from *relativizing* any given present, the eschatological aspect of any Christian theology *links that present to the absolute*. Absolutization is necessary for all effective human mobilization. What the Christian eschatological aspect does, then, is prevent that mobilization from degenerating into human rigidity, petrification, and a sacralization of the existing situation merely because it does exist.

2. It follows, then, that the eschatological aspect does not define the *content* of Christian theology vis-à-vis secular ideologies nor the function of the ecclesial community in the midst of society as a whole, contrary to what

seems to be the implicit or explicit view of European political theology. The eschatological aspect is simply Christian theology's *way* or manner of accepting absolute commitments. The stress placed on the eschatological aspect depends on a proper, constantly reconsidered evaluation of the *kairos,* of the opportunity for liberation at a given moment. The critical space cleared by eschatology is not rectilinear but dialectic.

3. We are making an improper extrapolation when we take Luther's rediscovery of personal justification by faith without works and make it the key to all biblical exegesis, particularly insofar as cosmic and ecclesiological themes are concerned. In other words, we cannot move logically from Paul's demand that we avoid a paralyzing preoccupation with our own personal justification to the communitarian demand involved in the construction of the kingdom. To do that is to throw Scripture as a whole out of balance. What is it that effectively and definitively builds up disinterested love in the cosmos? What exactly is involved in the practical violence that snatches the kingdom from utopia and plants it in the very midst of human beings? Those questions, biblical questions par excellence, make no sense at all if we start from the a priori assumption that the kingdom is already completely fashioned and is simply waiting for everyone to enter it through faith.

4. Christian theology will have to be grounded much more on sensitivity to what liberates concrete human beings *here and now.* This of course would be in marked contrast to a science that starts out from the assumption that it can foresee and preclude any future dangers or errors with the help of an adequate model, or which presumes to criticize and relativize every historical step that does not provide such guarantees. Theology has sought to be the science of the immutable in the midst of human vicissitudes. Like the theology of the gospel message, it must get back to being the theology of *fidelity*. Grounded on the Immutable, such a theology offers guidance to the venture of history that is subject to all the corrections dictated by real facts and events.

5. Consequently the eschatological horizon does not offer theology the possibility of soaring aloft and maintaining its distance equally from the political right and the political left. The right and the left are not simply two sources of social projects that are subject to the evaluation and judgment of some reason located right in the center between them. As Martin Lotz points out: "The objective of leftist radicalism is to open up society permanently to its future. In the sixteenth edition of the Brockhaus one can find the following definition of the left: 'domain of that which has not yet found form or realization, of that which is still in a state of utopia.' "[16] Thus the sensitivity of the left is an intrinsic element of any authentic theology. It must be the form of any reflection in which historical sensitivity has become the key.

6. What about the relationship between a liberative event in history and the definitive kingdom of God? By virtue of the power of God who lies

behind it every such happening, however ambiguous and provisional it may be, stands in a causal relationship to the definitive kingdom. The causality is partial, fragile, often distorted and in need of reworking; but it is a far cry from being nothing more than an anticipation, outline, or analogy of the kingdom. We definitely are not talking about the latter when we are talking about such options as racial segregation versus full community of rights, laissez-faire supply and demand in international trade versus a truly balanced marketing process, and capitalism versus socialism. In however fragmentary a way, what is involved is the eschatological kingdom itself, whose revelation and realization is anxiously awaited by the whole universe.

By way of conclusion, then, my feeling is that Latin American theologizing is moving in the direction that I have just described. I fully realize that anyone who carefully examines the above guidelines will conclude that I have just delivered a radical criticism of all European theology, even its most progressive currents. I do not deny that, though I grant there are exceptions. It seems to me that over the course of centuries theology struck out on its own paths; that, like the church itself in many instances, theology did not allow itself to be judged by the word of God. The hope of many of us Latin Americans is that theology will draw close to that word once again, becoming a form of human thought deeply committed to human history.

PART II

UNMASKING THE IDOLS

CHAPTER 3

Conversion and Reconciliation in the Perspective of Modern Liberation Theology

Here Segundo is at pains to demonstrate that true reconciliation is possible only if it is preceded by genuine conversion. The conversion must clearly recognize the true causes of conflict and take objective action to eradicate these causes. Otherwise, premature reconciliation could function as an ideology concealing the continuing existence of conflicts, thus making their solution impossible.

Source: "Conversão e Reconciliação na Perspectiva da Moderna Teologia da Libertação," *Perspectiva Teológica* 7 (July-December 1975): 163–78.

Permit me to begin by delimiting my responsibility for the title selected for this essay. It is folly, of course, to attempt to do battle with a title. Nevertheless, if my contribution is to be understood here, I must observe that, *for me*, "liberation theology" either means simply theology—good theology, correct theology—or it means nothing at all. It certainly does not mean a theology that *deals with liberation*.

In terms of such a reduction, then, the correct title of this address would have been: "Conversion and Reconciliation in a Theological Perspective"—which, unfortunately, would have little meaning, since all the contributions of this meeting bear on the same theme from this same point of view, the theological.

I see no way out of my dilemma. I can only point out that, as all living theology is a rereading of the same font of revelation vis-à-vis a precise historical context, what I can offer here is precisely a biblical rereading—or, better, a New Testament rereading—of the theme of reconciliation with explicit reference to the context in which the said rereading is to be done—that is, the current Latin American problematic.

Now to my task. The proclamation of a year of *reconciliation* will fall on a "biblical" ear like a thunderbolt. It is as if someone had said, "This is the year of the *end of the world*." After all, if we were to hear, "This is the year of the recapitulation of all things in Christ," we should surely reply, "History is over! The parousia is upon us!"

True, the word "reconciliation," unlike "recapitulation," has a secular content, attested at least once in the New Testament. But its normal usage in the latter denotes an "eschatological" blessing—that is, a final, meta-historical reality.

When it comes to eschatological blessings, we do not accept the dichotomy, peculiar to a goodly part of European theology—mostly Protestant, but also Catholic—between a history that would be the work of the *human being alone*, and an eschatology that would be the irruption of the deed of *God alone*. Consistent with the theology of Vatican II, most Latin American theologians conceive of the eschatological as an interaction of both causalities: that of God and that of the human being.

To refer to reconciliation as an "eschatological" blessing, then, is not to deny that it must be sought within history itself. Even so, however, the question remains whether eschatological blessings are secured in history via the *same route as indicated by their final reality*—in other words, whether we cooperate in the final recapitulation whenever we recapitulate something historically—whether we cooperate in the final reconciliation whenever we reconcile any persons in history—whether we collaborate in the construction of the future city, which, as the Book of Revelation tells, will have no temple, whenever we destroy a historical, concrete temple.

If there were to be a continuity of this simple kind between the historical and the eschatological, it would be easy to understand a "year of reconciliation," since, even though reconciliation is eschatological, any accentuation of that direction in history would constitute a furtherance of its definitive realization.

If, however, there is no such simple continuity, then we shall be obliged to reflect somewhat more deeply on the possible sense and meaning of a year that, while in itself being merely a year of history, nonetheless bears upon the final reconciliation.

In what has been said up to this point, then, three problems seem to be posed, which I propose to subject to some development, however modest:

1. Reconciliation as an eschatological blessing.
2. Human collaboration in the realization of eschatological blessings.
3. The manner of executing this collaboration with the eschatological.

I

In the major Pauline letters—Romans and Corinthians—we find the verb *katallassein*, "to reconcile," used only once in a profane, or if you prefer, merely historical, sense. It occurs in the passage from First Corinthians in

which Paul speaks of a possible reconciliation of estranged spouses (1 Cor.
7:11).

In all other cases, both the substantive *katallagē* and the verb *katallassein* — "reconciliation" and "to reconcile" — denote in the New Testament
the reality characterizing the new age, the "now" of Christ, in contradis-
tinction to the old age, the "before."

Thus, in Romans we are told:

> *Now* . . . if, when we were God's enemies, we were reconciled to him
> by the death of his Son, it is all the more certain that we who have
> been reconciled will be saved by his life. Not only that; we go so far
> as to make God our boast through our Lord Jesus Christ, through
> whom we have *now* received reconciliation. [Rom. 5:9–11]

And the text goes on with the great comparison of the two ages: the old,
the Adamic, and the current, the Christic (Rom. 5:12–19).

Later in his letter, Paul examines the (momentary) lot of the Jewish
people in the light of the Christ event. Until the totality of that people
recognizes Christ, it shuts itself out of the work of Christ. Now, continues
Paul, "if their rejection has meant reconciliation for the world, what will
their acceptance mean? Nothing less than life from the dead!" (Rom.
11:15).

Finally, in Second Corinthians (5:17–6:1) — in the key text for our subject, the year of reconciliation — we read:

> If anyone is in Christ, he is a new creation. The old order has passed
> away; now all is new! All this has been done by God, who has rec-
> onciled us to himself through Christ and has given us the ministry of
> reconciliation. I mean that God, in Christ, was reconciling the world
> to himself, not counting men's transgressions against them, and that
> he has entrusted the message [or, according to other manuscripts,
> "the gospel" — that is, the good news] of reconciliation to us. This
> makes us ambassadors for Christ, God as it were appealing through
> us. We implore you, in Christ's name: be reconciled to God! [2 Cor.
> 5:17–20]

The *first* element that calls for our reflection, then, is the fact that reconciliation always appears in the past, as something given already, given
now, in virtue of a historical deed that has occurred with Christ. It is an
element of the *new* creation realized in Christ.

This could be disconcerting, inasmuch as reconciliation pertains to the
eschatological — were it not for the fact that we have two other elements
clearly present in the passages that we have read, and for that matter,
common to the New Testament (at least beginning with Luke, taking

"beginning with" not strictly chronologically, but in function of a process of complexity of thought).

The *second* element, then, is the explicit reference, in the passages cited, to realities that are eschatological by definition. To begin with, the first text that we have studied, Romans 5:10–11, shows us a reconciliation that implies *salvation*, a concept that is exclusively eschatological in the New Testament: "We who have been reconciled will be saved."

The second text, Romans 11:15, declares the definitive reconciliation — that is, the reconciliation destined to include the totality of the Jewish people, who for the moment remain unreconciled — to be a "life from the dead." In other words, it identifies the definitive reconciliation with the final resurrection, which is the eschatological blessing par excellence, something incomprehensible within the limits of history.

These two passages necessarily provide the hermeneutic framework for the third, dealing with the (current) "ministry" of reconciliation. Nevertheless, even the passage from Second Corinthians, 5:17–21, as we see when we regard it closely, contains unquestionable allusions to eschatology, perceptible to any ear attuned to the language of the Bible. In the first place, the whole of the new creation to which Paul refers is an eschatological blessing. The Book of Revelation, employing the same words, relates this new creation to the apparition of the future Jerusalem. After its description of the latter, it recounts: "The One who sat on the throne said to me, 'See, I make all things new!' " (Rev. 21:5). But among the new things that make Christ the Omega of the universe is, according to Paul, reconciliation.

On the other hand, although the word "ministry" (*diakonia*) is frequently used in its profane or secular sense of service, like the word "economy" or "administration" (*oikonomia*), it is employed in the New Testament in the sense of God's comprehensive plan, from the viewpoint of the cooperation supplied by the human being. And in this sense, Paul recognizes only two ministries: that before Christ, called the ministry of death and condemnation (2 Cor. 3:7–9), and the one after Christ, which is also the final one, that of life and salvation, resurrection and reconciliation — that is, the one that clearly bears upon the eschatological blessings.

And thus we arrive at the *third* element, one of the most essential in the New Testament, at least from Luke's degree of complexity onward: ever since the Jesus event, that which is eschatological is at one and the same time *past and future*. Conversely, when one and the same thing is asserted as simultaneously past and future, we can be sure that we have to do with the eschatological world.

This, to all evidence, is the case at hand. However one may prefer to interpret the eschatological, at all events the latter is conceived, at least from Luke onward, as an "already, but not yet." And this is what we have with reconciliation.

In the first of the texts cited, Romans 5:9–11, the accent is on the Christian conviction that "we have now received reconciliation." Nevertheless, the direct effect of this reconciliation—that is, salvation, without which reconciliation would have no meaning, and would remain frustrated—appears in the future: "we . . . will be saved."

In the second text, Romans 11:15, the "already" is expressed by the past tense in which "reconciliation for the *world*" with God is spoken of. The "not yet" appears as well, however, in the fact that this reconciliation must include a future: that of the "whole" of the Jewish people (Rom. 11:16).

The third text, 2 Corinthians 5:17–6:1 likewise combines an *already*— "the old order has passed away," "God . . . has reconciled us to himself through Christ," "has entrusted the message of reconciliation to us"—and a *not yet*, since this message is (also) a word of "appeal" to do something which, at the same time, is supposed already to have been done: to "be reconciled to God." Indeed, while God has reconciled us to himself, he still has need of cooperators (*sunergountes*) in that reconciliation (Rom. 6:1).

II

Perhaps you will say that we have spent too much time establishing too obvious a fact: that the only reconciliation to which the New Testament refers in a theological context constitutes an eschatological blessing.

That may be. The only valid excuse would be that familiarizing ourselves with the principal New Testament texts referring to reconciliation can help us in this second problem: *whether the eschatological blessings are realized to any extent in history.*

Two kinds of arguments could seem to suggest a negative response to this question. The *first* is the familiar argument that, the more nearly we approach the historical Jesus, the more clearly we find a conception of the eschatological as the imminent irruption of the reign of God and the cessation of Christian history. Only when the realization of eschatological hope begins to be postponed beyond the expectations of the historical Jesus and the primitive Christian community does the process begin, especially in Luke, of filling in the intervening time with a view of an intermediate history between the present time and that of the eschaton. This intermediate time, neither conceived nor foreseen by Jesus, would be the time of the church.

The *second* argument, related to the former, surely, but much more dependent on theological presuppositions, identifies history as the domain of a causality dependent on the human being alone, with the eschaton and its realization, the reign of God, depending on the divine will and causality alone. Thus, eschatological hope becomes the relativization of history, and therefore an openness to a hope placed in the irruption of the power of God, who will build the reign regardless of the development given by human beings to history.

Either of these two arguments, and a fortiori the convergence of the two, is sufficient to lead us to a very specific conception of reconciliation as an eschatological blessing: that of a profound relativization of the *con-flicts* that, in history, oppose this reconciliation, in the name of a historical efficacity. There is neither space nor time here, of course, to discuss both problems in detail.

As for the *first*, we need only point out that the hope of an imminent eschaton appears in many key passages of the New Testament, and not only in the Gospels antecedent to Luke — for example, in the Pauline letters to the Thessalonians.

Furthermore, it cannot be denied that the Jewish apocalypticism of the age constituted the historical framework of the first Christian thinking and its corresponding language.

And finally, biblical exegesis, at least over the past hundred years, especially at the hands of liberal Protestants, has suffered the impact of a rush for ever more Copernican revolutions, frequently at the expense of the *regime of the hypothesis* that holds sway in more scientific areas. We might almost say that, the more scandalous an interpretation for the naive reader of the gospel, the greater have been its chances of impacting exegetical opinion, gaining scientific status, and finding partisans.

Hence, the hypothesis that Jewish apocalypticism had completely deceived Jesus himself regarding the sense of his mission, and that it was only the Christian community, especially as we see that community in the works of Luke, that had finally surrendered to the evidence that the time of hope would probably be a very long one, becomes extremely seductive.

Too seductive, perhaps — to the detriment of another, more economical hypothesis for explaining facts of this sort. If we keep in mind the distance in creativity separating Jesus and his disciples — constantly attested in the redaction of the Gospels — it would appear far more credible that it had been the disciples who reduced Jesus' much more complex and rich thinking to the apocalyptic categories of the age that impregnated, as exegesis like-wise evinces, their popular religious mentality.

This would enable us to explain, for example, the fact that even before Luke, we find in Mark himself, the most primitive and least developed of the synoptics, as well as in Matthew, a message of the prepaschal Christ of a complexity that is structurally incompatible with simple Jewish apocalyp-ticism, and diametrically opposed to, for example, the "interim morality" preached, we are told, by John the precursor (Luke 3:7–18).

Keeping in mind the comprehensive thought structure with which we are dealing, and even prescinding from passages like that in Matthew where the Reign of Heaven is proclaimed to be subject to violence, and snatched away by the violent (Matt. 11:12), a basic revision of the law and its situation with respect to the human being (Mark 7:1–23) is incompatible with a hope in an imminent eschatological judgment whose criterion would have to be this same law.

When I speak of thought "structure," I wish to make it clear that, inde-pendently of what Jesus may consciously have thought about the proximity of the end of the world, his message was, at bottom, incompatible with the prevailing notion of an imminent eschaton. Indeed, as this incompatibility was a subtle one, it is unlikely that it could have been a later interpolation. In the first place, it is pre-Lucan; and second, the synoptics wrote before it could have been evident that the message had to be reworked, given Jesus' "error" in calculating his second coming, or, if you will, the coming of the Son of Man.

If I have placed heavy emphasis on this point, it is because I believe it an essential one for a Latin American theology—that is, for a theology that will accord the human being's liberative toil in history its actual value.

As for the *second* argument—to the effect that in the New Testament the eschatological is presented as altogether withdrawn from human historical causality—it is interesting to note from the outset that the main text concerning reconciliation, cited above, from Second Corinthians (5:17–6:1), employs the clearest, strongest possible term for a *co-causality* on the part of the human being with the divine causality: *sunergos*, "cooperator."

To be sure, an interpretation can be maintained a priori, for preestablished reasons, that would empty the word of its obvious content. For example, we could always say that our "cooperation" consists in renouncing any pretense of changing things in history for ourselves, as Bultmann does in the beginning of his *Theology of the New Testament*.

This interpretation, however, does not stand up against a scientific critique. Paul uses the term "cooperator" at least eight times in its obvious profane signification of positive historical activities converging on one and the same causality (Rom. 16:3; 1 Cor. 16:16; 2 Cor. 1:24, 8:23; Phil. 2:25, 4:3; Philemon 1:24). On one occasion he moves from historical to eschatological toil by speaking of those who are "working with me for the [building of the] kingdom of God" (*eis tēn* basileian tou theou, Col. 4:11), where the object of the cooperation, highlighted by an *eis*, is nothing other than the final reign of God.

Indeed, in two other texts (1 Cor. 3:9 and 1 Thess. 3:2), the causality of the eschatological blessings is explicitly attributed (unlike that attribution in the last text we have studied, 2 Cor. 6:1, where the attribution is merely implicit, however evident) to the activities *of the human being and of God*. Human beings, then, under the pen of Paul, appear as *sunergoi tou Theou*.

Two other Pauline terms reinforce the interpretation I propose. One of them—*diakonia*, "service," or "ministry"—is particularly important for our case, since it is the nub of the text concerning our human mission with regard to the eschatological blessing of reconciliation. Thus we have the *diakonia*, the ministry, of reconciliation. This indicates that the eschatological activity of God *occurs by way of* the historical action of the human being, although the latter neither exhausts that activity nor is the principal activity.

It is interesting to note that this is not the only time *diakonia* is used apart from its obvious profane acceptation: an active cooperation with the interests or projects of another. Thus, in 2 Corinthians 3:7–9 Paul speaks of the service we render in the Spirit's realization of the eschatological blessing of justification, or realized justice. The same thing occurs in Galatians 2:17, where the word *diakonia* serves to distinguish the two ages: the old one, of sin, and the new and final one, of justification. True, the "deacon" here is Jesus. But on the one hand we understand that the term *diakonia* refers to God's comprehensive plan, and on the other hand, that historical actions "serve" that plan. (See also Rom. 15:8.)

The second term that reinforces still more the Pauline conception of the convergence of both causalities, the historical human and the eschatological divine, is *oikonomia*, "administration." Thus, the Letter to the Ephesians (1:10) speaks of a plan "to be carried out (*eis oikonomian*) in the fullness of time," thereby indicating that God's plan to recapitulate all things—in other words, to give meaning to the entire universe—consists not merely in an irruption of the metahistorical into the historical, but in a different disposition of the historical itself, depending on the age in question. Paul's *diakonia*, then, bears an intrinsic relation to this detailed plan, according to the same Letter to the Ephesians (3:3–9), so that this ministry of his constitutes him an *oikonomos* of the mystery of God—that is, of a mystery that can only move by way of historical mediations, to arrive at its eschatological realization (1 Cor. 4:1).

Once more, if I have overemphasized this point—considering its currency in Latin American theology—it is because the European theology regarded as the most scientific and progressive, like *political theology* and the so-called *theology of revolution*, in explicitly denying all convergence of causalities between historical activity and eschatological plenitude, only succeeds in transforming the eschatological into a neutralizing and (negative) relativizing agent vis-à-vis historical conflicts and struggles.

III

Almost by definition, eschatological blessings have two vectors. On the one hand, they are *blessings*. Their function as such requires them to be, in some manner, connected with the blessings that we recognize within history. Otherwise they would cease to attract, and the eschaton would appear simply as a catastrophe, an anticreation, rather than as God's final deed.

On the other hand, these blessings are *eschatological*—final, and not present. In other words, it is also their function to demonstrate the unsatisfactory character of their present realization—demonstrate God's negative judgment on history as human beings manage it—and thus to constitute a call to *conversion* issuing from history.

The distinction between these two contrary, complementary aspects of the eschatological is important, because it demonstrates that, in practice, neither is the eschatological a mere breach with the present (it must be connected with the construction of a final good), nor is it the mere pursuit of a historical good (there must be a breach, a conversion, in order for this good to be converted into the final good).

To be sure, in conformity with different interests, emphasis can be laid on one or the other line. But an integral conception requires the presence of both.

Perhaps the clearest example is furnished by the two versions, in Matthew and Luke, respectively, of the Beatitudes, whose eschatological character is beyond doubt.

Let us begin with the Lukan version — without prejudice to a determination of which of the two is the more primitive — since it is the clearest in its literary construction. According to Luke, four classes of persons are or will be happy or fortunate: the poor, those who hunger *now*, those who weep *now*, and those who are mistreated on account of the Son of Man. By contrast, four classes of persons are or will be unfortunate: the wealthy, those who have their fill *now*, those who laugh *now*, and those who are well treated by all.

The cause of this happiness and this misfortune, respectively, lies in the fact that eschatological reality consists not only in a breach with, but even more, in a reversal of these situations. To begin with, those who are hungry *now* will have their hunger satisfied, and those who *now* have their hunger satisfied will be hungry. Those who *now* weep will laugh, and those who *now* laugh will weep and mourn. The reversal of the situation is more complex, but no less evident, in the other two cases. The poor will have as their recompense the possession of the reign of heaven, while the wealthy have already had their recompense *now* (and will be deprived of it). Those persecuted by others and those well treated by others will be judged according to the criterion of the fate of the prophets: the prophets were persecuted on earth (although supposedly rewarded afterward), while their persecutors were applauded by all (although supposedly condemned by God afterward).

In other words, the eschatological is conceived almost after the fashion of a "reprisal" in behalf of those who, all blameless, have had to suffer in history.

This interpretation is precisely reinforced, in Luke, by the "eschatological" parable of the contrasting lots of the rich person and Lazarus. To the protestations of the former, Abraham replies: "My child . . . remember that you were well off *in your lifetime*, while Lazarus was in misery. *Now* he has found consolation here, but you have found torment" (Luke 16:25).

Matthew, on the other hand, in his Beatitudes, accentuates, although not right up to the end, the continuity of the eschatological blessings with values already present in history.

First of all, this appears in the suppression of the second term (the woes, the misfortunes), so essential to the Lukan version, and precisely setting the stage for the eschatological reversal. Thus, in Matthew the Beatitudes act rather through continuity with and in culmination of existing *values* than by the reversal of current *situations*.

Thus, a *situation* in Luke, such as poverty, is transformed into a *value* in Matthew—the "poor in spirit" (Matt. 5:3), or the spirit of poor persons—and into a value that can rightly be supposed to continue to be a value even when the reign of heaven is possessed. Thus, the Beatitudes are to a large extent transformed into a list of virtues having an eschatological culmination. *Spiritual* poverty, hunger, and thirst *for justice* replace the simple situation of poverty-versus-wealth, hunger-versus-satiety. And other virtues appear: the merciful (who, without ceasing to be such, will obtain mercy); the pure of heart (who, precisely by being such, will see God); the friends or agents of peace; and so on (Matt. 5:3–12).

Nevertheless, the structure of an eschatological reversal appears in the Beatitudes of Matthew, as well, which may be an indication that Luke's version is the original one. The reversal appears in Matthew in three very clear cases: that of the lowly who will inherit the land, the sorrowing (who will cease to be sorrowing and be consoled instead), and those persecuted for holiness' sake (who will pass from persecution to its opposite: possession of the reign of God).

What conclusions can we draw from these two lines, that we may be true *sunergountes*, collaborators, in the eschatological blessings?

The *first* line, that of the reversal by which God will make, for example, the poor rich and the rich poor, evinces that the will of God is opposed to the prevailing order, that it calls for conversion, and that consequently we do not collaborate with this plan by multiplying the number of the poor and hungry or by introducing tears and persecution in order thereby to augment a future happiness. At the same time, it will be appropriate to take a position in favor of those whom God's plan favors, which does not constitute a mere historical reversal of the current situation. To make the rich poor and the poor rich does not prepare the eschaton, seeing that what God evidently wishes is that the division of labor not produce oppressive differences of this sort. This is where the second line comes in, with its continuity between hunger and thirst for *justice* and the fact that those suffering them will have their fill *of justice*.

The *second* line, then, that of continuity, is important, inasmuch as it enables us to grasp more concretely and powerfully the dimension of the eschatological blessings as realizable here and now. In isolation from the first line, however, it could be completely deceptive, in that it might seem to indicate that the mediations for arriving at such ends are of the same nature as the end itself. For example, the spirit of poverty does not mean that the generalization of poverty, or even the relativization of material goods, is the mediation by which human beings cooperate in the divine deed of the eschaton at each moment in history. The Beatitude does not unambiguously indicate what attitude to take with respect to concrete poverty and wealth, and the economic causes that produce them. Taking this line of reasoning could lead one to say—and it has actually been said—that one should not struggle to emerge from, or draw others from, poverty or to destroy the economic structures that produce it, since, after all, the poor are blessed!

That peace is an eschatological blessing is beyond all doubt. But peacemaking is not an unequivocal mediation. Jesus himself declares to his disciples, "Do not suppose that my mission on earth is to spread peace. My mission is to spread, not peace, but division" (Matt. 10:34). In other words, concrete peace actually diminishes with the work of Jesus, the eschatological "peacemaker."

We must conclude from this that the mediations of an evidently eschatological blessing, such as peace, are not necessarily or even primarily pacific, or of the same immediate nature as the end toward which they tend. To put it another way: the historical *oikonomia* of peace is not a series of pacific acts, or if you prefer, of acts whose *immediate* object is to introduce peace where there is conflict. In fact, if we attend to the gospel passage just cited, Jesus, the peacemaker par excellence (Col. 1:20), takes as his historical mission the undoing of peace and the introduction of conflict:

> I have come to set a man at odds with his father, a daughter with her mother, a daughter-in-law with her mother-in-law; in short, to make a man's enemies those of his own household. [Matt. 10:35–36]

This deliberately secured enmity is at the service of peace, of course, true peace, since a facile, immediately rewarding peace—exemplified here in family situations—can present precisely the greatest obstacle to a deeper, more universal peace.

The eschatological blessing of the universal recapitulation offers us another, equally enlightening, example. Recapitulation, as we know, is not a "recap" or summary of anything. "To place the same head" on all things is to join them together in a single meaning or significance (Eph. 1:10). To this end, it is necessary to collaborate with the plan of God, who seeks to suppress the uselessness or "vanity" of all seemingly meaningless things on earth, as Paul tells the Romans (Rom. 8:20). It implies a reversal of the order of things that causes such uselessness. In other words, it is necessary to introduce conflict into the false "recapitulation" that reigns in the world (or that *is* the world, in Johannine terminology):

> Brothers, you are among those called. Consider your situation. Not many of you are wise, as men account wisdom; not many are influential; and surely not many are well-born. God chose those whom the world considers absurd to shame the wise; he singled out the weak of this world to shame the strong. [1 Cor. 1:26–27]

What Paul means is that there is no possible "recapitulation" as long as meaning is assigned to things by those who are currently wise and powerful.

Thus, while the eschatological—according to the version more emphasized by Matthew—would have no drawing power or positive value unless it were possible to have a foretaste of it in some historical good, nevertheless its realization in history consists not in a sum-total of those same goods, but in a conflictive mediation that seems to take the shape of the negation of this same good—hence conversion—in order to settle it upon its true basis. To put it in what may be rather high-sounding words, the eschatological and its historical mediation stand in a frankly *dialectical* relationship.

IV

Considered from this viewpoint, which seems to be the only one consistent with the New Testament message, the Holy Year, if it is to fly the banner of the eschatological blessing of reconciliation, ought to be a revolutionary, conflictive year par excellence, the destroyer of all premature, forced, imposed reconciliations that leave the actual basis of human discord untouched.

Therefore I should like to devote the last part of this essay to an examination, in light of the exegesis done in the foregoing paragraphs, of the interpretation and application of the theme of reconciliation in certain recent church documents from Latin America.

In the proclamation of the Holy Year by his Holiness, Pope Paul VI, we read:

> Our life is disturbed *by too many breaches, too much discord, too much disorder*, for us to be able to enjoy the gifts of personal and collective life in conformity with the ideal finality of that life.

This is true, beyond any doubt, just as it is true that this reality moves us to direct our gaze, with desire and hope, toward the eschatological blessing of reconciliation.

The problem arises when, from this altogether correct general orientation, we pass to a consideration of concrete mediations in the particular context that is Latin America today.

For example, the apostolic nuncio in Uruguay, addressing the Uruguayan bishops' conference meeting to plan the implementation of the papal directives for the Holy Year of Reconciliation, exhorted the bishops to strive "for the elimination of the *reasons* for tension and struggle, and for the conciliation and unity of the exponents of the *various positions* within the church" (summary published in the official organ of the Uruguayan Bishops' Conference, *Vida Pastoral*, December 1973, p. 367). Assuming that the quotation is accurate, and citing it only by way of example, I find in it a notorious ambiguity, which we shall see repeated in a thousand ways in other ecclesiastical documents on the same subject.

On the one hand, no one is ignorant of the fact, and church authorities point it out, that the divisions among human beings have *objective* causes, and do not proceed only from a *subjective* rejection of reconciliation. There is no denying the importance of these objective causes. Hence the nuncio's reference to the *elimination of the reasons* for tension and struggle, and not simply to the elimination of all tension or struggle. Nevertheless, the second objective in the formula is precisely the elimination of the tension and struggle themselves: "the conciliation and unity of the exponents of the various positions within the church." In fact, it is obvious that intrinsic church differences in Latin America are intimately bound up with positions taken toward the *reasons* for tension and struggle in society: injustice, misery, exploitation, dictatorship.

A profound, realistic elimination of the reasons for intrinsic church tensions, then, will consist in a demonstration both of the evident irreconcilability of certain positions with the gospel message, and of the fact that conversion is the only path to an actual reconciliation. In a word, conversion is required *in order that* Christians be reconciled. Conversion does not consist *in* a reconciliation of Christians by way of a minimization of the objective, evangelical reasons for tension and struggle.

Whether or not the nuncio's exact words have been cited, the same ambiguity is reflected in the document "Pastoral Reflections of the Uruguayan Bishops' Conference on the 'Holy Year.'"

That document is altogether clear regarding the importance of the *objective* reasons that divide Uruguayans. The bishops write:

> Social peace, *national reconciliation*, will not come from the dominion of some groups by others ... but necessarily requires ... the full recognition of all rights. Justice demands it, and only upon justice can peace be cemented.

It is not baseless to suppose that this paragraph contains the only allusion to political events of five months before: the elimination of parliamentary representation and the suppression of the human rights of assembly, free expression of thought, right to strike, and so on.

But what is remarkable in the document is that, after these strong expressions concerning the need to eliminate reasons for division, and the need to implant justice with a view to reconciliation, the practical conclusion is drawn: "*Therefore*," the document continues, without a hiatus—and let us take careful note of this "therefore"—"in the face of the division and hatred that threaten to destroy the community, the church proclaims the necessity and utmost urgency of *reconciliation*." When it would seem that the church ought to proclaim the necessity and extreme urgency of *conversion*, in order that, according to its own declaration, a reconciliation may be possible based on justice and on the recognition of all rights, it calls for reconciliation without further ado—that is, without the recognition of these rights.

And that this is not a mere lapse, or too subtle an interpretation on my part, is clear from other paragraphs, such as the following:

Hatred, rancor, mistrust, fear, suspicion, and slander have been sown everywhere. The fruit of this recklessness is the breach, today, dividing, as if it had been *a whetted sword*, Uruguayans into seemingly irreconcilable factions. The situation is becoming grievous in the extreme. It painfully divides the family. It renders dialogue in any social group difficult or impossible.

It is instructive to observe, in this passage, besides the allusion to the whetted sword (a Christian metaphor precisely of the impact of the divine word, and not of evil), a description of the dissolution of family unity, as if the eschatological blessing of reconciliation were to be obtained by the contagion of lesser reconciliations—that is, by an incremental process beginning with the easiest, the reconciliation of the family. On the contrary, the mission of Jesus the "eschatological reconciler" is strikingly reminiscent of the very situation that the bishops declare grievous:

Do not suppose that my mission on earth is to spread peace. My mission is to spread, not peace, but *division* [lit., "the sword"]. I have come to set a man at odds with his father, a daughter with her mother, a daughter-in-law with her mother-in-law: in short, to make a man's enemies *those of his own household*. [Matt. 10:34–36]

It is to be hoped that the bishops will carefully analyze whether the division prevailing in the Uruguayan family is not somehow connected with the values proclaimed by Jesus.

In referring to the class struggle (in quotation marks), the text makes explicit allusion to the Marxist conception of the process that, according to that conception, ought to lead to a classless society. This supposes, in the first place, that the class struggle is a fact (and certainly not something introduced by Marxism), rather than a slogan or mediation utilized by Marxism. Indeed, where there is oppression of one human group by another, there, whether Marxists denounce it or not, is class struggle. It supposes, in the second place, that this already existing conflict ought to become conscious and emphasized, in order that authentic solutions be actually sought. Otherwise, in the presence of a minimization or concealment of the conflict—and a reconciliation that wafts above it—the oppression will tend to perpetuate itself.

The bishops, however, seem to conceive reconciliation as the concealment, not the solution in depth, of conflicts. Here once more, if by social classes we understand the poor and the wealthy, Jesus the reconciler centers his preaching on a radical division of the "social classes." According to the gospel, the poor, the hungry, those who weep, and the persecuted, are happy; the wealthy, the satiated, the satisfied, and the applauded are cursed. It is difficult to imagine that, in thus emphasizing the radical difference between one group and another, Jesus would be striving for a reconciliation among them, or at any rate a reconciliation that would not come by way of the conversion of the second group.

A similar example, perhaps a more tragic one, appears in some recent documents from the Chilean episcopate. In the first year of Allende's government, in an interesting working document called "Gospel, Politics, and Socialisms," the bishops declared:

> *The Church makes no option* among the various human groups. In and with Jesus Christ, the church decides in favor of those for whom Jesus Christ himself has decided: for the whole people of Chile, whom he calls *to be converted*—by way of acceptance of his Gospel—to being a people of God.

Once more, one is surprised by the invocation of the name of Jesus in the adoption of behaviors precisely opposed to his. The first thing Christ did, if we may credit the synoptics, was to opt for human groups, and to say why. Indeed, there is a patent contradiction between a refusal to opt for any human group and *conversion*, inasmuch as conversion, in the language of the gospel, is a change of attitude in the form of the rejection of a sinful situation. And when the latter, as the bishops say at Medellín, is translated into social grouping and structures, how can a person be converted without making an option? If Christ had refused to make an option for certain human groups, and had opted, in the Chilean episcopate's terms, for the whole of the Jewish people, he would have died a natural death.

But at least the Chilean bishops are consistent: with their whole people deprived of its human rights, and half of it even more so deprived—a situation which the Holy See itself has denounced— that body of bishops, while protesting the situation, issues a call not for *conversion*, but for *reconciliation*, in the framework of the Holy Year. The trouble is, it seems as if that reconciliation will have to be achieved on the basis of the rejection of the essential evangelical values. And we say that this is not coincidental, because it is impossible to see how the eschatological blessings could be realized except through a dialectical mediation, without which eschatology is irremediably transformed into a conservative ideology.

I have cited these few examples, among so many that I might have used instead, in order to show that one must exercise caution in appealing to an eschatological blessing like reconciliation. True, human beings cannot live divided by *too many* conflicts, as his Holiness Pope Paul VI indicates. We must not seek to be awash in conflict. Reconciliation must seek to reduce the number of conflicts to the basic ones, the decisive ones, in order that, by way of a conversion provoked by these conflicts, one more step may be taken in the direction of the eschatological blessing.

To take an example from the gospel itself: Christ's reconciliation constitutes a call for the concrete reconciliation of all of those on one side of the dividing line of the Beatitudes—which are the central values of the gospel—the poor, the hungry, the exploited, and the persecuted, in order that the radical conflict of the gospel with the opposite categories may be a universal, mighty call for the *conversion* of persons and peoples.

CHAPTER 4

Human Rights, Evangelization, and Ideology

In this article, Segundo probes into some neglected aspects of human rights, especially the ideological manipulation of human rights discourse by countries in the West to justify the maintenance of unjust economic systems on a global level. He also pursues deeper implications of the relationship between human rights and evangelization.

"Derechos humanos, evangelización, e ideología," *Christus* (November 1978): 29–35.

In addressing the relationship between human rights and evangelization, I think it important to underscore certain characteristics of the evangelization that has actually occurred in the Latin American context.

First, what, precisely, is meant by "gospel" (Spanish: *evangelio*) or "evangelization"? We know that St. Paul spoke of his "gospel"—referring to the entire Christian message communicated through a whole catechesis. That is, for Paul the "gospel" is his own interpretation of what Christ was, said, and meant for human beings (see, e.g., Gal. 1, 2, passim). We also know that the title of "gospels," bestowed on the four narratives of the life of Jesus, means something very much the same. However, the noun "gospel," and still more the verb "evangelize," are applied with greater frequency, as their etymology would suggest, to a first encounter, generally brief and sudden, with some good news—in this case, the good news that is Jesus himself and what Jesus represents for the human being.

Mark gives us the paradigm of an "evangelization" when he expounds the content of Jesus' preaching in Galilee: "The time is accomplished and the reign of God is near: be converted, and believe in the good news!" (Mark 1:15). What good news? Obviously the following: that "the time is accomplished and the reign of God is near."

Accordingly, we may assert as a principle that, strictly speaking, good news ceases to be such, and becomes information and catechesis whenever it moves on to further development of the news, unless that development sheds new light on the triumphal aspects of existence. Only in this sense could Paul properly apply the word "gospel" to the entire content of his preaching.

Secondly, nothing is good news in itself, as the church so often seems to believe that it is, or as an apologetics thinks when it pretends to present Christ "in an attractive way" independently of the situation in which human beings find themselves. All the evangelizing initiatives to be found in the New Testament are located in, and limited by, spatio-temporal circumstances, and set in a relationship with concrete expectations. For example, the fact that the time is accomplished and the reign of God is near can be "evangelizing" only in the perspectives of Israel, and the Israel of that era — since the expectations of Israel were concretely based on specific messianic promises, and on a concrete image of the restoration of the Davidic kingdom.

In Athens, then, St. Paul, in turn — seemingly rather fruitlessly — began to devote himself wholeheartedly to the work of evangelization. His discourse in the Areopagus deals with the supposition that Jesus could function as "good news" in confrontation with any divinity at all, even the most hidden, and this in terms of the importance of a divine judgment that would be equitable for all human beings. The administrator of the queen of the Ethiopians, of whom we read in chapter 8 of Acts, was interested in knowing of whom the prophet Isaiah was speaking in singing of the Servant of Yahweh. And here it is recounted that the deacon Philip, "opening his mouth, evangelized Jesus to him, beginning with that part of the scriptures" (Acts 8:35). The apologetical or "evangelizing" intent of the fourth Gospel (unlike that of the others) is expressed in the intent to present Jesus in terms of the actual expectations of Hellenistic thought, a good deal more on the basis of a knowledge of the essential than in historical hopes.

Third, as a consequence of the foregoing: there is no such thing as an evangelization that would be equally and directly the same for all persons. This is true not only because, in a limited, situated world, expectations are different, but because in a conflictive world, expectations are often contrary. This explains why the Beatitudes, which are actually the proclamation of good news (the divine judgment upon certain human values) in Luke have their inevitable parallel in correlative "woes" (the proclamation of bad news). God declares blessed or fortunate the poor, those who suffer hunger, those who weep, and the persecuted. And next, in all logic, God also declares unfortunate those who find themselves in the contrary situation. Unless they are converted — and this implies a mediation, sometimes a painful one — the good news is addressed to them not directly, but by way of a call to conversion.

The surprising thing about this sorrow, this bad news, which must necessarily, and concretely, be associated with the gospel, with the good news, is exemplified in Jesus' dialogue with the rich youth (or the magistrate). I do not have time to bring out all the elements of an exegesis here. I wish only to emphasize the fact that the young man, who thought that he was protected and insured by the observance of the commandments when it came to eternal life, "went away sorrowing," because he had received from Jesus the bad news that such observance was insufficient. The disciples are astonished, understandably astonished, at the fact that the good news of the gospel, instead of opening a more universal door, seems to make that doorway even narrower than before. Indeed, they ask one another: If not even the rich can be saved, then who can? According to the moral theory of the time, practically only the rich might enter into the luxury of licit pleasures. They alone might purchase with their goods the pleasures allowable within the framework of the commandments. And according to the "good news," not even for them were the gates of the reign open, the gates of life!

Finally, I should like to emphasize a fourth characteristic of New Testament evangelization—one intimately connected with the first three and with the subject with which we are concerned here. From what has been said, we must conclude that there is no such thing as good news that is valid for all human cases; or, if you will, that this "only" good news is Jesus, but that, in order for Jesus to come to be good news in the concrete, we have the obligation of discovering his relationship with a sensible, critical point in the current situation, and the expectations of each person or group.

An even clearer demonstration of this is the fact that not even the evangelists are in accord as to who are declared happy in Jesus' Beatitudes. Owing to limitations of time, once more, I can only sketch the exegetical conclusions that seem to me to be the most solid and most important. We have two extant versions, and one reconstruction, of the Beatitudes: the versions of Matthew and Luke, and the reconstruction of Q—the presumed common font of Matthew and Luke. These three versions are different— even, to some extent, with regard to the object of the Beatitudes, the persons or groups whom Jesus regards as "happy" or privileged by God.

According to Matthew, Jesus pronounces happy those who possess a particular series of virtues: spiritual poverty (however this is to be understood), a thirst for justice, mercy, loyalty, the desire for peace, and a justice subjected to persecution.

In Luke, unlike Matthew, Jesus declares happy or fortunate the Christians of his time—despite their poverty, hunger, tears, and persecution. In Luke, the moral quality of the addressees of the Beatitudes consists in the fact that the social condition in question is being lived by Christians. This explains why unlike Matthew, Luke puts the Beatitudes in the second person (rather than the third). The "you" suggests, to the readers of his gospel, an obvious identification with the disciples of Jesus.

If we regard as valid the research that has been conducted into the common font of Matthew and Luke, Q—and I think that it is—we find ourselves before a version of the Beatitudes rather nearer to Jesus' own version. And precisely according to this version, the "happy" would be—

in the third person, as in Matthew—those who find themselves in the social conditions singled out by Luke: poverty, hunger, sorrow, persecution, period. Jesus would be presenting to us, then, the judgment of God as contradistinguished from the current judgment of the world, which regards as happy the wealthy, the well-fed, those with smiling faces, and the prestigious. And this strange divine favoritism would constitute precisely "the good news according to Q."

If this is the case, and I think that there can be little doubt about it (even if the hypothesis of Q is not admitted), it would seem at first sight that Matthew and Luke have retreated from the radical element in Jesus' Beatitudes. Perhaps they thought that it was impossible for God to declare happy certain persons by the simple fact of their participation in a particular social condition, without taking account of their internal dispositions. Hence Matthew's virtues, and Luke's participation in the Christian community.

However, I think that it is not out of a fear of the radical that Matthew and Luke have introduced their alterations. Rather it is owing to the exigency noted above. Each evangelist—like ourselves—is obliged to re-create the good news in terms of what Jesus would say today to the people of the time and place in which we live. In other words, the various versions of the Beatitudes do not represent failed attempts to understand Jesus. Indeed, we know that, in the course of his ministry, Jesus added a great deal to what is asserted in the Beatitudes. But he wished, it would seem, that his first, jubilant encounter with the addressees of his most direct good news would be the 'am-ha'arets—that is, in the words of the Fourth Gospel, with "this lot, that knows nothing about the law" (John 7:49). But, as we have said, Jesus also preached what Matthew will call "spiritual poverty." Matthew is not being unfaithful to the good news of Jesus when he synthesizes it, in different circumstances and for another audience, in the first Beatitude: "How blest are the poor in spirit . . ." (Matt. 5:3). He is only recreating, as one should, a *situated* good news.

There is no magical, ready-made formula, then, for evangelization—no "checklist" for the elements of evangelization. The encounter with the good news depends not only on a most demanding fidelity to the gospel, but furthermore, on our interior, committed knowledge of the persons to whom we are to give this message.

What should be our approach to human rights, on the basis of this New Testament concept of evangelization?

After what we have seen, it should come as a surprise to no one that something seemingly so nonreligious, so "lay," might be an essential part of evangelization for today.

However, before examining this point in terms of the exegesis I have presented, I think it will be important, at least for our topic, to draw a clear distinction between (1) human rights as human ideals, and (2) human rights as rights, or as juridical, and juridically valid, instruments.

Although these two vectors generally lie adjacent, one can nevertheless hold the same human ideals without seeking their concretion by way of law (for example, in the French Revolution); and on the other hand, these same human rights can be made to function de facto in a society without everyone in that society having the same ideals with regard to what the human being should be. (For example, human rights can de facto be respected partly because some gain an advantage in this way and partly because others sincerely respect them.)

Let us examine, then, separately and in their relationship with evangelization human rights as human ideals, and then as juridical rights—that is, as an instrument of law.

HUMAN RIGHTS AS HUMAN IDEALS

The fact of a certain agreement, and in a sense a universal agreement, on the rights of the human being, presupposes, implicitly, a particular conception of what human beings are, in their very essence as such: that is, what they should be. There must be an implicit agreement on what human beings should be in themselves and in their relationship with their neighbors and society. Beyond any doubt, then, there is an ideal at the basis of the proclamation of human rights. Before being conceived as rights, they are conceived as ideals. In principle, then, it is perfectly in order to demonstrate that, in the function of evangelization, the God of Jesus Christ endorses these human ideals and personally adopts them, since it is precisely God who has sown them in human hearts. In the original version of the Beatitudes, Jesus, omitting any mediation in terms of favorable religious conditions or subjective dispositions, declares that God endorses the right that accords priority in the reign to the poor, the suffering—in a word, to the socially rejected.

But, from what we have seen earlier, we must deduce that, in order to evangelize in the strict sense, the mere defense of human rights (as ideals) on the part of the church is not enough. These rights must be plausibly associated with the God of Jesus Christ, and with the paschal mystery.

It is not enough to say that it is good news—in fact, it is even strange, in a way—to see the church rush to the defense of those whose rights the powerful seek to trample underfoot. Not all good news is "evangelization" in the New Testament sense that we have seen. In this rigorous, New Testament sense, it is important to show explicitly that what is proclaimed is contained in the "gospel," in the good news par excellence.

I have not the slightest doubt that what is done without this explicitation is useful, decisive, supernatural preevangelization—anonymous evangelization, or what you will. But, even at the risk of using terms in such a way as to occasion grave misunderstandings, in conformity with what we have seen earlier, I think that by "evangelization" we must understand only (and any) proclamation of good news that appears as a consequence precisely of the content of the good news of Jesus.

There is no doubt that human rights as ideals—inasmuch as they reflect an image of the (ideal) human being—constitute something that, at least at first sight, seems intimately linked with the gospel message. The relationship is evident if we consider very carefully, for example, the absolute, divine value of every human being as alluded to in Matthew 25:31–32, in the good news of Christian freedom so stoutly maintained by Paul (Gal. 3–5), and so on.

Thus, we are in for a first surprise when we observe how the church in recent times has been approaching the ideals contained in the Declaration of Human Rights. To be sure, someone might say that its own history, in which these rights were often violated, had predisposed the church to a certain prudence in these matters. But let us examine the facts. True, the Pastoral Letter of the Brazilian Bishops' Conference (October 25, 1976) declares that "Christ was the great defender of human rights" (followed by a few lines of explanation to serve as a bridge to subsequent applications). However, the official documents of the church that best develop this point—the relationship between the Christian message and human rights—the so-called social encyclicals, have much more explicit and frequent recourse to a timeless human nature than to the content of the gospel! This is well known—and much criticized, especially in Protestant circles—and I shall not pause to establish it factually. No, what I am interested in is *why* this is the case—since, at bottom, we are dealing with a dissociation between evangelization properly so-called and the defense of human rights as human ideals.

It seems to me that the most probable hypothesis, from a theological viewpoint, on which to explain this phenomenon is that the authors of this document understand very clearly that human nature provides a far stronger basis upon which to establish a human ideal that must be supposed to be invariable. Furthermore, it is obvious that, in order to be effective, the proclamation on human rights must rest on a basis such that no group, government, or power will be able to claim that the human ideal has changed overnight and that consequently human beings can no longer demand the same rights.

It is by no means easy for exegetes to demonstrate that the New Testament contains a human ideal similar to the one that today lies at the basis of the proclamation of human rights. They all know that the ideal proposed by Paul for slaves, who comprised the majority of the population of the Roman Empire, was not to try to escape their situation, but rather to live in it as spiritually liberated "in Christ":

Let each continue as he was when the call of God came upon him. Were you a slave when you were called? Not to worry. And even if

you could have your freedom, [your condition of slavery] is better."
[1 Cor. 7:20–21]

After all, it is in that condition that the "will of God" is found (Eph. 6:5–6).

Of course, one might argue that only with the passage of time did the church gradually discover "Christ [as] the great defender of human rights," as the Brazilian Bishops' Conference puts it. But precisely, this would imply the practical concession of the decisive importance of revelation on the one hand, and of social and material conditioning on the other, since it was only when it became economically viable that the relationship was discovered between the gospel and the abolition of slavery. We must ask, then: Are there human ideals that need not be proclaimed as rights—perhaps not even as ideals—until certain conditions are present? And will these conditions be universal and irreversible?

On the other hand, the New Testament is not an island. Jesus presents himself as continuing and bringing to perfection the revelation of God in the Old Testament. Even after the break between the Jewish religion and Christianity, the Old Testament was by no means transcended or corrected. Strangely, if you will, Jesus adopts it. He does not invalidate it or "go beyond" it. If we qualify both Testaments homogeneously as revelation, it is easy to see that the people led by God lived, throughout the centuries, very different ideals from those we find canonized today in the proclamation of human rights, and lived them not only as God's actual revelation, but later as revealed in Jesus Christ as well: the de facto and sacralized supremacy of some peoples and races over others, the total extermination of peoples holding other religious beliefs, intolerance on the part of those who possessed the truth vis-à-vis any attempt at dialogue outside particular limits, and so on.

Of course, all of this can—and should—be seen as steps in an educational process. And by way of culmination of this process, Christ can be posited as the potential—not yet the actual, as we have seen—defender of human rights. But then at once we comprehend a hesitancy to appeal to a biblical basis for the rights corresponding to the proclamation of human rights. The tendency is understandable, consequently, to prefer to base human rights on the immutability of a supposed human nature (which God of course did not reveal from the beginning, or even in the gospel).

Still further: if the entire Bible represents an educational process, then part, and a positive part, of this process will be the fact that these same ideals have not been accepted at certain stages. Unless we are dealing with an "absolute relativism," we have to suppose that only beginning with particular cultural and religious achievements do certain values begin to play a positive role.

Let us examine just one example. What would have been fatal, and therefore was prohibited, for Israel in the time of its first coexistence with the native population of Canaan—tolerance and dialogue—became something positive after the monarchy and the exile, making it possible to assimilate Hellenistic elements into the process of the divine revelation. It is to this peaceful, enriching assimilation that we owe a goodly part of the (protocanonical and especially the deuterocanonical) Wisdom literature of the Old Testament, and nothing less than the fourth Gospel and a considerable part of Paul's teaching in the New.

This presents us with a crucial question. Only a historicist view can explain the Bible as a revelatory process. Are we then to think that this process has come to an end, and that we can today formulate the ideals underlying human rights invariably and universally? If this were to be the case, is this situation due to certain conditions suddenly at hand today that make possible what would have been impossible or harmful in other ages? Or is it rather due to the fact that the revelatory process has ended, and that we are today only drawing universal, timeless conclusions from it?

It seems essential to answer these questions when dealing with "gospel" and "human rights." As we see, then, the relationship is not easy to define. An indication of the difficulty is precisely the tendency of the church to seek a relationship between these rights and the timeless "nature" of the human being. But we cannot proceed without entering into the second point of our *status quaestionis*: that the proclamation of human rights refers not only to human ideals, but to a juridical means of putting these ideals in force. It is not a matter of ideals alone, but of rights. It is to this point that we now turn our attention.

HUMAN RIGHTS AS HUMAN RIGHTS

Indeed, just as, implicit in the proclamation of human rights, we find an ideal of what the human being can and should be, we also find, and explicitly, the means by which this ideal should be attained: law.

The fact that the ideal is presented with a particular means to attain it does not, at least in principle, preclude its being good news, in the strict sense of an "evangelization."

In fact, any evangelization, if we regard it attentively, at the same time as proclaiming something joyful, should, implicitly or explicitly, in order not to remain in the abstract, allude to concrete means by which the human being may appropriate this exultation. Indeed, we have already referred to the diversity of means in which the various versions of the Beatitudes, for example, are incarnated. The virtues to which Matthew alludes, like the Christian condition in Luke, are means proposed by the gospel whereby people may become believers of the good news by which God judges them blessed. An intellectual participation in the mindset of a Hellenistic culture seems to have been the indispensable condition for the fourth Gospel to discharge its function of founding faith in the good news of Jesus. Today, for example, what we might call John's "arguments" fail to convince, precisely because we are without the mediation of a Hellenistic culture.

Accordingly, as we have also seen, this diversification of the good news relativizes, up to a certain point, each version of that news. No version can be removed from its context and applied to another without losing its "evangelizing" function, precisely because it would thereby cease to constitute good news precisely for the new context.

What is the actual scope that one could reasonably wish the application of human rights to have? A facile answer—too facile—would be that, as these rights are universal, they consequently constitute good news for all who find themselves deprived of the goods proclaimed in them. When I say that this would be a too facile answer, I am referring to the perfectly obvious fact (and one recognized in every other area of the juridical) that every right, to be effective, requires enforcement on the part of authorities, and that this enforcement, in turn, requires the existence of courts disposing of the necessary autonomy and authority to put recognized rights in effect.

Thus, all problems relative to human rights will be felt not only by individuals, but by states as well. It is states that are called to account, and what is precisely at issue in the case of many of them is their structural manner of administering justice. It is a well-known fact that, in the area of the most fundamental human rights (such as those, for example, bearing on survival), in almost no country of the world, not to mention the international sphere, are there courts to guarantee the legal force of such rights. If two-thirds of humanity suffer hunger, this obviously indicates a serious deficiency in the effective recognition of human rights. Nevertheless, with the exception of only a few countries, no court, national or international, will entertain a complaint of hunger.

At the same time, the problems that constitute the object of debate in the area of human rights nowadays, and that give rise to investigations and denunciations of the administration of justice in various countries, painful as they are, are de facto limited to far more sophisticated cases, occurring much less frequently than those cited above, which affect two-thirds of humanity.

For example, take the case of the treatment of political prisoners. Does not this inverse proportion between basic human rights on the one hand, and juridical protection and attention on the other, perhaps indicate that we are slipping into a gigantic trap? Is the proclamation of human rights not leading us to maximize, as an assault against freedom of thought and expression, the closing down of a periodical or the imprisonment of a writer, and to minimize, as if they were the consequence of "natural causes," the economico-social conditions that produce, throughout an entire population, the deprivation not only of expression, but also a lack of instruction, and consequently a deprivation of thought?

Let me give you a historical example. The North American "Wild West" was long under the "law of the gun." What would we have thought if some propagandists or other, back then, had counseled people who had been violently stripped of their goods and were in danger of their very lives, not to have recourse to arms, but to "go to court"—when they knew full well that no such courts existed? Would we not have suspected that such propaganda either were incredibly stupid, or else had been invented and paid for by the gunslingers and desperados themselves?

My country has been internationally criticized for the systematic violation of human rights. In some small, insignificant measure, my own human rights have been violated there. Nevertheless, in principle, I agree with the response my government has given to these accusations. It has rightly claimed that respect for individual human rights, in all honesty, is based on the defense of collective human rights. For example, the right of every human being to instruction and education is based on the right to have a country not systematically exploited and robbed, but possessed of the economic wherewithal to offer instruction and education. The right to work is based on the right to have a country where the product of a person's labor may have a just place in international exchange. And so on and so on.

And this brings me to something else—perhaps the most inhumane and anti-evangelical element in the defense of human rights. Somehow we have introjected a guilt that is not ours. Even we, in the poor countries, fall into the ideological trap of imagining that, owing to some genetic defect in our Latin American makeup, all the authorities of our countries are somehow inclined to the insolence of office, sadism, and torture; and that the wealthy countries, doubtless endowed with better genes, give us an example of how to respect a person's human rights. What those wealthy countries are not willing to see is that we are the ones who have to pay the cost of their respect for these rights, with the economic and political crises provoked by the plunder of the planet, which oblige our governments to maintain a minimum of order by means of more and more barbarous and inhumane methods. We are accused of not being democratic, when we are prevented from being so. If my country could apply to the rich nations the economic and political measures that are applied to us today, it would be we who would go and investigate, today—hypocritically, of course—the violations of human rights in *those* countries. The tragic thing about the situation is that those who shape and control the defense of human rights—despite undeniable individual good will—are the same persons who make that defense impossible on three-quarters of the planet.

And there is still more. Our Latin American local churches have to ask the churches of the rich countries to insist on the observance of human rights among ourselves. In the rich countries, even the churches project this false sense of guilt upon us. Through ignorance or impotence, they are somehow unable to denounce the loss of all prophetic sense within themselves, and are apparently content to teach an abstract, universal good news that has no effects on anyone in terms of conversion.

To return to the gospel: a person who is wealthy enough to be able to keep, let us say, almost all the commandments, or, let us suppose, observe almost all human rights, approaches Jesus to ask him what he must do to win eternal life. Apparently there is no Christian church community that will muster the courage to give that person the bad news, the only news that can found the good news for the poor: that you cannot win eternal life this way.

CAPITALISM VS. SOCIALISM IN CHILE

A final observation, one in the area of pastoral theology, will serve to conclude this presentation. It is a well-known fact that, by virtue of good theology or bad (it matters little, for the moment), the church shows a great deal of respect for public power, because it thinks, correctly, that the latter can be decisive for the religious practice of the multitudes. We know, furthermore, that, between this respect for the powers that be and the prophetical function of the church there has been a certain tension in Latin America for some centuries. Nor could it have been otherwise. And the word "tension" is the most moderate word I could use to describe this relationship between political commitment and prophetism.

The Latin American church whose hierarchy has most explicitly and "theologically" renounced prophetism has been, without any doubt, that of Chile. In the Latin American countries, in nearly all of them, there have been moments in which a historical opportunity for a new kind of society, with new economic, political, and cultural bases, has presented itself. It has been necessary to make an option, since the fate of almost the entire population of these countries would depend on the course selected. The Chilean church, in its hierarchy, has refused to make this option, alleging that to do so would divide Christians in matters less important than the gospel. Here we may read the working document of the Chilean bishops entitled "Gospel, Politics, and Socialisms."

Accordingly, if we admit, as we find ourselves obliged to do after what we have seen earlier in this essay, that prophecy and evangelization are intimately related, it is astonishing that there could be persons who imagine an evangelization that would not divide—who think that there could be a "Beatitude" that did not entail its counterpart, a "woe"—in the face of what the gospel itself tells us: "I have come not to bring peace, but the sword. I have come to divide a man from his father, the daughter from her mother, and the mother-in-law from her daughter-in-law; and a man's greatest enemies [will be] the members of his family" (Matt. 10:34–36). Inevitably, good news and bad news are correlatives in any real historical context.

Paradoxically, but also quite symptomatically, the very Chilean episcopate that had been the most explicit and incisive in refusing the historical option, is now perhaps the most committed to the defense of human rights. No especially keen eyes are required in order to suppose that the underlying attitude has not changed. It is just that the Chilean hierarchy no longer sees anything in the defense of human rights that would be divisive!

I surely do not wish to belittle the risks of such a defense. I only wish to emphasize that any church accused of being politically beholden can simply say that it is not making an option, it is only reminding the powers that be of certain basic moral obligations. It does not condemn the system, only its excesses.

Let us be perfectly clear here. I have not the slightest doubt that there are heroic individuals who have had to suffer and even die in defense of human rights. I have not the slightest doubt that, for some persons whose human rights are attacked (a tiny minority, surely), the position of the church has often been good news. I have not the slightest doubt that, had I been tortured, I should have counted myself happy and fortunate if the church had come to my defense, even by simply appealing in behalf of my human rights.

But I will not and cannot lose sight of the great proportion of human beings who lead a subhuman life and to whom no one pays any attention, let alone affords the juridical instruments—national or international—to mount an effective attempt to claim their rights (be it only by reason of the simple fact that the media are precisely in the hands of those who violate those rights).

In other words, to the extent that, by its words and actions, the church intimates that the gospel today is identified with human rights, it conveys the sorrowful news of its attachment to international capitalism. Capitalism exists to the extent that its game rules prevail—rules introduced independently, we may suppose, of any concern for human rights. But the moment these rules become rights, no one can attack the actual essence of the regime without changing its game rules, without violating the law, without attacking the rights that have been declared "human," although so few benefit from them in terms of any privileges deriving from the rules.

In Chile, then, the very bishops who, in the name of the gospel, have declared themselves against abandoning capitalism and moving toward socialism, are the ones who today defend—with all sincerity and courage, I have no doubt—human rights. It is the same position, the same rejection of the real commitment that divides and opposes: committing oneself to a particular societal model, whatever others might think.

In other words, if, as we have seen, revelation has always been an educational process in which everything collapses if the necessary steps are omitted, if ready-made answers are preferred to flexibility, then a determination of the exact position of the historical human being in any given case becomes a key question for theology.

Allow me to use an example—this time some theological fiction. Moses was on his way back from the burning bush. Only he stepped into a time machine and found himself among the hearers of Jesus Christ, God's own Word in person. Thus, he was able to include elements of what he had heard from Jesus in his own message to the Jewish people. He now goes to the Jewish people, and tells them that God declares happy the poor of spirit, and the meek, and that when struck on one cheek, they should turn the other. Centuries pass. The Canaanite population still occupies Palestine. No David, no Solomon, no Isaiah appear in history. Neither does Jesus Christ. Then, in the year 2700 from the foundation of Rome — today — a party of Mongol explorers discovers, in old Egyptian ruins, a relief depicting a group of foreign slaves offering gifts to a pharaoh. This people, now lost to history, seems to have been called "Jewish." Nothing of theirs remains but this inscription.

To any of you who may be accustomed to the solemnity of academic theology, my little piece of theological fiction may look somewhat sacrilegious. And yet it is terribly serious, especially if we think of theology from a pastoral standpoint, as our subject obliges us to do.

The great question for the task of evangelization, posed by the fact of human rights as rights, at least in Latin America, is that of the logical condemnation it implies of those who fail to respect these rights, even if they do so only in order to protect the people from greater evils, or to attain more effectively the ideals contained in these rights — ultimately even to consecrate them precisely as rights. In other words, these rights, for the moment only proclaimed, unconsciously function as an ideological weapon, diverting into harmless byways the rebellion of the people who are paying with their inhuman situation the price of respect for these rights in the wealthy countries.

In all probability, the good news that God considered them happy, and would make them actually happy, was addressed by Jesus to the poor as such, even though that category also included petty criminals and exploiters. What was important in the judgment of God was above all the status of these persons as poor and outcast. For tactical reasons, and certainly "respectable" ones, it would appear that the church is responding to Jesus today in the same terms as did the religious authorities of his time: Cursed are the poor who neither know nor respect the law. God grant, then, when the gates of happiness finally swing wide for the poor, the doctors of the law will only be able to stand in awe at seeing even torturers precede them into the reign of heaven.

Let me briefly recall the line of argumentation I have taken in this essay.

After an examination of the New Testament's presentation of the task of evangelization, we saw that there is an inescapable, intrinsic relation between the gospel to be transmitted by the church and the human ideal underlying the proclamation of human rights. But we have also seen that the gospel is not some timeless declaration, universally valid once proclaimed: the good news is couched in a historical process, and occupies a particular place in that process. Otherwise it could not be called good news, since ideals appear in a positive manner on the horizon of the human only in particular stages of human promotion, and not before.

And this brought us to our second point. When something is granted as a right—as something that can be demanded in justice—this normally occurs because a sufficient abundance of goods has been amassed and juridical tools exist for the enforcement of such rights. By contrast, we see the current state of humanity so deprived of the goods allegedly erected into rights, and of the juridical tools that might ensure their enforcement, that we readily conclude that, while they morally correspond to the ideal, the juridical formulation of that ideal constitutes an ideological trap set for the most deprived countries of the earth.

When human rights are violated without reason, this would always be a crime, and its denunciation by the church is good news that ought to be related to the gospel. But when human rights are violated because the game rules governing relations among peoples, races, and social classes demand it, even the most recent social encyclicals agree that the denunciation ought not to be aimed so much at the violations (under pain of disqualifying the weak and the oppressed) as against the structures that provoke the systematic commission of these violations.

Only the latter denunciation is "evangelical" and "good news," and it requires the courage to make an option, without divine guarantees, for those systems of social coexistence—national and international—in which these violations, even when they might occur, are no longer necessary, or at least not with the same ironbound necessity.

CHAPTER 5

The Shift within Latin American Theology

In a lecture delivered at Regis College, Toronto, in March 1983, Segundo stressed the importance of a shift in approach that had taken place among some liberation theologians during the 1970s. Instead of the intellectual task of deideologizing in dialogue with the social sciences, these theologians began to look to the poor as the primary locus or source of theology. The author provides reasons for his belief that such a shift is seriously mistaken.

Source: *The Shift within Latin American Theology* (Toronto: Regis College Press, 1983).

There are so many and at times such ridiculous commonplaces about Latin American theology, especially about so-called liberation theology, that it should be clear from the beginning that I do not want to bore you by trying to correct them. For instance, I will not try to show that this theology has nothing more to do with violence than the traditional theology one learns, and which was used in the northern hemisphere to allow Christians to kill without regret millions of people in World War II as well as in other battlefields following it. I do not pretend either, for it would be naive and unrealistic, to deny that within what is labeled Latin American liberation theology there could be and surely often are superficial, boastful, and excessive features.

Rather, I prefer to deal with an important shift which, after the middle or even the early 1970s, has clearly divided theologians and, more generally speaking and taking account of the receptivity and creativity of lay people, has changed the way of doing a liberative theology in our continent.

I will speak then of at least two theologies of liberation coexisting now in Latin America. And, given the fact that they did not appear simultaneously, I will try to give you a historical account of their respective causes, the context of their appearance, their aims, their methods, and their results. In so doing, it is my hope that this historical view may help to avoid a superficial view of what is happening in Latin America, as well as global misconceptions about the development and different viewpoints during these twenty years of theology in our continent.

I

Contrary to the most common assumption, Latin American theology, without any precise title, began to have clearly distinctive features at least ten years before Gustavo Gutiérrez's well-known book *A Theology of Liberation.* This was a kind of baptism, but the baby had already grown old.

The real beginning came simultaneously from many theologians working in different countries and places in Latin America, even before the first session of Vatican II. In any case, these developments began some years before the Constitution *Gaudium et Spes* in 1965, which, to a great extent, was used afterward as an official support for the main views of this liberation theology.

Let us, therefore, go back to the early 1960s. Something was happening, more or less at the same time, all over Latin America, something which established a new context for understanding our Christian faith and, hence, for doing theology. It is, I believe, of great importance to precisely understand the social, political, and theological context of this event.

Until 1964, when the military takeover of Brazil began to foreshadow a reversal of privileges afforded to universities within society, the state universities at least were ruled by a students' movement created at the beginning of this century in Argentina. This movement, which was successful in almost every Latin American country, was aimed at giving the university the necessary freedom it needed over against political governments and other pressures.

It did not mean a depoliticization of universities. On the contrary, by making students the principal rulers of university life (together with faculty members and groups of professionals), and by gaining political autonomy the state university became a sort of parallel power in politics. It was, so to speak, a state within the state. It became free to support any kind of political ideas, and above all to unmask, through all kinds of intellectual tools, the mystifying ideologies used by our governments to hide and to justify the inhuman situation of the majority of our population.

It was precisely in this context, however one may evaluate it, that a new approach to Christian faith developed among students. It involved a kind of Christian conversion as far as the social consequences of our faith were concerned. Without taking this context into account, one easily falls into the mistaken notion that liberation theology is a specific branch of theology, recently created and somehow inflated, dealing with "liberation," whatever this term may mean. Another mistake coming from the lack of knowledge of this context consists in believing that liberation theology in Latin America came from a particular understanding of European political theology.

Before knowing anything about political theology, if it existed at all at this time, the university student, using above all the notion of the social function of *ideologies,* had already discovered that our whole culture, whatever the intention in constructing it may have been, was working for the benefit of the ruling classes. It was not, of course, necessary to be a Marxist to make such a commonsense discovery, but it is also true that many Christian students at the university were led by their Marxist fellows to this realization and to be concerned with this fact.

Furthermore, Christian students could do nothing except include *theology* — the understanding of Christian faith — into the ideological mechanisms structuring the whole of our culture. And when I say "the whole of our culture" I mean by this that even though ideologies are consciously or unconsciously developed in the ruling classes which benefit from them, they also pervade the whole of society, since they are introjected even into the minds of those who are their victims. Unlearned and so incapable of utilizing developed tools of ideological suspicion in a culture considered impartial and the same for all social classes, poor and marginalized people were led by the culture to accept distorted and hidden oppressive elements which justify their situation, and, among all these elements, a distorted and oppressive theology.

From Christian students to theologians working with them, this ideological suspicion thus became a source of a new vision about what theology should become and about how a theologian was supposed to work to unmask the anti-Christian elements hidden in a so-called Christian society.

In order to give some concrete flesh to this quite abstract reflection, let me give you an example. Among thousands of possible examples, I will choose one, since the same example will be helpful later on in my lecture to show the shift between this first trend in liberation theology and the second.

I suppose that you are familiar with the name of at least one of the outstanding Latin American theologians today, Leonardo Boff, a Franciscan from Brazil. In an article written two years ago after one month of pastoral experiences in one of Brazil's poorest states, the state of Acre on the frontier between Brazil and Bolivia, Boff, trying to reflect on the Christian faith — that is to say, trying to theologize with those poor and uncultivated members of Basic Christian Communities — experienced some difficulties in dialogue and communication between such different levels of culture. But he tells us in his article that once, at least, the dialogue was set in motion when he asked: How did Jesus redeem us? Many people answered: "through his cross." Others put the same idea in slightly different terms: "through his suffering."

At this point Boff recalls his reflection on those answers of grass-roots Christian people. His reflection can be meaningful for us since it shows, in a particular *theological* case, the global attitude of suspicion which a university student is supposed to have about popular religion and its function in an oppressive society like ours. Boff writes: "I asked myself: Why do (grass-roots) people immediately associate redemption with the cross? Undoubtedly because they have not learned the historical character of redemption—that is, of the process of liberation. Perhaps it is so because their own life is nothing but suffering and crosses, the cross that society has managed to make them carry on their shoulders." And the consequence for theology develops in the article: "A Jesus who only suffers is not liberating; he generates the cult of suffering and fatalism. It is important *to re-locate within the mind of (common) people the cross in its true place.*"[1]

I think that this example can provide a good indication of both the method and the aim of this first theology of liberation.

No amount of subtle argument can conceal that the only relevant methodological feature of Latin American theology is, as a matter of fact, to start thinking not from a systematic listing of theological problems linked by an inner logic for the sake of an orthodox and credible answer to every problem, but instead, in the precise context I am describing, to start both from a commitment to think for the sake of poor and oppressed people, and from a consideration of their praxis every time we perceive that this praxis is linked, through theology, to the oppressive mechanisms of the whole culture. This consideration of praxis aims at reformulating a Christian theology capable of transforming this praxis into a more liberative one—that is to say, aiming at orthopraxis; in this example, it aims at preventing passivity and fatalism.

The context I am describing should prevent one from falling into two superficial and mistaken preconceptions. The first one is that liberation theology comes out of practice. And the second one is that it makes orthopraxis, instead of orthodoxy, the main criterion for its solutions.

In the example I presented, one can see the true role of praxis in theologizing. Of course, as we understand it, the passivity and fatalism of common people belong indeed to the practical side of their lives, insofar as they are not intellectual problems about their faith calling for theoretical solutions. Praxis means, therefore, a starting point based on a systematic suspicion which tries to perceive any possible link between some oppressive and inhuman behavior, and a similarly oppressive and inhuman understanding of Christian faith. In this sense, and only in this sense, has the first line of liberation theology stressed the relevance of the hermeneutic function of praxis. And I am not trying to belittle it. But at least serious theologians in Latin America, as one can see from the example proposed, do not aim at reducing theology to more or less superficial and spontaneous answers to the problems which Christian people *perceive* in their everyday life and which they bring forward when they meet in Basic Christian Communities.

Secondly and accordingly, when theologians in our continent stress the relevance of orthopraxis over against orthodoxy, they are not saying that they prefer the former to the latter, or that they are not concerned with the historical development of Christian dogmas as a true criterion in theology. They are as concerned with orthodoxy as everybody else. They cannot, however, deny that the starting point of their task as theologians is closely connected with the concrete facts of *heteropraxis* that are clearly discernable, like the cult of suffering and fatalism Boff was alluding to in the example. Do not forget that we live at the same time in one of the most Christian lands and in one of the most inhuman ones. We cannot escape the question of the connection between both facts. And, of course, what appears at the beginning as a heuristic starting point, leading our theological inquiries, must also appear at the end as a relevant though always vague and elusive focus — namely, orthopraxis. Humanization and liberation in real people should measure to some extent our theological achievements, no matter how provisional and ambiguous these achievements are.

That is why the aim of this first theology of liberation from the beginning was to remake, to the extent of our possibilities, the whole of theology. Being faithful to both, orthodoxy and orthopraxis, we felt the necessity of deideologizing our language and our message about God, the church, the sacraments, grace, sin, the meaning of Jesus Christ, and so on. We were not interested at all in creating a new kind of branch of theology *that spoke of liberation,* or in making liberation the explicit center of the whole of theology, instead of any other theological theme. In this sense, the title this theological trend received after Gustavo Gutiérrez's famous book *A Theology of Liberation*[2] made us perhaps quite fashionable, but helped also to distort to some extent our aim and to push us toward a useless battle against many European and North American theologians, and finally to create suspicion among church authorities about our supposed intention of substituting "supernatural and vertical salvation" with a historical and political liberation.

In any case, deideologizing our customary interpretation of Christian faith was, for us, the necessary task in order to get the whole church to carry to our people an understanding of our faith both more faithful to Jesus' gospel and more capable of contributing to the humanization of all people and social classes on our continent.[3]

Of course, this theological liberation was supposed, through pastoral activities and agents, to reach *at a different pace* different social classes, thus becoming universal with the same kind of universality that can be attributed to the conflictive gospel of Jesus. As I have already said, the context for this new trend in Latin American theology was the university, or, in other words, middle-class people. Now, the middle classes are usually considered by sociologists as the most mobile and creative part of society, inclined either to provoke rightist upheavals when they feel their interests or social order threatened, or to be involved in restructuring and liberating society when they feel guilty.

Thus it was not the oppressed people, but the middle classes, beginning with students, who received the first features of this liberation theology as a joyful conversion and a new commitment. As middle class, they clearly perceived that they themselves belonged to the side of oppressors and were more or less linked with an ideology fostering their interests. As Christians, they felt increasingly concerned with fighting for the liberation of poor and marginalized people, but also blocked by many oppressive elements which they had always considered constitutive parts of their faith. A new theological vision of faith was thus assumed by a wide range of middle-class Christians as a liberative force so that they accepted and fulfilled a new type of Christian commitment to liberation, even against their own material interests and privileges.

As theologians, we believed at that time, and some of us still believe, that this movement among the most active and creative members of the church could eventually reach, sooner or later, all oppressed people on our continent, through the pastoral activities of a church following a new line and carrying a new message. Thus the first theology of liberation was committed to a long-term and far-reaching goal. . . . But something different happened.

II

Now, as I examine the second line in liberation theology, I believe that it would be useful to recall the elements we have brought forward in the first line, namely: the origin of a theology of conversion among middle-class groups, the methodological trend to suspect that the customary way of understanding Christian faith was distorted at all levels of society by ideological bias that concealed and justified the status quo, and, finally, the long-term aim of providing the pastoral activities of the church with a new and deideologized theology capable of speaking about the common themes of Christian faith as they were at the beginning—that is, a revelation of the humanizing and liberative will of God and of God's own being.

Let me briefly look now at a new context for theologizing: the common people. This context was already there in most Latin American societies, but it was discovered, so to speak, with the help of some popular or populist movements which came to public attention in the early 1970s and still more openly in the late 1970s. I would like to call attention to the fact that in this new context for theologizing it is important that one depart from the customary view of two things: the intellectual foundation for theologizing and the usual and culturally simplistic view of Third World countries as only economically underdeveloped and poor societies.

Let us follow very briefly one of these powerful popular movements in Latin America, the so-called Peronism of Argentina. As you know, perhaps, Perón was freely elected and reelected president of Argentina, and his government lasted for more than ten years until a military takeover in the late 1950s. Perón went into exile and remained in Spain for almost twenty years. And, then, another free election gave him the presidency again for a new term, one which terminated with his death.

This is the rough historical outline of political events which will provide us with a central fact and with an excellent example of the shift within Latin American intellectuals in general and within the theology of liberation in particular.

What happened among intellectuals and theologians during those twenty years of Perón's exile? When Perón went into exile, Argentina was deeply divided politically. For different and understandable reasons, the upper classes, the upper middle-class, intellectuals, and the majority of the Catholic hierarchy were utterly anti-Peronist. The lower middle class and the working classes, both in urban and rural areas, remained fervently Peronist during these two decades.

It is perhaps worth noting that the intellectuals' disaffection with Perón during his first presidential period was clearly caused by the liberal ground of Perón's vague political ideology, rightist nationalism, linked with elements akin to fascism and anti-Semitism. Intellectuals were against Perón for the sake of democracy and for the sake of the people themselves.

In any case, the successive failures of many military and some civilian non-Peronist governments made both intellectuals in general and Catholics in particular reflect on their former political position. They seemingly discovered the mechanism of their political mistake, and they were converted to Peronism for the sake of the same popular majority, who suffered oppression from every regime but was always faithful to its old leader. Thus when Perón came back from exile, he had at his disposal besides the old and monolithic popular support the new support of the majority of intellectuals and particularly of a "new" theology of liberation.

I guess that this conversion of intellectuals and, hence, of theologians (since the latter belong by definition to the former by their task, *intellectus fidei*) had its roots in a painful experience intellectuals often have. In Latin America and everywhere else they try to think and to create ideas for the sake of the common good. They sometimes speak against their own interests in the name of a voiceless people supposedly incapable of recognizing where their actual interest is. And finally they discover not only that they are not understood by the people for the sake of whom they have tried to think and to speak, but also that the main stream of history leaves them apart from popular victories.

Conversion means, then, for many intellectuals a kind of self-negation. Instead of teaching, they should learn. And in order to learn from common people, they should incorporate themselves, even mentally, with these common people, and give up the chronic suspicion among intellectuals that common people are always wrong.

Given this background, let us consider, from this example, the crisis of the mid-1970s in the Latin American theology of liberation, and the following shift from the first to the second one.

Something was obvious: the rise of popular or populist movements either outside or inside the church had shown that common people had neither understood nor welcomed anything from the first theology of liberation, and had actually reacted against its criticism of the supposed oppressive elements of popular religion. They resisted the new pastoral trends trying to correct it. The first theology of liberation had raised hopes, enthusiasm, and conversion only among the middle classes which were integrated into a European culture. It is true that their concern for the poor and oppressed had made them dangerous for the status quo, but the persecution of middle-class leftists all over Latin America did not fill the gap between them and grass-roots peoples.

It appeared then that if theologians were still to be the "organic intellectuals" of the common people—that is to say, useful as intellectuals charged with the understanding of popular faith—they were obliged to learn how oppressed people lived their faith. Thus Enrique Dussel coined for theologians and pastoral agents the expression, *the discipleship of the poor.* And Leonardo Boff spoke about a new "ecclesiogenesis," *a church born from the poor.*[4] And Gustavo Gutiérrez put as the title of his new book *The Power of the Poor in History.*[5]

Theologians, wanting to be in religious matters the "organic intellectuals" of poor and uncultivated people, began then to understand their function as one of unifying and structuring people's understanding of their faith, as well as grounding and defending the practices coming from this faith.

Of course, not all Latin American theologians agreed with this shift. Some still refuse to give up the first critical function which comes out of a suspicion that theology, like other all-pervasive cultural features, can and perhaps should be considered an instrument of oppression and, hence, as a non-Christian theology. Facts point so obviously in that direction that theologians belonging explicitly to the second line cannot but raise the same central suspicion.

Let us recall here as an example the experience of Leonardo Boff trying to dialogue with members of Basic Christian Communities in Acre about Jesus' redemption. He cannot but conclude that theologians must (in his own words) "relocate within the minds of (common) people the cross in its true place." In saying that, Leonardo seems to naturally act as a theologian of the first line of Latin American liberation theology. But at the beginning of his article we find a brief introduction containing the methodological principle of the second one. He writes there: "In a church that has opted for the people, for the poor and for their liberation, the *principal learning of theology* comes from the contact with (grass-roots) people. Who evangelizes the theologian? The faith witnessed by faithful people, their capacity to introduce God in all their struggling, their resistance against the oppression they customarily have to suffer."[6]

I do not know if you perceive that there is an undoubtedly involuntary contradiction here between the claim of having been evangelized by the poor and taught by them, and, on the other hand, the pretension of relocating in people's minds the true meaning of the cross and suffering. How can a passive and fatalistic conception of God evangelize the theologian?

I believe that at this point we both grasp the meaning and appreciate the difficulty in the shift in Latin American liberation theology I was alluding to in the title of this lecture. No doubt, both share the same global intention of liberating and humanizing those who suffer the most from unjust structures on our continent. But this cannot conceal the fact that we are faced here with two different theologies under the same name: different in scope, different in method, different in presuppositions, and different in pastoral consequences.

III

Let me now conclude this lecture by listing some of the opposite characteristics of both liberation theologies now existing and working simultaneously in Latin America.

If we look at their *scope,* both lines seem to have failed, to a considerable extent, in fulfilling the expectations raised by them.

It is clear by now that the first line of liberation theology failed in providing the Latin American church with a new and deideologized theology dealing, in a liberative way, with the customary themes of pastoral activities: God, sacraments, grace, and so forth. I think that three principal causes were influential in this failure.

The first was the *title.* Instead of taking over the old theology by slowly giving a new content to every field of theology, the new title sounded as if it were pointing to a new and dangerous kind of theology more concerned with politics than with a serious improvement of theology taught in universities and seminaries. To this inner danger was soon added the pressures and threats of civilian or military authorities on the church to make it avoid any activities explicitly connected with the theology of liberation.

Secondly, the new theology, identified by its title, to the extent that it reached not only theologians but also large segments of the middle-class lay population, raised all over Latin America a wave of doubt and strong criticism about *popular religion* (otherwise and perhaps more aptly called "popular Catholicism") as being oppressive and, all in all, non-Christian. It provoked a growing reaction against liberation theology among church officials striving to keep the masses within the church. The accusation of being more or less influenced by Marxism in this analysis of the relationship between religion and oppression was an easy although unfair reason for preventing the majority of theologians in this line of thought from teaching in institutes, seminaries and faculties destined to prepare pastoral agents for the church in Latin America.

Thirdly, many Latin American theologians, under this banner which made them fashionable in the international market, if not fully appreciated in their particular churches, engaged in relentless and quite useless battle with their European and North American peers comparing methods and theological loci. As a result, twenty years later, Latin American liberation theology is more a repetitive apology for itself than a constructive theological discourse.

It is far more difficult to determine to just what extent the second line of liberation theology has achieved its objective, not only because it has been functioning for a more limited time on the continent, but, above all, because of a certain modesty in the very objective proposed. Actually, I believe it should be clear that this modesty is part of the conversion which is required of the intellectual confronted with the interests and way of thinking of the people themselves. To some extent this conversion demands a renunciation of critical and creative characteristics which intellectuals can draw out of themselves, in order to be freely engaged as an instrument of the people.

It is not odd, then, that a theologian in this precise context cannot present serious works, or better, works which would be considered weighty by other intellectuals who are working in the same area of thought. Thus, for example, the second theological work of Gustavo Gutiérrez, his book *The Power of the Poor in History*, could not be considered, even by a long shot, to be of the same intellectual quality that characterized *A Theology of Liberation*. Anyone who ignores the context and shift we are studying would think that the theological quality of Gustavo had markedly diminished and that the work does not rise above a certain sort of debatable propaganda, although it is of a quality beyond that which characterizes ordinary people and what they do. The same comparison could be made of certain books of Leonardo Boff such as *Jesus Christ Liberator,* but above all, *Passion of Christ — Passion of the World,*[7] in relation to more recent works such as those which deal with new ecclesial forms and a church which is born of the people.

As a result, trying to indicate exactly to what extent the second line of liberation theology has succeeded or not in its own quest, I would say that, considering the context, it can only be said that it has only achieved its objective halfway and on two levels.

In the first place, it is true that this second line of thought has had more success in winning over for liberation theology an important part of the ecclesiastical hierarchy. We have already indicated that the resistance to the first line came from a criticism of it vis-à-vis popular religiosity, or simply, because of its way of conceiving Christian religiosity in Latin America. In that regard, the second line dissipated many suspicions when it accepted the religion of ordinary people as a generally liberating element. Where the church felt itself strongest in protecting ordinary people, even against governments and their repression, as in the case of Brazil, the second line was widely accepted. From this point of view, the Puebla Conference would have been, if not an acceptance of this line, at least a compromise between it and those who wanted a global condemnation of liberation theology.

Nevertheless, it is impossible to ignore, whatever our opinion about the justification of popular religiosity might be, the political aspect of this second line which is just as or even more accentuated than that of the first. Actually, the first line of liberation theology came in contact with political concerns through a redefinition of faith which paid close attention to the influence of faith on the political activity of Christians. However, the second line accepts, up to a certain point, the control and design of a political posture for liberation from the people themselves. When theologians become part of the people, they lend even more political support for the political revindication of the people. It is not in vain that a theology linked with Peronism is even more political than an attempt to reformulate theology in general in a deideologized way. The same thing could be said about Brazil where the bishops of several dioceses distributed political guidelines for the last election to teach people how to make a political option among different parties. And the same thing could be said about the relationship between Basic Christian Communities and politics in the whole process which characterizes the present situation in Nicaragua.

Furthermore, there is another level where the objectives achieved by the second line of liberation theology should be considered, although as very modest achievements. As intense as the theologian's conversion to ordinary people might be, this intellectual cannot totally renounce the exercise of a certain criticism. We have already seen that sort of "lapse" or contradiction between the pretension of learning theology from common people and the attempt of relocating in people's minds the true meaning of suffering in the example of Leonardo Boff. But generally speaking, this second line of theology has tried to provide more balanced principles despite its seeming lack of criticism toward popular phenomena. It sees the issue as one "of rescuing and promoting Christian values in popular culture." To that end, obviously, one has to be immersed in it, but not with closed eyes. Beyond doubt there are negative elements in a culture, while at the same time a theologian discovers magnificent liberating aspects. It is a question, then, of distinguishing one from the other and, to the extent possible, of promoting some while restraining or repressing others.

I think it is imperative to explain briefly why the results on this level have been much less than were expected. And I believe this explanation is more necessary here since the Latin American context at the cultural level could be unfamiliar.

As opposed to North America, Latin America is a mosaic of cultures to a degree and depth difficult to imagine outside that context. It is not a question of the existence of immigrants from western or central Europe — they certainly exist as well — or even of immigrants from cultures developed for centuries in Asia. Rather it is a question of very ancient cultures from the time of the conquest and colonization by Spain and Portugal, pre-Columbian cultures like the civilizations of the Aztecs, Mayas, Incas, and other indigenous civilizations (like that of the Guarany who made up the old Jesuit reductions), who have remained as enclaves in a Western civilization introduced and imposed by Occidental conquerors. And to this one should add the introduction in many countries of African slaves who were violently deprived of their own religion and obliged to accept Christianity.

The most important thing here is to recognize that these African or American indigenous people managed to preserve for centuries under Christian names, rites, and creed their ancient cultures and religions. These enormous efforts of the ancient cultures to survive the growing impact of modern Western culture, supported by a market economy which does not recognize any cultural differences, have only very recently been acknowledged by the church. And this struggle has been given a liberating character. It is, in reality, the right of these peoples to maintain their own cultures. Furthermore, those cultures, closed in on themselves, display certain values which can be considered very Christian as opposed to the consumerism and growing individualism of Western urban culture.

The second liberation theology we have spoken about has given great importance to those values. But perhaps it has not taken account of an important anthropological element of these cultures—namely, their monolithic character. They are such, in part, because they are primitive and, in part, in order to defend themselves better. Many efforts to "rescue Christian values" from values in these cultures which are not Christian, and especially the religions of these peoples, have failed because they have not realized that everything is bound to a unitary understanding of existence. It is a question of survival where any change (for example, in religion) is considered terribly dangerous.

Thus, partly as a result of this second liberation trend, we now see a great amount of energy unleashed in pastoral work with these people from ancient cultures. But in trying to slightly modify rites, places, and instruments of worship, the idea of the religious, and so on, all in the name of rescuing the most valuable and liberative Christian elements, this energy is not generally producing the hoped for results.

Let us now consider certain elements relative to the *method* in both lines of liberation theology. For this purpose it will be interesting to consider some observations of Jon Sobrino, another of the liberation theologians who has passed through the same shift from the first to the second position.

In an article given as an address to a meeting precisely on theological method, which took place in Mexico in 1975,[8] Sobrino refers to the context in which liberation theology was born—namely, the Latin American university—as something closely related with its methodology. He says that the founders of this theology were not professional theologians, but rather people that "had become theologians as counselors of action groups, such as priests involved in pastoral work." From this context arises an important methodological characteristic to which we have already referred and which Sobrino introduces with these words:

We think that Latin American theology is more conscious than European theology of its very status as *awareness.* Obviously, *this is the problem of the ideologization of theology,* in regard to which Latin American theology is more sensitive than European theology.[9]

And precisely because of this sensitivity, according to Sobrino himself, the *social sciences* are used in a way similar to the use theology made of philosophy in past centuries. The social sciences provide the theologian who wants to carry out a deideologizing task with valuable cognitive tools, but tools which, because of their complexity and subtlety, are beyond the grasp of the majority of people.

But in a later article Sobrino goes on to the second line of liberation theology. The subtitle of this article is quite interesting: "The poor: the theological locus of ecclesiology." And there he writes:

Thus the Church of the Poor finds the historical site of conversion, *the place of the other and the force to become the other.* And the most important thing, although it is apparently trivial in terms of mere conceptual reflection, is that it consequently happens in good measure.[10]

The process of becoming the other in the church thus occupies the theological position that the social sciences and their instrumentality for deideologization held in the first variety of liberation theology. Up to a certain point it is interesting that the second line returns to philosophy in a certain way, because it finds in philosophy the means to establish the theological rationale for becoming other among common people. One can observe, for example, the profound influence of the philosopher Emmanuel Levinas as much in Enrique Dussel as in Juan Carlos Scanone, two of the outstanding theologians of the second line.[11]

To conclude this lecture, I realize that many central questions are still unanswered. And it is true that I have no answer for many of them. For example, are these two lines complementary? Are they opposed? Of course, as attempts to liberate and to humanize the same people through the same Christian faith, they should be considered complementary. Nevertheless, they are based on opposite presuppositions, they have different strategies, and their methods are not easily compatible in reality. Perhaps the only thing we can take for granted is that, after twenty years at work, liberation theology is profoundly alive on our continent, although taking different forms in different classes or groups of society. It is our common hope that those different forms will prove to be convergent. In any case, with this amount of data, one can perhaps have a better and more accurate picture of what is happening in Latin America with liberation theology or, more simply, with theology.

But in trying to focus attention on the important shift which took place on our continent in the middle of the 1970s, my aim has been not only to provide a surer, more complex and balanced account of something abstract and remote. My purpose, whether or not I have succeeded in accomplishing it, was also from the beginning to challenge. The challenge is not to do the same thing as we are doing, for this would not make sense. But certainly it is to fight creatively for the same cause in your own context, with your own tools and, above all, with your own hearts.

PART III

FOCUS ON CHRISTOLOGY

CHAPTER 6

A Note on Irony and Sorrow

*What Has Happened to Liberation Theology
in Its More than Twenty Years?*

*It seems clear that the chef-d'oeuvre of Segundo's career thus far has been
the three massive volumes of his christology (or "antichristology"), El hombre de hoy ante Jesús de Nazaret (1982); English, 5 volumes, Jesus of
Nazareth Yesterday and Today. This article and the next contain the most
extensive responses of Segundo to equally lengthy critiques of his work by
the Brazilian Hugo Assman, and the Mexican Javier Jiménez Limón. The
first article is concerned with the critique of Assmann, who objected to
Segundo's criticism of other liberation theologians such as Jon Sobrino (El
Salvador), Leonardo Boff (Brazil), and Gustavo Gutiérrez (Peru). In his reply,
Segundo continues the discussion of the previous chapter regarding the
correct method of a liberating theology.*

> Source: "Nota sobre ironias y tristeza: Que aconteceu com a Teo-
> logia da Libertação em sua trajetória de mais de vinte anos
> (Reposta a Hugo Assmann)?" *Perspectiva Teológica* 15 (no. 37,
> 1983): 385–400.

In the preceding issue of this periodical, my good friend Hugo Assmann
undertook and completed the "mission impossible" of reviewing the three
thick volumes of my *El Hombre de Hoy ante Jesús de Nazaret*, which
appeared a year ago in Spanish.[1] Mission impossible indeed, had it not
been undertaken by someone who knows me as well as does Hugo; we are
close friends, and Hugo has an extraordinary talent for allowing the authors
he reads to express themselves (in his own thoughts).

This may not have been readily apparent. The reader may have thought,
paging through Hugo's notes, that Hugo has gone on the attack, with all of
his compiling of quotations from my work instead of tracing my line of

thought in his own words and then evaluating it. But while the reader may be deceived by this (only apparent) attack, the author is not. With every citation, he recognizes the exact point at which his thought adds a new building block to the edifice of the work under construction. And thus he joyfully perceives that Hugo's procedure is not one of mere talent, but the fruit of a meditated strategy, and of a profound comprehension of each of the steps I take in my book.

I cannot imagine how readers (or nonreaders?) of my work may react to this accumulation of citations, at first so disconcerting. Doubtless they will want to ask questions. And I suppose that they would ask Hugo these questions. Hugo, meanwhile—not to escape having to answer them—would pass them on to me.

And here is where I have a practical problem. Suppose that, in the present article or note, following upon Hugo's, I now strike a dialogue with what he has said in his. But it happens that Hugo's article or note—by an author, then, who understands marvelously well what I wrote—has me speak for myself. So what do I do now, dialogue with myself? This time it is I who would have the "mission impossible"!

I think, for reasons that the reader will perceive in these few pages, that the best thing for me to do will be to take as the subject of my reflection and dialogue a friendly observation that Hugo has made at the conclusion of his review, and attempt to explicitate its meaning.[2]

The second last sentence in Hugo's review—the one that the reader will doubtless remember best, if only because of the questions and suspicions it might arouse—runs as follows: "I think that Juan Luis is harming himself . . . by certain biting or ironic criticisms of Jon Sobrino, Gustavo Gutiérrez, and others."

What is the meaning of this observation of Hugo's? What is the meaning of such criticisms in themselves? What do they mean in me?

I

I have an advantage here, which I am not sure that it will actually be fair to use, but I shall use it all the same. In order to make this observation at the end of his reading, Hugo has doubtless had to have recourse to his memory. Well, I happen to have, in manuscript, an Index of Authors Cited, which I hope will appear in subsequent editions of my book.[3]

I begin, then, by looking in my index to find my references to this other close friend of mine, for nearly thirty years now, Gustavo Gutiérrez. I find seven in all. Among them, one (*El Hombre de Hoy ante Jesús de Nazaret*, 2:46) merely alludes to the fact that, along with Hugo and myself, Gustavo was the recipient of a critical "open" letter, addressed more specifically to José Míguez Bonino, and more generally, to Latin American theology, by Jürgen Moltmann. Three other references (ibid., pp. 575, 582, and 616) simply support things I say in my book. (The first, situating Gustavo's *A*

Theology of Liberation chronologically, enables me to explain the fact that it cites European political theology, which was still unknown to Latin Americans when, before Vatican II, what would later be called liberation theology began to be developed.)

Three references remain, and I leave it to the reader to make the necessary judgments:

> Indeed, it has been suggested that we must have a theology of *captivity*. Surely, as an alternative to a theology of liberation, this suggestion must be rejected. No one claims to canonize captivity because liberation is so long coming. But the proposal acquires a certain sense in view of the triumphalism with which certain Latin American theologians speak of liberation as if it were within arm's reach; whereas comprehensive Latin American reality, the increasing misery of the poor, their evident disorientation, and situations (and forecasts of situations) of still greater repression and oppression, are calling for a bridge between theology and reality. We confess that this is the impression we gather from the very title—despite all critical rectifications and qualifications—of the selection of Gustavo Gutiérrez's writings, *The Power of the Poor in History*. What "power" is being referred to? Where has this power been hiding itself for lo, these four centuries of Western colonialism or this century and a half of independence? Why not analyze the how, the why, and even the where, of the *weakness* of the poor in history? [*Hombre de Hoy ante Jesús*, 2:583]

> There is a great deal of rhetoric in superficially brilliant formulas in vogue in Latin America, like the invitation to enter "the service of the poor,"[4] or the one that, despite the tragic history of Latin America, exalts a supposed impermeability on the part of the authentic "people" to the ideologies of the dominant class. Gustavo Gutiérrez himself—in a nuanced form, to be sure—uses a brilliant argument that will later come to be employed in its more realistic and demagogic form. He refers to "the intelligence of the intellectual, of the theologian who thinks the faith without reference to those from whom the Father has precisely concealed his revelation—'the wise and prudent.' Annihilation of this intelligence, but not of that that comes from the 'least ones,' the poor, because to them alone has been given the grace to accept and comprehend the reign" (*La fuerza histórica de los pobres*, p. 175). [*Hombre de Hoy ante Jesús*, 2:593]

> We find a more nuanced formulation than this in one of the collected essays of Gustavo Gutiérrez on the "power of the poor in history," in the volume of the same name: "The gospel read from among the poor, from within the militancy of their struggles for liberation, con-

vokes a popular church—a church born of the people, born of the "poor of the land"—a church that sinks its roots in a people who snatch the gospel from the hands of the great ones of this world and prevent its utilization as an element of justification of a situation that is contrary to the will of the God of liberation" (*La fuerza histórica de los pobres*, p. 382). From the hermeneutical viewpoint, one is surprised at Gutiérrez's not wondering why Jesus, in his time, did not succeed in having his own people, that of the poor, likewise snatch "the law and the prophets"—God's revelation—from the hands of the mighty ones of Israel. [*Hombre de Hoy ante Jesús*, 2:598–99]

Apart from whether these criticisms are justified (obviously they are criticisms—this is how Gustavo and I always let off our critical steam), does the reader observe any "irony" in them—that is, humor at Gustavo's expense? Can I be the only one—or am I deceiving myself on this point?—to think that, if there is anything there, it is purely and simply sorrow at having to disagree with a friend? Must it be taken as a mere artifice of language, an artifice at the service of irony, that I observe that Gustavo's formulas are generally "more nuanced" than those of other theologians, inasmuch as Gustavo can certainly be rhetorical when he wants to, but he will never be a dunce?

Let us look at the alternative Hugo indicates: that these criticisms are "biting." In virtue of the common origin of our Iberian languages, I suppose that this adjective has the same sense in Portuguese and Spanish, and that the Spanish dictionary, too, then, defines it as "hostile, wounding, or offensive."

Obviously the capacity of someone to be "wounded" by a criticism can depend to a huge extent on that person's sensitivity. When it is a matter of a friend of long standing, I am not oblivious that this definite possibility might be verified in a high degree. But the effect that the criticism may have on the one who is its object is not enough to make the criticism "biting." This adjective indicates rather the intention of the one making it: the criticism would have to be "hostile," in its source. Thus, it not only causes pain; it offends.

In the criticisms before the reader's eyes, in order for them to be examples of "biting or ironic" criticism, seeing that there is no irony, there must be hostility. Where does Hugo perceive this hostility?

Here we touch on what has moved me to write this note. The reader will perceive—I believe—that the critical elements appearing in the citations above are not points of honor between rival intellectuals. They refer to what the Latin American people can or cannot do for their liberation— nothing more and nothing less. And it is difficult to imagine that the words of Gustavo himself (were they a criticism directed against my position), or mine (which, yes, are a criticism of his) could proceed from a hostile intent to wound or discredit. We are both of us plunged in something far more important — and Hugo as well, of course: in something over which we can disagree (especially on strategy), but which consumes our lives. Without superfluous solemnities, let us say that we are confronting enormous human suffering, that has prevailed among us for four centuries.

What with this common commitment of ours, how can I help but be saddened when, unless I am mistaken, I observe that we are becoming less and less critical when it comes to the power of the ideology victimizing our people, even in the religious elements transmitted to them by their culture. For example, in our reading of the Bible: incredibly, with huge ideological naivety, fundamentalist positions are reappearing. I cite one example (*Hombre de Hoy ante Jesús*, 2:598), and then I hedge: we must take into account a possible distortion or oversimplification on the part of the press in transmitting what this particular author has to say in this concrete case. (Not so in the case of other, less important authors, who sign their articles or works, and whom I could cite.) And then I say that even Gustavo's "more nuanced formulation" concerning biblical hermeneutics, while it is surely beautiful, for me is not enough, or perhaps is naive. He alludes to the example of Jesus, but Jesus does not seem to have "abolished the intelligence" of the "learned" so that they would follow a person who comes from among the "little ones." On the contrary, how shall we explain that not even the little ones followed him, or thought as he, but delivered him up to his fate? Have circumstances changed so very much since then? The burden of proof rests with the affirmative. And if the truth rests with the negative, it is difficult to escape the impression of triumphalism or of rhetoric.

When Leonardo Boff, in his article, "A Theology that Listens to the People,"[5] introduces his reflections on his theologico-pastoral praxis in Acre, he employs one of these formulae that I consider "rhetorical":

> Theology's great apprenticeship is at the hands of the people. Who evangelizes the theologians? Precisely the faith witness of a believing people, their capacity to inject God into every struggle, their power of resistance to all the oppression that they must constantly suffer.

Nevertheless, when the Christian poor of the base communities of Acre answer his question, "How did Christ redeem us?" with, "By the cross," and "By suffering," Leonardo, unless I am mistaken, precisely questions the ideological element in their reply, thereby striking at the root of the very rhetoric to which I allude:

> I have to ask myself: why do the people instantly associate redemption with the cross? Surely because *they have not been taught* the processual character of redemption — that is, of the process of liberation. Perhaps it is because their own lives consist mainly in the suffering and cross

that society has laid on their shoulders. A Jesus who only suffers does not liberate. He *generates pessimism and fatalism*.

From this reflection, Boff concludes the following as to the nature of the theologico-pastoral task: "One must *restore* the cross to its *proper place in the mind of the people.*"

Is there not a contradiction here? The theologian has not learned this last concept from the people. As he himself says, this is *not* how the people think. Nor has he been evangelized by the "God" that the people inject into all their struggles, who is, if we accept what he writes, a pessimistic, fatalistic God. And his proposal is nothing less than to "restore to the minds of the people" a theological element of central importance calculated to effect a radical *change* in the "faith witness of the faithful people." Well, I think that Leonardo is honestly paying the price of his emergence from rhetoric and triumphalism: that of a formal contradiction, which, when all is said and done, does him credit.

Now, in a matter this serious, this crucial—would I be engaging in irony merely because, in order to express my disagreement with Gustavo on this point, I use words like "rhetoric" or "triumphalism"?—indeed, in a sentence in which they do not directly refer to Gustavo (although I could include him), and are accompanied by nuances and argumentation?

And so, Hugo, my friend, do we agree that, in the three volumes of *El Hombre de Hoy ante Jesús de Nazaret*, there is no "biting, ironical criticism" of Gustavo Gutiérrez—*not a single one*? Whence this lapse, Hugo?

II

The index of authors cited in my three volumes lists four references to Jon Sobrino.

One of them (*Hombre de Hoy ante Jesús*, 2:577) is in support of what I assert. The other two are criticisms of the way in which Sobrino deals with the christology of the *Spiritual Exercises* in his well-known *Christology at the Crossroads: A Latin American Approach* (*Cristología desde América Latina*). Here are the two criticisms:

> Thus we observe the interesting fact that certain very radical theologians, capable of rejecting christologies ancient and modern as inadequate or not well founded, become surprisingly uncritical—ignoring or dismissing problems with the value of the christology at the core of the *Spiritual Exercises* of St. Ignatius. [Here there follows a footnote: The clearest example, to our view, is in *Christology at the Crossroads*, "The Christ of the Spiritual Exercises of St. Ignatius."] [*Hombre de Hoy ante Jesús*, 2:621]

> To our view, it is completely useless to dissociate from christology (or at least to evaluate independently) the conception of God, as Jon

Sobrino seems to do. True, Sobrino declares that "Jesus' God is different, and knowable only from a point of departure in Jesus." Nevertheless, when it comes to the use of God made in the key loci of the *Exercises*, as in the First Principle and Foundation, his argumentation consists in remarking that our dissatisfaction with it is due to the fact that "our current situation is, in large part, culturally profane, and not sacral." Why throw out the criterion, and approve a christology that is incapable of affecting in depth the concept of God? To our view, Sobrino does not indicate the deficiencies of christology in its task of revealing the being of God. [*Hombre de Hoy ante Jesús*, 2:762]

Readers will be the ones to judge here. But I do not think that they will discover irony in these paragraphs. They will indeed perceive — I hope — a serious and important hermeneutical consideration in the first observation: a consideration on how our own situation (and I might add, spirituality) conditions us as theologians. Just as so many Dominican theologians — especially in the recent past — found it difficult to accept criticism of Thomism, in which they had been formed by the great tradition of their Order, so also it is painful even today for many members of the Society of Jesus — without imputation of opportunism — to question the solidity of certain theological elements in the Ignatian spirituality they have imbibed ever since the days of their Jesuit novitiate. (And of this, I myself attest.)

As for determining whether or not Sobrino experiences this difficulty, I think it will be enough to ask the reader to read the chapter cited from his *Christology*. Furthermore, the second criticism presents a concrete example of this difficulty. Instead of irony or biting, the reader will perceive nuances of respect for the author that may even be exaggerated: ". . . seems to do. True . . ." The fact remains, however, that if we expect to see how the God of Jesus is different, precisely by being the God of Jesus, we cannot then turn around and say that certain presentations of God that are basic to the *Exercises* sound bad to us because we live in a nonsacral world. Is this "biting irony," or simply a convincing critical argument?

Actually, there is some biting irony. It will be found in the remaining citation, which, by the way, is the first one in textual order (*Hombre de Hoy ante Jesús*, 2:27). There I take it upon myself to say that, "despite the author's well-merited esteem" (Why would I have written this, if not even Hugo believes it?), Sobrino's christology — in the first and last *work* of Sobrino to come into my hands, since the other that I have is a collection of articles — should be called *A European Christology for Latin America*.

Biting irony? Right, Hugo! No doubt about it. But there are extenuating circumstances — you know? — for this slip, which, for now, is only *a* slip, and not "biting or ironic criticisms" in the plural.

You know me too well to be ignorant of the enormous distance between my long and deep friendship with Gustavo and the almost complete absence of a personal relationship with Jon Sobrino, whom I only met for the first time in a congress in Mexico, at which you were also present. And this is important. If, after so many years of deep friendship with Gustavo, as also with you, Hugo, and, besides, owing you both so many valuable things in my life and my thought, I were to heap "ironical or biting criticism" upon you, I should not be a friend. I should be either a neurotic individual, or a person of evil character.

Let us suppose, then—surely a safe supposition—that my relationship with Jon Sobrino is neither one of long friendship, nor, on the other hand, of any enmity whatever. Meanwhile, you think I "harm myself" with this irony. But look, Hugo. Do you think Sobrino's christology is a *Latin American* christology? The reason I ask is that I recall your stating in theological congresses (Detroit, Switzerland) that we could never engage in dialogue with European or North American theologians, because they would never understand us. I do not believe you are ignorant of the basic dependency of Sobrino's book on Moltmann and Pannenberg, whom he cites at every turn (no less than eighty-five times); nor do I believe that your thinking has changed on the christological problematic of these authors not being ours.

If Sobrino's book, to which I allude, is, as I suppose, the fruit of his European studies, will the title not be a bit pretentious on the author's (or editor's) part? What would you have said, Hugo, had I wished to christen my doctoral dissertation, also done in Europe, and on Berdyaev, a European thinker, "A Christian Reflection on the Person: A Latin American Approach"? Would you not have told me that I was being a ridiculous pedant? Perhaps not, out of friendship—although in you, thank goodness, sincerity has always prevailed over courtesy. But at least you would have thought it.

And this is my point. There is something we easily lose sight of with age, and it is something important. It is that we are seeing a new generation now, one that is studying in manuals what for us was creation. And the theology of liberation, at a distance of over twenty years from its inception, is overlaid with myths today. In my trips across the continent and abroad, I have had the occasion to engage in dialogue with this new generation, who have received or who know liberation theology on the basis of bibliographies listing everything carrying "liberation" in its title and written by a native or naturalized Latin American.

In christology it has become a firmly ensconced element of this myth that christological research began here in 1972 with Leonardo Boff's *Jesus Christ Liberator*, continuing in 1976 with Jon Sobrino's *Christology at the Crossroads*. This can all be found in any bibliography. But there is not the slightest effort to find out whether it was well defined in those days, and defined in depth, what it means to do christology, and to do it here; what was positive and what was unsatisfactory in European hermeneutics and exegesis; what capabilities, theories, and material we had for an analysis of the context in which our christology was to be enfleshed.

If all this is kept in account, a christology like, for example, Christian Duquoc's would be far more "akin" to Latin America than other works, written here, but indebted to theological and exegetical presuppositions far more ahistorical, such as those of Moltmann and Pannenberg. Why not admit that José Comblin's *Jesús de Nazareth* (1976) contains numerous accents tied to Latin American reality, even though this continent is never named in the book? Or that a mature Latin American christology is better represented in Boff's work by reason of his (partial) christology, *Passion of Christ, Passion of the World?*

To dismantle commonplaces both entrenched and superficial one must sometimes apply energetic remedies—call them depth charges. And what cannot be achieved by a simple explanation is sometimes achieved by a piece of irony that will knock readers out of their chairs. And for fear of the irony being applicable to them, they start doubting the myth. But what you say, Hugo, is also very true: I harm myself this way. Myths are hardy. They go on living. And sometimes they wreak vengeance.

I plead guilty, then, to this crime—in the singular—of a biting, ironic criticism: in a single case, involving a theologian whom, once more, I "respect" without knowing him personally, and whom I suppose to be intelligent enough to perceive that the irony is not directed against himself so much as against anyone who would take a work of his youth as the finished expression of a Latin American christology. But, Hugo, whence this unnuanced *plural*, and the explicit citation—as explicit as it is mistaken—of *Gustavo* and "others"?[6]

III

Can it be a matter of a mere lapse of memory, after reading such a long book? Knowing you, I doubt it could possibly be an attempt to accentuate the distances among theologians who, each in a particular way, are all working for the same cause.

And so I set myself to formulating hypotheses. And I get the feeling that you, as is your wont, read this book so well—too well—that, perhaps without your even being completely conscious of it, you perceived something implicit in the whole course of my argumentation.

In a work intended to begin at the beginning in the matter of Jesus of Nazareth, and to combat any facile commonplaces in this regard (that is, what is commonly accepted), my entire argumentation—especially if one gets down to concrete examples—ought to give the general impression of constituting a "biting or ironic criticism" of anyone feeling caught in one of these commonplaces, even if not cited, and in direct proportion to the objective force of the argument.

How is one to make oneself heard in any other way, when swimming upstream against what is today accepted almost as dogma, and held for the most original and precious theology on the continent? Hugo, you yourself, at the beginning of your note, do me the honor of pointing out that my book is not the fruit of any circumstantial "reaction," but is in continuity with my thought and my premises, now long maintained. Keeping all this in account, would it not be more faithful to conclude to, not black humor, but *necessary sorrow* at having to think and speak rather in isolation?

And if this were to be the case, then what can I do to defend myself against your admonition? If you could see into the depths of me, perhaps you would perceive a certain sorrowful irony, hovering not precisely where you seem to see it, Hugo, but in a simple "why?" or perhaps just a question mark placed where any Latin American theologian of today—not precisely Gustavo, Jon Sobrino, or "others"—would see nothing amiss. This is the handicap of limiting oneself to the formulation of certain questions, and to raising certain suspicions with regard to the recognized theology of this continent. And even were I to accept these handicaps on the conscious level, it would not be surprising if my unconscious were to betray me.

To put it another way: if I cannot oblige you, at least not directly, in the matter of the penultimate sentence of your note, I think that, once more, in the course of our friendship, something I have received from yourself becomes an aid to my reflection, and helps me to see more clearly for myself and to speak more clearly for the reader of my book.

Let me explain what I mean. What has happened to liberation theology over the course of the more than twenty years of its existence? The reason I ask is that I think that, as of this date, one of the most tremendous misunderstandings and commonplaces is the notion that we have won over, first, the North Atlantic theologians, and next, Latin American theologians themselves (despite the fact that the latter, according to Sobrino, are so much more aware than the former of their theology being "situated"); and that liberation theology is still saying what it always said—that liberation theology is one and indivisible, at least in Latin America.

Meanwhile, I recall that, in the first theological meeting at which a clearly distinct hermeneutics was employed, Gustavo and I, each of us on our own initiative, and without any previous agreement, used parallel methods in our addresses. It was a matter of analyzing the impact of two theologically key, but impoverished, concepts bearing on relations between the church and the people: freedom (Gustavo) and salvation (myself). Each of us sought to show that, conceived in the habitual manner—the classical, or academic manner—these two concepts have a dehumanizing impact on the praxis *of* the people *for* the people. And we tried to show how a more liberative—and surely more orthodox—theology must assign them both the character of a historical process.

These two addresses and their intrinsic method are no fantasy of mine. The reader can find and read them in the collective work containing the addresses of that 1966 meeting in Santiago, Chile: *Salvación y Construcción del Mundo*, by Gustavo Gutiérrez, Juan Luis Segundo, J. Severino Croatto, B. Catão, and José Comblin.[7]

I insisted that the only possible liberative — and orthodox — concept of salvation would be of salvation as a historical project, where a central role would be played by human intelligence applied to the building of the world.[8] Gustavo showed that this same liberation — and orthodoxy — implied a theological criticism of the classic concept of freedom used in theology, where it was reduced to the minimum below which an act is no longer a human act. In the "Final Conclusions" of his presentation, Gustavo shows how far a study apparently without reference to Latin American praxis can nevertheless have its deepest roots here:

> The subject takes on . . . a special urgency in countries where there is a Christian — or baptized — majority, whose great problem is precisely the promotion of the masses, their slow insertion in the process of personalization, and their difficult, frail access to an adult faith, as is the case in Latin America. Ultimately it is a matter of — let us limit ourselves to emphasizing this — how to conceive the respect due to the freedom of the process that leads the human being to a relationship with God. This service to and respect for religious freedom must be studied, of course, taking into account the concrete conditions of the Latin American human being, taking care not to transplant to this continent various series of problems not our own. But we should be deceiving ourselves were we to imagine that, by virtue of the mere consideration of these local factors, we shall move forward. Current nonsituated reflection on and clarification of the theological questions cited above — salvation, the mission of the church, and secularization — must supply us with elements that will indicate to us the lines of an authentic fidelity to the word of God on our continent.[9]

A great deal of time has passed since these assertions, which I have allowed myself to cite at length. And I would be willing to bet my shirt that, had the names of the two authors been removed, no theology student today, of the many who frantically search for bibliographies to do a monograph on liberation theology, would include these two articles in that monograph. They would be disconcerted were they to be told that this was the method practiced by those then laying the foundations of what today is called liberation theology.

And what is painful to me is that I no longer know whether Gustavo himself would endorse what he said then, or whether he would consider it a mere sin of his youth. Would he recall the impact his address made on us in that meeting, when we saw that, by different routes, we had arrived at a new theological method, which promised to change such important things on our continent?

And when I say I do not know, it is because so much water has flowed under the bridge since then. For example, what, at that moment, was the "praxis" in which theological thinking took its point of departure and which was thereupon achieved? Not, surely, as can be seen in Gustavo's same contribution, what today is called the "people's practice of faith."

In the first place, "praxis" is not a pedantic use of a Greek word to denote "practice." "Praxis" denotes a richer conjunction of practice *and theory*—and in the case of theology, of human (or inhuman) practice and hermeneutic theory. Via the latter, we suspected—and we operated on the basis of this suspicion—that the practice of faith, when manifesting dehumanizing signs, reflected the "cross that society has laid on [the] shoulders" of the poorest and most exploited (to use Leonardo's expression, cited above)—*having recourse for this purpose* to seemingly neutral and orthodox theological concepts, like (extraterrestrial) "salvation," or "freedom" (sufficient for an act to be "human" and have salvific value).

Thus, "praxis" became a central theological locus. But not in the sense that people had to be asked what practical problems they had. It is this latter, superficial, understanding of the function of praxis in the construction of a Latin American theology that occasioned European criticisms—like Moltmann's—to the effect that a local coloration was missing from Latin American theology: that it cited Marx, without at the same time "describing" the sufferings of the people of this continent. As if that were the task of theology! And as if this "description" did not already sin by excess, without, often, managing to see what theological reflection might add that was radically new! What the most serious theological reflection sought to do when it began, was, as I recall, not to describe the situation that the sociologist, the economist, and the political scientist were already portraying with perfect exactitude. It was trying to do something, yes, but what it was trying to do was to *verify* the "praxis" of faith—to take account of the impact of theological concepts or beliefs on dehumanizing practices, and thence—on a solid basis—to produce a liberative theology.

Ten years later, however, a very different language was being heard. The praxis to be theologized was the faith practice of the "believing people." And in Latin America the believing people and the people were equivalent. Nor was it any longer a matter of discovering in this practice an introjected ideology, which dehumanizes. Now what was "discovered" here was an "authentic faith," which "liberates."[10]

In all logic, the original theology of liberation was criticized, and the criticisms were "biting or ironic" indeed. It had been the product of displaced, elitist, bourgeois intellectuals, who, in ignorance of the popular wisdom, pretended to go and instruct the people concerning the way to liberate their Christian faith. You allude to these criticisms yourself, Hugo, at the beginning of your note, and you observe that I have been the object of these criticisms myself. Only, these criticisms do not seem to have "harmed" their authors, as is supposed to happen in my case.

Be this as it may, the consequence, to my view, was that popular religion became a pastoral and theological shortcut—the mainspring of a theology and a pastoral approach *already* free and liberative. The church need no longer radically question its theology, but only preach liberation, offer its services and power to the people, and lead them by the hand to the political options recognized by a paternalistic church as being more representative of the popular interests.

In the vast Latin American panorama, Argentina was the first to make the switch, and its conversion was so wholehearted that, at the meeting of the Latin American Bishops' Conference Theological Committee, Methol Ferré, a collaborator of Cardinal López Trujillo, then secretary of the conference, declared that the actual founder of liberation theology had been Argentinian theologian Lucio Gera, who had bestowed upon it its indigenous base, while Gustavo, while writing earlier, had thought in European categories. He was wrong, of course, on both counts.

What Peronism produced in the theological evolution of Argentina developed shortly thereafter in every kind of base church community in Brazil. Toward the end of the 1970s, this—new and different—theology of liberation had come to dominate the Latin American scene.

And by osmosis, European theology followed suit, as I had the opportunity to experience recently in Germany. This was partly due to the fact that the attention of the "liberal" theologians of the old continent had gradually been drawn to the universal problem implied by the Third World, and within the latter, especially Latin America. And I think it was partly due to the fact that the more autochthonous a Latin American theology, the less it questions the domination implicit in the concepts manipulated by European theology. While the latter had originally been oppressive, arriving here as a tool of the oppressors, now, by a kind of reciprocity, wisely mestizoed by the subject native (or African) cultures, it became an instrument of liberation—which proves that it was oppressive only *per accidens*.

I am saddened—I do not deny it—at seeing theology take this course on my continent. I am saddened at the sight of a once common labor taking another track (from which I feel aloof today), letting elements fall by the wayside that, I think, are still crucial. I am saddened at the sight of a people, at one of the moments at which its cause is most difficult, trying, and unsure, being used once more, unless I am mistaken, as tools for triumphs not their own.

I understand the difficulty of distinguishing this sorrow from irony. Even without realizing it, one often defends oneself against the former by means of the latter. It is quite possible, Hugo, that you have discovered an important reading key for a book that strives to remain within a theological line that may have become strange today (relatively strange, at any rate, just as, surely, my isolation in the line I am following is also only relative). Working in Brazil, as I so often do, I have encountered everywhere, especially among a laity not unfamiliar with matters theological (because they greatly concern them), the most profound attention to these problems. These persons raise questions that are not even expected, let alone adequately answered, by the dominant theology. Only these laity fear to confront that theology.

To be sure, this note is not the place to embark on a theological discourse. But I have simply had to continue my dialogue with you, Hugo —with the same rigor, friendship, and gratitude as ever.

CHAPTER 7

On Absolute Mystery

In his review of Segundo's christology, Javier Jiménez Limón expressed his "suspicion" that various reasons had prevented Segundo from "redis-covering and vigorously expressing an openness to absolute mystery." Considering this an extremely important issue, Segundo replies that, since the incarnation and revelation of Jesus Christ, the Christian God can not be considered absolute mystery and thus to speak of a direct or mystical openness to absolute mystery would not be theologically correct.

Source: "Disquisición sobre el misterio absoluto," *Revista Lati-noamericana de Teología* 2 (1985): 209–27.

A young Mexican theologian, Javier Jiménez Limón, has written an excellent review,[1] the best that I know, of my *El hombre de hoy ante Jesús de Nazaret*.[2] I think that I can be objective in calling it excellent, and pre-scind from certain laudatory judgments in the review. The writer's extraor-dinary accomplishment, I acknowledge, is to have condensed, with remarkable insight and clarity, the large ideas of a hodgepodge of a work that I should like to rewrite in a more orderly manner.

At the conclusion of his review, Jiménez Limón indicates "three points calling for discussion," and formulates certain negative, or at least inter-rogative, criticisms. I have already had the occasion to address one of these—the one referring to concrete judgments in my book of other Latin American theologians—in a response to Hugo Assmann in the Brazilian theological journal, *Perspectiva Teológica* (Belo Horizonte, 1983), no. 15, pp. 385–400, under the title, "Note on Irony and Sorrow" (see chapter 6, above). Another of these criticisms bears on the use of the political key for the historical exegesis of the synoptics. I think that this criticism is founded on the misunderstanding that *I* selected this key. The only thing open to discussion, to my way of seeing, is whether or not the historical Jesus selected it, to communicate his prophetic message concerning the reign. Did he himself use this key, or did he use another? After all, if *the key*, however limited, constitutes an obstacle to understanding his message, then that message is not that of someone who can be called the "true human being."

But Jiménez Limón's third criticism, I think, calls for a bit of friendly dialogue — an inquiry that could contribute to a clarification of one of the most crucial points of my book. That criticism reads as follows:

> *A deficient meaning for absolute mystery?* This is the most hypothetical intuitive criticism. Let us simply record our suspicion that its exemplary hand-to-hand combat with positivistic thought, and its more than justified criticism of "religiosity," has prevented Segundo from rediscovering and vigorously expressing an openness to absolute mystery. It is present, doubtless, in his insistence on transcendent data, in the importance he ascribes to eschatology in the strongest sense of the word, in his interpretation of Chalcedon. Here we should simply like to express our hope that, in his subsequent theological writings, Juan Luis Segundo will explicitate what he has here, perhaps justifiably, soft-pedaled.

Very well, then, let us explicitate.

Jiménez Limón has the delicacy, in his criticism, to make it clear that the treatment of this subject in the context to which my book seeks to do justice is a matter of appropriateness — indeed, that this appropriateness bears not so much on whether or not to treat of mystery, since I do treat it in various places and in various ways in the book, but on whether to treat of it still *further*. Unerringly, he perceives that this could be done only by broadening and clarifying what the book says about Chalcedon, or the manner in which Jesus of Nazareth, perfect human being and perfect God, reveals this mystery to us (John 1:18).

I sense the danger that Chesterton felt: ask me a good question and I may write a book! I hope that this will not happen here, but I cannot avoid my obligation of going back and addressing once more the chapter, in *The Christ of the Ignatian Exercises* devoted to this subject (Chapter 1, "Jesus and God: Approach to the Council of Chalcedon"), in an attempt to formulate its content more clearly and succinctly, and then move on to discuss its relevance for the subject at issue: openness to absolute mystery — the mystery of God.

I

Why go back to the fifth century? In the book under consideration, the answer given to this question was that we were led there by the suspicion that, far from being mere "ancient history," the Council of Chalcedon, which dealt with the correct manner of speaking of the divinity of Jesus Christ, had not yet been sufficiently understood and applied. Vatican II refers to a *twofold* mystery revealed in Jesus: the mystery of the Father, and the mystery of the human being:

> Christ ... in the *very* revelation of the mystery of the Father and of his love, *fully manifests* the human being to the human being himself. ... This is the great mystery of the human being, which Christian revelation *illuminates* (*illucescit*) for the faithful. [*Gaudium et Spes*, no. 22; emphasis added]

Here we are confronted with the case of a mystery that would "remain" absolute in (or despite) a revelation that "illuminates all with new light" (ibid., no. 11). And it is precisely this antinomy that justifies the following search.

The search calls for certain brief preliminary observations. The first is that we shall be supposing, by way of a heuristic hypothesis, that, from Nicaea to Chalcedon, the dogmatic course followed was dominated by a central problem: not so much that of (the datum of) the divinity of Jesus, but (as we have said) that of how to conceive and express that datum correctly. In other words, granted the fact that Jesus is somehow divine, how ought his divinity to be conceived and expressed so that his humanity will remain intact? If I insist on the word "express" it is because I think I perceive that, I might almost say, the most important thing in the problematic is generated by a *linguistic* crisis. From Nicaea to Chalcedon, neither the divinity nor the humanity of Jesus was ever under discussion. But it was gradually more clearly realized that it was difficult to speak a *language* that would do justice to both.

The second observation, then, consistent with the foregoing, is that the — modest — search undertaken here prescinds, by heuristic right, on its own responsibility and at its own risk, from the antecedent data concerning how the New Testament arrives at the certainty that Jesus, while not "the God," is "God." In other words, our search begins with the Council of Nicaea. And it ends with Chalcedon. And it does so in full knowledge that later councils were concerned with other data regarding the twofold nature of Jesus. It seems to us that, with Chalcedon, the problem concerning us, the "linguistic" problem, was solved—well or ill, but solved. And it was not posed again for centuries.

The third observation is that we take as the field of our search, and as milestones in the treatment of our problem, three ecumenical councils: Nicaea, Ephesus, and Chalcedon. We are not unaware that, in the background, behind the conciliar events themselves, is an immense field for investigation, constituted by the data of patristics and even of church history. Our heuristic wager is that what issued from these three councils (it does not seem to us that the second ecumenical council, Constantinople I, contributed anything to the matter under consideration here) constitutes the necessary and sufficient *development* of the problem—sufficient, surely, to explain what later occurred, over the course of centuries, in this material. And for another thing: I am altogether aware that the history that I leave out of account in my investigation can in principle invalidate my conclusions. It can be argued that personality conflicts, like that of Cyril and Nestorius or Eutyches, determined certain councils in such a way that it would appear naive to regard them as milestones in the development of the problem. Obviously this can be matter for discussion. My hypothesis, however, is that, whatever the virulence of these controversies and their short-term influence, the result, on the level of the "meta-history" of dogma, is tantamount to that of the posing and solution of the problem alluded to above: how one may speak coherently of Jesus' divinity and humanity.

Thus, I shall be concerned in the first instance with how to recognize this development in the three councils cited. Then I shall attempt to translate this same development in terms of the implicit (although at times it is also explicit) linguistic problem it contains. And finally, based on the results of this investigation, I shall pose the problem that has occasioned this article: how and where the "absolute mystery" of God remains after its revelation in Jesus Christ.

II

The essentials of the christology of the Council of Nicaea (325) have been expressed in that faith formula or creed that, as we all know, is recited in the Christian liturgy even today, in the so-called long creed. As is equally well known, the council formulates, in positive terms, a condemnation of Arianism, which conceived the divinity of the Son of God as an inferior, created divinity, subordinate to that of the Father. From the viewpoint of digital language, one word leaps out at us as crucial: "consubstantial." The rest consists of iconic expressions like "begotten, not created," or "God of God, light of light," and so on.

Someone might say that, apart from solving this problem of the supposed "substantial" inferiority of the Word, Nicaea only repeated more or less naive formulas employed since New Testament times to express the notion that the Jesus of the first century of our era was both a human being and God.

But as the word "consubstantial" indicates an intent to transcend this innocence, the terms in which Nicaea expresses itself were by now impregnated with a problem that would lead, in the following century, to Ephesus and Chalcedon. With a view to grasping this implicit element, it will be in order to review the central part of this creed, the part devoted to Jesus Christ:

> We believe . . . in one Lord, Jesus Christ, Son of God, only-begotten
> of the Father, that is, of the substance of the Father, God of God,

light of light, true God of true God, begotten, not made, of one substance with the Father, by whom all things have been made, in heaven
and on earth, who descended for our salvation, became incarnate,
and became a human being, suffered and rose the third day, ascended
to the skies and is to come. [Denzinger 54]

The first thing we notice is that directly—*in recto*—the Council of Nicaea
wishes to define that the divinity attaching to Jesus, since Jesus is identified
with the Word, or the only-begotten Son of God, is "substantially" equal
to that of the Father—that is, in no way inferior, whatever reason in terms
of creation or incarnation might be set forth for an alleged inferiority to
that of the Father, or "the God."

But secondly—perhaps less obviously, but it is the commencement of
the linguistic problem—there is a relevant phenomenon in the construction
of the phrase. The complement of the verb "we believe in," which then
becomes the subject of all that follows, is: "one." This *one*, of course, is
Jesus Christ. Why does the formula speak of "one," when its appositive is
immediately specified? At first sight one might think that this "one" is no
more than an obligatory repetition of the other "one," at the beginning of
the creed: "We believe in *one* God the Father." But such is not the case.
In the former instance (although we are not given to know how the phrase
would be punctuated for pronunciation), the "one God" is obviously an
assertion of monotheism. Today, we rightly place a comma between "God"
and "Father": "We believe in one God, the Father." The "one" applied to
the Father, refers to the "unicity" of God. But it would be meaningless to
assert such a "unicity" of the Son. And indeed we observe that the creed
does not speak of "one" Holy Spirit. The "one" preceding "Jesus Christ"
cannot refer to his "unicity." It refers to the specific problem presented by
Jesus Christ: his "unity." In other words, in linguistic terms, the reference
is to the unique phenomenon by which, in the formula that we are analyzing,
this "one" subject receives, *without breach of continuity*, divine predicates
("consubstantial," "God of God," "begotten of the Father," creative cause
of the universe, and so on) and human predicates ("became man," "suffered," "rose again," and so forth).

Third, and last, between these two lists of predicates, one after another,
with a single subject, there is a difference, destined, as the event would
show, a growing importance. It is not a matter of the divine and the human
considered in themselves. It is a matter of what we might call, in terms
more familiar to biblical exegesis, the proper "literary genre" of these levels. The "divine substance" is expressed in terms that, while they cannot
be eternal—because human language contains nothing of the kind—are at
any rate intended as atemporal. Generally speaking, they allude to an
abstract nature or substance. By contrast, the human predicates (while they
could refer to the abstract nature of the human being) are, in the formula,
historical predicates, concerning Jesus' life, death, and resurrection. Thus,

in succession, divine substance and human history converge in "one" Jesus Christ.

The Council of Ephesus, despite all, despite even the difficulty of knowing what can have that appellation, has decisive importance for the problem before us. And that importance resides in the fact that, more than is evident in Nicaea and Chalcedon, the "Anathematisms" or "Capitula of Cyril," subjoined to the canons, serve notice that the problem of theology that was to be solved concerning Jesus Christ was originally linguistic. To put it another way: at Ephesus, the point of departure in the posing of the problem consisted explicitly in a difficulty of language.

This appears altogether clearly in the key anathemas:

> Should anyone distribute between two persons or hypostases the vocables contained in the apostolic writings or gospels, or stated concerning Christ by the saints or by himself concerning himself—applying some of them to the human being understood as such, apart from the Word of God, and others, as worthy of God, only to the Word of God the Father, let that one be anathema. [Canon 4; Denzinger 116]

From this principle derive two further canons, which favor us with examples of the principle just enunciated: "If anyone does not profess that the Word of God suffered in the flesh and was crucified in the flesh, and tasted death in the flesh . . . let that one be anathema" (Canon 12; Denzinger 124).

As we see, we are awash in the unexpected linguistic consequences of that seemingly innocent "unity" in which a divine substance and a human history converged. This convergence does not seem "compatible" or "condign" with such opposed realities as the human and the divine. What fits one does not fit the other. The human cannot be "worthily" predicated of God. Therefore, compatibility of language requires a distinction, in Jesus Christ, of two subjects. This seems to be the only logical consequence. But let us see what the council (or Cyril, at least), would have us accept.

In the first place, "God is truly Emmanuel," which, translated, means the "God with us," is a reality such as ought to have its own language, a language "worthy" of the incarnation. Thus, the use of "vocables" that, in order to preserve the divinity from flaws too human, separate predicates that seem proper respectively to the human being and to God, is forbidden. At the same time, it is insisted that the Nicene "one" be explained as unity of *subject* for everything, divine or human, that is predicated of Jesus Christ.

In the second place, we must explain what we mean by unity of "subject." The expression as such does not occur in Ephesus. Ephesus forbids, in this specific, unique case, the reference of expressions to "two persons or hypostases." This is obviously tantamount to saying that we are dealing with *one person*, or *one hypostasis*. Neither of these words offends the truth. But "person" was a term still too new at the time to convey all the deep meaning of which it is the vehicle today. There was no term, in the language of the era, to have the semantic wealth of our own substantive, "person." The term thus translated—*prosopon*—at that time denoted the mask an actor might wear in theatrical presentations to facilitate identification of his role.

As for *hypostasis*, its ambiguity is perceived even in its modern equivalent, "substance." The latter, as we know, can designate the being or the essence of a concrete singular, and in this sense it is akin to "person," or at least, "subject." But it can also denote the abstract being, the nature (generic substance), of several similar things. Therefore I think that, for purposes of what is actually at stake in the problem before us, it will be advantageous to substitute the word "subject," with its etymological base, for "substance" or *hypostasis*, as well as (for the reason already given) for "person."

This *subject*, the Word of God or Jesus Christ, is one, then, not two. And it is likewise to this single subject that the terms attaching to the divine and human elements predicated of it are to be referred. This is the only language "worthy" of Emmanuel, the only language appropriate to the reality of the incarnation.

In the third place, however, Ephesus (amid a world where Greek culture still dominates) is aware that all of this calls for a linguistic tour de force. If we are to meet the demand of the fourth canon, we must admit the tremendous realism (or humanism) of the incarnation. The prologue of the fourth Gospel itself had shown this. Greek has two verbs to express the notion of being, depending on whether we are dealing with an eternal, essential "to be" (*einai*), or with a created, perishable one (*ginesthai*). Perhaps we ought rather to translate the former as "to be" (of itself), and the latter as "to come to be" (by virtue of another). Throughout the Johannine prologue, the Word systematically receives the verb "be," while the rest of creatures—John the Baptist, the children of the Spirit—receive, as is only fitting, the verb "come to be." But the fourteenth verse, the one that enunciates the incarnation, creates a linguistic wonder: "The Word *came to be* flesh and pitched its tent among us." The Word not not only took on human reality: it likewise took on the *language* proper to human beings and creatures.

In the fourth place: now we understand that the incarnation establishes a communication of realities; and that this communication of realities, when it is to be expressed, must likewise become a "communication of languages" between God and the human being. God experiences—we have to use some term—human realities in Jesus. God experiences what it is to have a mother, what it is to suffer and to die. Those who would spare God such contingencies and miseries simply are not Christians. But there is a strange thing about this communication of languages. It would appear that, in perfect logic, it ought to be a two-way street. One way should mount to God, and the other descend to human beings. However, we are suddenly struck by something unexpected. The examples presented to Christian faith by Ephesus go one way only: up. Would the "communication of languages" then be only a one-way street? Summoning all my courage, I respond that all theology, and especially the liberative power of theology, hangs by a thread here. On the response—yes or no—to this question depends all. Thus, Ephesus leads to Chalcedon.

Only twenty years elapse between Ephesus (431) and Chalcedon (451). This might appear to support the thesis that Chalcedon is a *reaction* to Ephesus, and not, strictly speaking, its continuation or culmination. My hypothesis, as I have already indicated, is the contrary. Whatever may have been the explicit intent of the actors in this dogmatic drama, it would seem that a kind of "artfulness of reason," if not without these personages, then at least in spite of them, brings the problem to its logical denouement.

The basic question, in this case, is: What has Ephesus left undone? As we have seen, we are struck by a certain imbalance. If the unity implied by a single subject or persona founds a communication of languages (as this phenomenon will later come to be called, in tribute to its linguistic origin), then why are only one-way examples cited in the text (the way "up")? In other words, why must one say that God had a mother, suffered, and died, and not say, conversely, that the human being who is Jesus is changeless, inaccessible, immortal, omniscient, and all-powerful?

This question conceals a deeper problem. If what is known of Jesus' human history must be introduced (by way of communication in language) into the concept of God, it would appear that, in like manner, the divine attributes would have to attach to the concept of what this human Jesus is who experienced a human history. But—and this "but" is a formidable one—if the attributes mentioned in the last sentence of the preceding paragraph are predicated of Jesus, then the entire history of Jesus as perceived by the witnesses of his life is *false*. His changes are false, the relationships he had with other human beings are false, his agony in the face of pain and death is false, his very suffering and death are false!

To put it another way: the human "condition," or human "nature," such as it arises from our experience, *contradicts* these attributes. The various predicates that this (descending) communication of languages would imply would not reveal God, because, were we to seek to mingle them with the predicates that arise from what a human being necessarily is for us, they would dissolve Jesus into a ghost, into someone who only "played human," without really being such. Why? Because the concept of human being is *already filled with concrete content*.

But why does the same thing not occur with the "way up"? How does it come about that predicates proceeding from human history, altogether human history—such as to have a mother, to suffer, and to die—can be introduced into the concept of the divine "condition" or "nature" without destroying the very concept? If the concept of human being resists this linguistic "communication" because it is already full, then is the concept of God, which (according to Ephesus) likewise receives that communication, *empty*? In order to take seriously the wild Pauline metaphor of the "emptying" (*kenosis*) of the divinity in Jesus according to Philippians 2:7, shall we have to understand it metaphysically?

Let us read and analyze the most pertinent elements of the lengthy Chalcedonian formula:

> We unanimously teach that one and the same Son is to be professed, our Lord Jesus Christ, the same perfect in divinity and the same perfect in humanity, truly God, and the same truly a human being of rational soul and of body, consubstantial with the Father as to divinity, and the same consubstantial with ourselves as to humanity . . . in two natures, without confusion, without change, without division, without separation, without the least effacing of the difference of natures on account of the union, but rather with each nature preserving its property and joined in a single person and in a single hypostasis, without separation or division into two persons, but one and the same only-begotten Son, God the Word, the Lord Jesus Christ. [Denzinger 148]

In the interests of brevity, I omit explanations, biblical citations, and perhaps more importantly, certain confirmatory allusions to the "Anathematisms of Cyril" (such as the assertion of Mary's "divine" motherhood).

First of all let us note that it is Chalcedon that first employs the classic formula: one person, two natures. Hence, although what we have said of Ephesus concerning the terms used to express what we today call "person" (at that time, *prosopon* or *hypostasis*) holds here as well, I prefer to use the word that has likewise become classic: "nature." I add "subject" only to indicate that, in those days, this term would perhaps be the one that would come closest to saying what the council meant. In turn, what previously had no specific name now has one: "nature" (in Greek, *physis*). Before Chalcedon, the reader will recall, divine attributes (substance was mentioned) and predicates issuing from his human history (like the "fact" of being born, suffering, dying, and so on) were attributed indistinctly to this single subject (the Word of God, Jesus Christ). Here what are *two* are identified with one substantive, and unfortunately, that substantive is too suggestive of the "reifying" tendency of a Greek philosophy that at first was precisely a search for the essence of the most elementary things. Nevertheless, despite all, and for better or worse, naming what the *two* are will serve to call attention to the respective *concepts* that are at the origin of the linguistic problem: the divine and the human.

In the second place, it has been said, not without reason, that Ephesus places the accent on nonseparation. The communication of languages is its strong point, its discovery. Chalcedon, on the other hand, is said to place the accent on, if not separation, at least distinction. That natures are never mingled in Jesus will be the great epistemological principle of Chalcedon's solution to the problem posed by Ephesus.

In the third place, indeed, Chalcedon, in denying all mixture or confusion, closes an important door to the concept of the divine: experience. Why do I claim such a thing? Very simply: if the natures never mixed, what was perceived in Jesus was *only* the human element. This conclusion, seemingly so simple, was not drawn. The notion that, even today, people have of Jesus is not so much that of Chalcedon, but the one that Chalcedon condemned: that of a demigod. I think that, in Jesus, human knowledge was mixed with the divine knowledge (which would mean that Jesus gave himself up to death knowing that he would only be a day and a half in the tomb). We imagine, or attempt to imagine, that the Jesus who sweated blood in the garden was simultaneously enjoying the heavenly delights, filled with the vision of his eternal glory and of the success of the reign of God. I think of a Jesus who is, constantly, aware of his divinity. And so on. In a word, I posit in Jesus things that do not come from what the experience of the witnesses perceived in him, but from what proceeds from our concept — our presupposed concept — of what a God should be. We practice — timidly, but we practice it — the "downward way" of the "communication of languages."

We must ask ourselves, however, a fourth question. Did the Council of Chalcedon in any way modify the state of the linguistic question? The answer can only be yes. It radicalized its terms. In dealing with Ephesus, we wondered whether we must think that the concept of God was empty, in order for predicates proceeding from the human history of Jesus to enter into it without absolute contradiction. And Chalcedon takes us still further along this road. It confirms this "emptying" of the concept of "the divine," since it obliges us to say that the divine was not perceptible — was not an object of experience — in the historical human life of Jesus. And now, yes, I may ask myself: With what concrete content do we endow this concept of what Chalcedon calls the "divine nature," or the concept of what God is by necessity? Where have we gotten our idea of what a "divine life" must be?

III

Here we must pause briefly in our analysis of Chalcedon. In order to proceed, we must take note of an obstacle on our path. The obstacle is the terminology used by the council — drawn, as we have indicated, from a "reifying" Greek theology. Let us attempt, then, to see what it is that is *meant* by "divine nature." After all, God is not an *ens physicum* or "natural being" — as the human being, up to a certain point, is nothing else.[3]

The order of being, or ladder of perfection of beings, begins — from the bottom — with a first rung on which beings are determined, and hence are ordered and known by the nature they possess — in other words, by their genus and species (and only to a far lesser extent, by their "particularities," so that the latter will be secondary on the level of cognition and use — for example, there is little of importance I can know about water once I have learned its essential natural constitution by chemistry).

A significant difference arises, however, even at the level of living beings—especially, as we mount the ladder of life above the animals called "adaptors" to the "regulators." The spontaneity of the latter is such that, for any practical end in our relationship with them, we can rely very little on a knowledge reduced to taking account of their nature. I do not know how to deal with a dog if the only thing I know about it is that it has a canine "nature." The higher the degree of an animal's internal determination, the more relevant is, if not the "freedom" of each dog, then at least its particular history, as an index of what can be hoped or feared of it.

Of human beings, Sartre has said, with evident exaggeration, that existence precedes essence. In plain language, we might say: freedom is antecedent to nature. If by precedence we were to understand a certain temporal order of precedence, the expression would be false, because, precisely in the first years of our existence, we human beings are dominated more by our "physical" element. But if precedence refers to the element that, at the close of our life, will be the one that most will have determined us as human beings, then we shall have to admit that human beings are to a large extent what they have wished to be. Our nature is only a kind of negative framework, indicating what our options cannot transcend. But no one in their right mind would consent to be joined in marriage with a spouse solely on the basis of knowing that that spouse is someone with a "human nature." It is far more important to know, to be acquainted with, my spouse's concrete freedom. But concrete freedom is visible only, up to a point, in its historical traits or results. I only really know a human being when I know that being's history. The sole "image" of a freedom is the history of its options.

And so we come to God. Here only the formality of God's *infinitude* in being can generate a certain cognition. But this infinitude is the formality of an unlimited freedom or spontaneity. This means that God is *entirely* what God has chosen to be. If "nature" denotes the limits a being cannot overstep, then we shall have to say that the only thing the "nature" of God gives me to know is that God cannot be limited in anything that God chooses to be.

What seems obvious to a philosophy no longer Greek, was not obvious at the time of Chalcedon. Thought that proceeded from philosophy believed it could move from the formality of the divine infinitude to a "concrete" content of the concept of God. An infinite being—an unmoved mover—could not move or change, because the reason for moving or changing would have to be the lack of something. Nor could it depend on anyone or anything, or hence be affected by the good or evil that befell any limited being. It could not love as human beings love—becoming dependent on the beloved, suffering with the sufferings and rejoicing in the joys of the beloved, and surrendering the lover's own being for the happiness of the other. This whole chain of speciously tautological deductions sprang from a supposed positive knowledge of the "divine nature." That knowledge seemed to indicate that the concept of divine nature was as full of content as was the concept of human nature. But this whole edifice, in which one thought to be able to house God, had been built in the crucial absence, in the Greek concept of God, of the infinite divine freedom. And this is Chalcedon's ambiguity: it uses the Greek term "nature" to refer to the concept of God; and yet everything indicates that the God it has in mind is the God of the Bible, the God become a human being, in the preeminence—here, yes, absolute—of existence over essence, of freedom over nature.

Now we come to the decisive thing. If God is absolute *freedom* exercised upon the whole of reality, then how can a "material"—that is, a concrete— content be given to the concept, let us say, of "divine nature"? If what we have been saying is true, then the only way we could ever know the options of this infinite freedom will be, once more, that of the "history" of God. And this, and nothing else, is the systematic view that the Bible holds of the cognitive way to God. This is how the God of the Hebrews imparted self-knowledge—as a God of history, not a God of nature. In the Old Testament, of course, that divine history is perceived through historical mediators who are not personally God, although they are indeed "images" of God. In the case of Jesus, it is the actual history of a divine person that enables us to fill the concept of God with concrete history. That by which we are enabled to know "what God is like" is meaningful to us in that fully human way in which Jesus lives his history: a way we need only thereupon strip—formally—of its limitations (its limitations in a reality, a created reality).

This is why the communication of languages has only an ascending direction, open to the descending love of a God become a human being and revealed in a human being's integral human reality. A philosophy of "natures" can only invent a God to the likeness of a perfect *thing*, or, negatively, speak of "absolute mystery." But we can and must say of the God of the Bible, and still more of the God whose concept is revealed to us through the utterly human history of Jesus, what Deuteronomy says (apropos of the God of a self-revelation in the law of Moses):

> The nations, who will hear of all these statutes [will say], "This great nation is truly a *wise and intelligent* people." For what great nation is there that has gods *so close* to it as the Lord, our God, is to us whenever we call upon him? Or what great nation has statutes and decrees that are *as just* as this whole law which I am setting before you today?" [Deut. 4:6–7][4]

IV

From a point of departure in the foregoing, we might now seek new theological conclusions from what we have observed concerning the formula of Chalcedon, especially in the area of the specific subject that we proposed to treat in the beginning of this article: that of the "absolute mystery" that, for us, is constituted by the divinity.

But I realize that a link would be missing—or at least, one link would be very weak—unless I attempt to offer, as briefly as possible, a version that would be intelligible to the modern human being of that "communication of languages" that has been established, but perhaps insufficiently explained.

If we accept on faith the divinity of the historical human being Jesus of Nazareth, we are confronted—even after understanding what Chalcedon wished to say—with a rather concrete problem of language. Or, if we prefer, and even more concretely, we are confronted with two problems or questions. We are faced with two assertions that Chalcedon will have us accept as completely true. (I understand that truth, vis-à-vis falsehood, admits of no degrees; I say "completely true" in the sense that the compound assertion is true in its totality, and not merely in one of its members.) The twofold assertion to which we refer is: *Jesus is a human being and Jesus is God.*

The two questions or problems to which I refer have nothing of the extraordinary about them, and can easily—and in many current cases of this kind, ought to—be asked: (1) In the proposition, "Jesus Christ [subject] is God [predicate]," which of the two terms adds information to the other? And (2) are the two propositions, "Jesus is a human being" and "Jesus is God," on the same logical level?

1. When we assert (as all Christianity has always accepted, with the exception of the docetists) that "Jesus is a human being," no one asks which of the two terms joined by the copula or "equal sign" "is" sheds (cognitive) light on the other. A proposition like this one usually supposes that the two terms are known. Usually too, the subject designates something more particular, while the predicate denominates a more general category. If this is one of those cases, it would seem evident that, in indicating a category in which Jesus is found, we are contributing, with the predicate (and the verb "is"), new knowledge to that already contained in the subject, "Jesus."

However, sometimes we have a different case. There are two very important areas of cognition in which the process flows in the opposite direction (without our having to change the order of the subject and the predicate in the proposition). One of these areas is that of our childhood apprenticeship in the area of categories. For example, if we do not yet know what the category "dog" means, or what specific animals it contains, we learn it from our elders through the attribution of the category "dog" to particular animals that we do know, and by the consequent negation of that category in the case of other animals. Thus, a child and an adult "read" the proposition "Fido is a dog" in exactly opposite directions. For an adult, this is information about Fido (the subject). For a small child just beginning to know the world, it is information about what a dog (the predicate) is. Thus, when this proposition has been asserted of many subjects, and if, furthermore, the negation is used as well, in propositions like "Mary is not a dog," or "Bossy is a cow" (a nondog), the child will register equalities (among dogs) and inequalities (between dogs and human beings, or dogs and cows), and will bestow content on the category or universal concept of "dog." In other words, by way of multiplication, the subject sheds light on the predicate. And it fills the latter with content.

Much the same thing occurs in the case of scientific discoveries. The first time that the proposition, "water is H_2O" was enunciated, the (partially) unknown term until then had been the predicate H_2O. Water, on the other hand, had already been the object of millions of experiments. Comparing these experiments implicit in the subject of the proposition, an equality was found, by chemical analysis, that could be generalized for all "water." Since then, and only since then, it has been possible to exclude from the concept of water other things that only "seemed" water—and that until then had had the semantic "right" to be called water. Thus, in some sort, science repeats, in more systematic fashion, the childhood experience of the formation of categories.

In good logic, then, we must inquire into the *direction* of the increase in knowledge, if any, in a proposition like "Jesus [subject] is God [predicate]." Indeed, we can say that the core of the dogmatic development from Nicaea to Chalcedon is precisely an attempt to solve this question.

The stock answer is that, since we already know from a "natural theology"—that is, from a metaphysical argumentation—what the category "God" contains, we ask ourselves whether Jesus has the right to enter into that category. But Chalcedon's answer is the reverse. If we can know what God is only from the history of a living God, then the category "God" is empty until we fill it with the unique case in which the living God grants us to assist at the actual divine "history."[5]

As we saw in analyzing the development of christological dogma in the councils from Nicaea to Chalcedon, the subject of the proposition "Jesus is God" shows us, as content (as material object), a freedom to be this and not something else, which imposes a certain value, an "ought to be," on the totality of being. In this choice appears that which is proper to the world of the person, and of freedom: the assignment of a meaning to one's existence. To this meaning selected for his existence Jesus gives a name— the "reign of God"—and thus this meaning structures his entire life. To say that God is love, to say that God is what the reign seeks to be, are both expressions of what the history of Jesus made manifest, and express the *only* content with which we can fill the concept not altogether felicitously denominated that of the "divine nature." In how Jesus lived his human life is his divinity, which was neither "outside" nor "mixed" with the former.

2. But if we were to stop here, the proposition "Jesus is God" would be simply reducible to the tautological assertion "Jesus is Jesus." In other words, cognition would not move from subject to predicate, because the predicate would say exactly the same thing as the subject. It is precisely

here, then, that the need arises for the second question or interrogation: Are the two propositions "Jesus is a human being" and "Jesus is God" *on the same logical plane*?

First let us see what we mean by this question, so little—too little—asked in theology. As is evident, communication does not transfer the thing itself that is under consideration, from the transmitter to the receiver. What is transmitted—and effects a cognitive contribution—is a message *in code*. Hence the need, in all communication, for two operations: one to codify the perceived difference; the other to decodify, or interpret, what is in code, for which it is necessary to remove the formal elements of the code, so that we may be left with the cognition of the "difference" perceived by the transmitter. Let us consider an analogy. Suppose that a machine perceives a difference in temperature (registered in its sensors). In order to communicate this difference, it does not transmit the "difference in temperature" itself, but first puts it in code: for example, "thirty degrees more." The person or machine receiving that message does not receive the change in temperature *itself*. The receiver can be chilled through and through, and the message will not change temperature. But in order to receive the communication, the receiver must know what "thirty degrees" *means*—that is, must extract the content of the communication from its code, which means first interpreting it and then discarding the elements proper to the code itself. After all, if we walk up to the receiver to see what it has received, we find no "thirty" anything. The "thirty" belongs to the code used for the communication, and not to that which is communicated.

The logical levels correspond to the various levels of abstraction from the codes employed to communicate some perceived difference. For example, the green color of the landscape of a particular terrain, and the red color with which this same terrain is codified on a map, cannot "mix." The green of the rural landscape is itself a code, of course (a visual one, transferred to language). But it possesses a "level of abstraction" below that of the map. Thus, the green of the landscape can mix with the temperature code or with the code of elevation above sea level. The map, however, is more abstract as a code. Thus, we say, logically, although the expression is not altogether precise, that "the map is not the territory." Its green is not a sign that the terrain is green. In the code that is the map, green is *only* a way of rendering more perceptible to the "decoder" where the boundaries of this territory lie and at what point of difference in the extension of the material translated one may move to a different territory (for example, to another nation).

The concept of "map" (like that of "degrees of temperature," "orographic relief," and so on) is a *formal* concept, in the sense that it alludes to a vacuum of material content. It designates an information code, not the content of the information. The "green" of the map does not designate a particular green on the terrain. Indeed, maps tend to explicitate their formality: they furnish us with a scale, in order to indicate how we are to interpret them—that is, how to decodify them. For example, two centimeters on the map may correspond to two kilometers of terrain.

I wonder whether the reader has already begun to perceive similarities with theological elements established by the christological councils with respect to Jesus' divinity. Let us briefly examine these similarities.

When we are told that the characteristics of Jesus' divinity cannot be "mixed" with those of his humanity, we are being told something similar to the logical advice not to take the map for the territory. Confusing the green of the map with the green of a terrain would be a logical blunder, since the map and the territory are on two different levels of abstraction.

When we are informed that the characteristics perceived in Jesus' history cannot be "separated" from the divine, we are being told something similar to the fact that the map cannot be "separated" from the territory, in the sense that only the concrete territory gives the map its "material" content. Otherwise a fictional map would lead me to the conclusion that I know a new territory.

When we are told that in Jesus' divinity there is no other content than what is perceived in his humanity, this does not mean that we must deny the "formal" content of divinity and its decisive importance. The case is similar to that of the scale that tells us what method to use in ascertaining (in the degree of abstraction proper to the map) the extent of the territory, which I could also ascertain by the more concrete code of traversing it on foot.

The proposition "Jesus is God" performs in language a function parallel to that of a map. It is the scale in which is fulfilled what Jesus decided to be and to accomplish. It is the scale that tells me to what extent reality yields to that reign of God that Jesus sought concretely and in limited fashion. And it tells me that, to all appearances, his project ended in failure. Thus, "Jesus is God" means that the limited freedom of Jesus as man is, in the unlimited being of God, raised to an infinite power of realization. The "formality" of the concept that Jesus fills with the content of his human history is the very infinitude of God. But it is none of the presumed logical conclusions that human beings have thought they could draw by directly converting formal infinitude into concrete existence, any more than a map can be transformed into a territory.

Thus, Chalcedon utterly and absolutely insists on the full validity of the Johannine theology that has Jesus reproach his apostle: "How long have you been with me, Philip, and you do not know me? Who has seen me has seen the Father (= "the God"). How is it that you say, 'Show us the Father'?" (John 14:9). Indeed, following the thread that has taken us back through the first ecumenical councils, we understand why there is *nothing* in the essence of the Father, in the being that "the God" freely chose to be, that is not visible in the "history" of the freedom of Jesus the "Son of God." Nothing "new" would be achieved by actually seeing the Father, as the "theologian" says who speaks through the mouth of Jesus in the Gospel of John. Surely the Father *is* what we see in Jesus, but in another dimension, which escapes us. However, Philip's request would have made no sense whatever if it had been a request to grasp, in human terms, the infinitude with which the Father possesses what becomes visible in the integrally human life of Jesus. Human beings would be unable to "see" what they would be shown.

V

I think that, after such a lengthy digression, the last sentence of the foregoing paragraph finally returns me to my starting point, and that I can finally respond to the desire of Javier Jiménez Limón that I explain "more" what I mean when I speak of the absolute mystery of God. After what I have said thus far, I think that this "more" can and should be very short, and consist of only a few brief suggestions that those who have read and accepted the foregoing will be able to implement and extend on their own initiative.

The conjunction of the terms "mystery" and "absolute" requires some brief precisions, lest we find ourselves engaged in a mere war of words. And let us begin with the first of the two. "Mystery," in theology, has a specific sense, which assimilates it to another, even broader term: "supernatural." Just as we cannot demand as a right that which is essentially gratuitous and outstrips our (natural) rights and capacity, so also on the level of knowledge: in the case of "mystery" we might say that mystery is the cognitive equivalent of the expression "grace of God," or "supernatural."

Hence we have what technically constitutes a mystery in theology: "Besides the things that natural reason can attain, mysteries of God are proposed for our belief of which, had they not been divinely revealed, one could not have been informed" (Denzinger 1795). But revelation is a fact. The "history of the divine freedom," which God alone could have made known to us (since knowledge of the "infinite nature" of God by reason would not have helped us to know anything of what God had decided to be), has been manifested to us in a thousand ways, first at a distance, so to speak, in the Old Testament, and then, in a person, in the Son or Word of God (Heb. 1:1–2). Thus far, however, we should have had to speak of mystery only in the past, since, in conformity with the same Letter to the Hebrews, and so many other texts of the New Testament, the *darkness* in which God was enshrouded has now become "spoken word," "discernment," "glory" — that is, *light*.

In the nineteenth century — perhaps in order to safeguard the nature of the religious in the presence of the exclusive claims of (positivist) science — there was an insistence on associating mystery, *even when it had been revealed*, with darkness. Mystery was supposed to be something so far above our capacity that, even when we knew it, we must give up any hope of

understanding it. (The story used to be told of a certain professor of theology that, when he had explained the Trinity, you understood it so well
that there was no mystery left!) Actually, the more revealing dogmatic
formulas of that period with regard to the mysteries are much more balanced. They place more emphasis on the light that has come, and less on
the darkness that still remains. To cite Vatican I, once more:

> The divine mysteries, by their very nature, so surpass created under-
> standing that, even when they have been taught by revelation and
> accepted by faith, they are nevertheless still cloaked in the veil of the
> same faith and enshrouded in a *certain darkness*. [Denzinger 1796;
> emphasis added]

The same entry asserts that "a certain intelligence, and a very fruitful one,
of the mysteries is attained" when "reason is enlightened by faith" (ibid.).

The "luminous" aspect of the divine mysteries, once they are revealed,
is, as we saw at the beginning of this article, emphasized by Vatican II,
which says that the revelation of the mystery of the Father and the Father's
love is likewise the revelation of the mystery of human beings and their
destiny, so that faith enlightens the entire human being with new light, a
light by which the problems that human beings must face can be solved in
a more human and humane manner (see *Gaudium et Spes*, nos. 22, 11, and
passim).

What, then, is being referred to when mystery is called "absolute"? God,
obviously. The sense of the expression—which has a certain nineteenth-
century flavor—is not so much that of absolute light as that of absolute
darkness. While there is no attempt to indicate a "total darkness," there
is an allusion to a limit beyond which the human being must give up—or
if not the human being, at least certain faculties of the human being, such
as that of reason. Vatican I itself alludes to this limit, speaking of the
"created understanding." We may therefore logically suppose that darkness
begins when this understanding or reason seeks to transgress the boundary
between finite and infinite reality; and that this occurs even after the Son
has given an account to the human being of the most intimate being—the
"bosom"—of the Father (John 1:18).

With all this *in mente*, let us return to the meaning of Chalcedon as we
have developed it above. What conclusions can we draw with respect to
"absolute mystery"?

The first, it seems to me, is that, due to its dependency—and the later
dependency of all Christian theology—on Greek philosophy, Chalcedon
failed to have the tremendous liberative impact it should have had. The
theology of subsequent centuries, with its implicit pastoral theory, continued to accommodate Jesus' history to its conception of God, and not its
conception of God to Jesus' history. The infinite continued to be sought
directly, as a cognition arising by deduction from the concept of the divine

nature. The immediate result of this was the sensible loss of Jesus' concrete particularity—not only, or not so much, as a human being, but as God. Jesus' historical partiality thus ceased to be part of "absolute mystery." That partiality had to be prescinded from in order to penetrate, somehow, to some extent, the "divine transcendence."

The second consequence, a result of the first, is the victorious rebellion of idolatry against the Christian message concerning God. Henri de Lubac says:

> Hypocrisy loves nothing so much as the idea of God. . . . Above all, human beings are, unfortunately, afraid of God. They fear they will be scorched on contact, like the Israelites of old who touched the Ark. Hence all the subtleties employed to deny God, all the cunning in forgetting him, and all the pious inventions to soften his shock. Unbelieving, indifferent, or believing, we are all engaged in a contest of ingenuity to protect ourselves against God.[6]

I should like to add that it does not require any exaggerated degree of mistrustfulness to suggest that, besides, we are all engaged in a rivalry to protect ourselves from one another by means of a "false" God. Or else from a God awaiting us in every nonhuman human being who awaits our love. What has made this idolatry possible? To a great extent, the loss of what I should like to call the "Chalcedonian brake." The emptiness of "absolute mystery" is available to human beings to fill with their human interests, without even having to disguise them very much. And when we ask how it is possible that God and the "values" of God seem so different from the Jesus who traversed our history, the answer is always: "mystery," "everything changes when we cross the line between the finite and the infinite," and so on. Contemplation—mystical contemplation—of absolute mystery, except when it has been contemplation in action, has been transformed into a parallel theology, which advances toward the interior of God in proportion as it diverts human sensitivity from what is occurring around us and in others.

In the third place, and in counterpoint with what I have been saying, the contemplation of God, the values of God, and the plans of God, throughout the earthly, conflictive history of Jesus, sheds light, not darkness, on the construction of a history, initiated even now (although it is only manifest in metahistory), of human beings' new earth and God's new heaven (*Gaudium et Spes*, no. 39). Obviously, our access to God occurs thus, and through history, and the light that dawns from "absolute mystery" does not "soften, rather it sharpens, our concern with the perfecting of this earth" (ibid.). Here the whole of liberation theology is at stake.

Fourth, and last, this conception of "absolute mystery" as light, and not as darkness, does not militate against the fact that, in the step from one formality to another, from the human to the divine, there exists a darkness that is none other than our inability to give any concrete content to the infinite. But I think that this formality, since that is precisely what it is, cannot be the object of contemplation. It would be useless to seek to imagine it, feel it, experience it, except as absolute confirmation of what we live and feel in the limited. We cannot know what the new earth will be like, once stripped of its limitation, since it is this limitation that makes it accessible and desirable to us. "We do not wish to be stripped naked," says Paul, "but rather to have the heavenly dwelling envelop us, so that what is mortal may be absorbed by life" (2 Cor. 5:4). "Absolute mystery" is not the absolute of an impenetrable darkness, but the absolute of a light that "enlightens all things."

PART IV

PATHS FOR THE FUTURE

CHAPTER 8

The Option for the Poor

Hermeneutic Key for Understanding the Gospel

Here Segundo makes the shocking assertion that for five centuries the church in Latin America has been interpreting the Christian gospel in "a way that kills not only the Christian who reads it, but real persons who die because others have interpreted the gospel in a particular way." He then proceeds to justify a hermeneutic based on an option for the poor that is essential to revealing the true meaning of the Word of God for the future.

Source: "La opción por los pobres como clave hermenéutica para entender el Evangelio," *Sal Terrae* (June 1986): 473–82.

THE GOSPEL CAN KILL

Let me begin with the following reflection. The gospel is used so much for discernment that the hermeneutic problem seems to have been forgotten—the problem of the interpretation of the gospel, an interpretation that presupposes an antecedent discernment. Why?

The gospel is letter, and not spirit alone, and we know from St. Paul that the letter kills and that the spirit alone gives life. Perhaps we do not sufficiently reflect on the fact that the gospel can kill. But of course it can, because it is letter, and not simply spirit. As letter, it posits a hermeneutic problem that, at least in Latin America, is no mere laboratory problem. In Latin America, literally millions of people are dying because for five centuries the gospel has been interpreted in a particular way. The hermeneutic problem of which I am speaking is not a purely speculative one, then. On this continent, the great Catholic continent of today, the gospel is read in a way that kills not only the Christian who reads it, but real persons who die because others have interpreted the gospel in a particular way. It is a very profound problem, then, and not an idle pastime. The gospel can be read apart from any relation to the liberation of the poor from their poverty, and this is why it has been read so long without the poor experiencing any change in their situation.

The phenomenon is not a new one. Nor is it exclusively Latin American. The problem of interpretation, and of an element antecedent to authentic interpretation, has arisen in the past, and with Jesus of Nazareth himself. We have the tremendous paradox of those in Jesus' time who knew the Word of God to the last jot and tittle, who were filled with scholarly zeal and employed methods of interpretation, and who watched Jesus walk right by without ever recognizing the presence and revelation of God in him. Cannot this same thing occur today? Are we sure that, were Jesus to appear among us today, the gospel as we read and interpret it would enable us to recognize him? The letter, unfortunately, continues to be the letter, and that letter can be lethal.

How, then, can we prevent this letter from killing us as Christians, and from killing those who in some way depend on our Christian responsibility in order to be human beings? Hence the evident existence of a hermeneutic problem, which, at least in Latin America, deeply affects us theologians who work here. I think that an understanding of, and minimal sympathy with, the theological work being done here will entail a desire to respond to this challenge.

AN ANSWER IN THE FORM OF A WAGER

Very well, I have an answer—my own—to this hermeneutic problem. My answer is: the option for the poor.

I shall approach the option for the poor not as a conclusion drawn by liberation theology, or as one of its favorite themes, but as a hermeneutic key—that is, as the antecedent element required in order to interpret the gospel and keep its letter from killing. In this sense, I propose this answer of mine as having universal validity—as valid not only for Latin America, but for the entire world. I call it "my" answer, not in the sense that it might not be as good as that of other liberation theologians, but because it is a wager.

I stake myself on this answer. I wager my Christian faith, not just my theological work. It is a bet I make, on how to understand correctly, and in a lifegiving way, the spirit of the gospel that speaks to me in the letter of the gospel. I do not have this answer in virtue of any scholarly argument to the effect that the option for the poor is the only one that permits me to read the gospel correctly. I cannot prove this from the gospel itself: this itself would be interpretation. I would be committing what the logicians call the fallacy of *petitio principii*, or begging the question. I cannot use the gospel to prove that the gospel must be interpreted precisely from a point of departure in the option for the poor. I have to assume this option as a risk. My option is something antecedent to the gospel; for, if the gospel were to tell me how to read it in order to read it correctly, I should thereby have this "letter" to interpret, as well!

There is more. Even though Medellín has said, and we continue to hear it said, that the gospel must be read in an option for the poor, the very expression "option for the poor" is letter, and once more the problem arises of how it is to be interpreted. As an example—of the fact that the very words in which the hermeneutic problem is formulated requires a hermeneutics—let me allude to the sad history of the expression, "option for the poor" in recent ecclesiastical literature.

Once upon a time we had learned to say: "option for the poor." But then along came Puebla, and suddenly we found that we had to say something a little different. Option for the poor now meant "preferential option for the poor." Why this tautology? When you have a preference for something, you make an option for it. When you opt for one thing, you give it preference over other things. Why must I say "preferential" option for the poor? It seems to me that the interpretive key, the cause of the change in this hermeneutic premise and its conversion into something different, is fear of conflict. By saying "preferential" option for the poor, I remove the potential for conflictivity from "option" for the poor. I opt for the poor because the poor are oppressed by the rich, by the powerful, by those who are invested with power. To opt for the poor means—as I think the Gospel of Luke somewhat understands it when after saying "blessed are the poor" it adds, "woe to you rich!"—opting against the situation in which the rich live today.

In order to avoid this conflictivity in the reading of the gospel, the expression "preferential option for the poor" is now used, which amounts to saying: out of every hour, I shall devote fifty minutes to the poor and the remaining ten to the rich, because they, too, are human beings, and deserve our Christian concern and care. In this hermeneutic key, the element of conflict is eviscerated; we shift to another key, in which, seemingly, there is more room for all human beings.

The Vatican's "Instruction on the Theology of Liberation," on the other hand, actually accuses liberation theology of citing Puebla incorrectly in constantly speaking of a preferential option for the poor, since the bishops at Puebla admitted—by way of a compromise, as I see it—that what was meant was a "preferential option for the poor and for youth." The instruction asks—with a question that doubtless includes a condemnation—why the theology of liberation forgets this datum. It forgets it simply because the young have nothing to do with the case.

The option for the poor derives simply from the fact that the poor are the abandoned, the marginalized of a society such as we know it; and therefore God makes an option for them, in order to bestow the reign upon them. This is the understanding of the gospel that we adopt. What are the young doing here? Simply removing the sense of conflict from the option for the poor (already degraded to the status of a "preferential" option) still further by converting it into a pastoral option. That is, the church is going to concern itself especially with the poor and young people, because the poor have so little attention paid to them, and the young have such important, typical problems that it would be dangerous for the church to ignore them. And there is still more. In order to conjure the conflictivity away completely, the Roman instruction proposes a third formula: "preferential concern." Now there is no longer even an option. I no longer choose.

As we can see, not even a phrase that implies a hermeneutics can escape hermeneutics, because it, too, is "letter," open to various interpretations and requiring an option.

I have already pointed out that the option for the poor is not a theme of liberation theology, but the epistemological premise for an interpretation of the word of God. As with any interpretation, I assume a risk here. I place conditions on what I hear in order to hear it — on what I read in order to understand it. In a sense, I assume the risk of conditioning my reading of God's Word, because that Word cannot be approached or understood without a determinate antecedent attitude — without my approaching it, before I hear it, with a particular understanding, an attitude that makes it possible for me to understand it. After all, were there to be complete disharmony between my attitude and what the Word will be saying to me, then I should completely distort the interpretation of that Word.

It is a matter, then, of a preunderstanding of who this God is who speaks to me, and what this God's plan is. I believe simply that this God is like a political figure who proposes to found a new kingdom — this is the image that Jesus used in speaking of his Father — and that this political figure is not going to be primarily concerned with judging people, with deciding who the good are and who the wicked are, but is going to start right out with those who suffer the most, with those who are most marginalized, most prevented from being truly human. This is the cause of everything that this personage is going to say to us, everything this figure will be revealing to us. And it is with this attitude, with this sympathy for those who suffer most, an attitude and sympathy like God's, that I shall read the Gospel, to see what it tells me about those persons to whom, and together with whom, I make my commitment.

THE GOSPEL ITSELF CALLS FOR AN ANTECEDENT UNDERSTANDING

I have already indicated that it cannot be proved from the gospel what the adequate "preunderstanding" for an understanding of the gospel is. I cannot go to the gospel to learn what preunderstanding I must have in order to read it aright. This would be a vicious circle. But I can indeed go to the gospel in order to somehow break into this hermeneutic circle. It can be proved, I think, that the gospel altogether clearly indicates the absolute urgency of a preunderstanding. Before saying what it wishes to tell us, the gospel informs us that a preunderstanding is needed—I make no attempt just now to say which—and that those who go directly to the gospel for the solution to a problem on the pretext of a "neutral approach" fail to understand the gospel. Thinking to spare themselves this initial wager, they fail to understand the gospel, because its letter has killed them in advance.

Who are these dead who approach the gospel? They are those who have a hard heart, with this neutrality of theirs—going to seek their answer directly in the letter of Scripture. These were the adversaries of Jesus—Jesus who had come precisely to continue the Old Testament Word of God and to render it explicit. Such is the content, for instance, of Jesus' three great disputes with the Pharisees in the Gospel of Mark, a content all the more important in that Mark is generally the least interested of all the evangelists in handing on to us the *logia* of Jesus. The three disputes are lengthy ones, and tense ones, central to Mark's Gospel, on the subject of the hermeneutics of the Word of God.

The first comes at the end of chapter 2 and the beginning of chapter 3, and bears on the use of the Sabbath. Jesus' adversaries have already gone to Scripture, seemingly with all necessary scientific apparatus and a neutral heart, to ask what may and what may not be done on the Sabbath. But Jesus begins with something else. He tells them that the Sabbath is made for the human being, and not the human being for the Sabbath. That is, whether the Sabbath is sacred or not is not in the word of God speaking of what is permitted or forbidden on that day, but in what God intends for the human being. God has made the Sabbath for the good of the human being, and therefore only those who seek the good of the human being understand what is written concerning the Sabbath.

Jesus thereby defends the disciples who have pulled off heads of grain on a Sabbath day as they walked through the fields. Then he goes on to heal in the synagogue the person with the paralyzed hand, and asks a most interesting question from the viewpoint of hermeneutics. To the Pharisees' stock answer on what could be done on the Sabbath, Jesus responds with this question: "Is it permitted to do good or evil on the Sabbath?" The question unmasks the hypocrisy of the response that was supposed to have been found in Scripture, since to say in the name of God that it was permitted to do evil on the Sabbath would be blasphemy; but to answer whether it was permitted to do good or evil on the Sabbath implies the possession of a hermeneutic key to interpret what Scripture says about the Sabbath.

The second dispute is over what makes a person clean or unclean. Jesus simply overthrows all the dietary laws of the Jews, in the name of the project of the human being. In a project where there is love, there is no impurity possible. It is what issues from the heart of a human being that makes the human being impure. From the heart of human beings issues the project of loving or not loving their neighbor, and so on. To what extent, therefore, in order to know the law of God, is it necessary to have already taken one's stand within a project that is parallel to, similar to, the project of God? We must make a personal wager for that project, before reading what the gospel says about purity and impurity.

The third dispute is even more clearly hermeneutical. It is the dispute on how to discern the presence of God in history, in Jesus. The Pharisees demand a direct answer from heaven. They take a completely neutral position. What Jesus does can in itself be ascribed, indifferently, to God or to Beelzeboul. They seek to have a clear word in the Bible and find none. They ask, therefore, that God provide them with a sign from heaven. But such a sign they shall not have. Jesus gives them, as an example of a sign of the times, and of a reading of the signs of the times, the pagan peoples who, in the sensitivity of their hearts, have attuned themselves to what God was trying to tell them. Meanwhile here are the Pharisees looking at Jesus, and out of tune with God, because they lack sensitivity in their hearts to interpret the word. The signs of the times somehow precondition the reading of the word.

It is important to see how the "Instruction on the Theology of Liberation" reverses this order of discernment. It says that the signs of the times with regard to where liberation is occurring must be discerned in the light of the gospel. Is this not the logic of the Pharisees, who sought a sign from heaven to solve the problem that a human being must actually solve by somehow placing a wager? "Why do you not yourselves judge what is just?" are the words with which Luke interprets the meaning of the signs of the times. He is referring to the preunderstanding required in order to understand what God sends as Word. This is clear in chapters 3 and 8 of Mark.

The other synoptic evangelists, too, furnish us with what we might call "hermeneutic parables." We have the parable of the Faithless Steward, who, while breaking the letter of the law, finds himself miraculously in tune with what the landowner wanted to do with the estate and his money. We have the parable of the Last Judgment, in which openhearted persons have done what Jesus' adversaries have been unable to do: find God in the suffering, in the hungry, the thirsty, the isolated, or the imprisoned. And we have the parable of the Good Samaritan, in which a person who neither knew nor understood the law, but whose heart was open to an option, to an attitude, interpreted the law. This parable is situated in a context of interpretation of the law. It is not a parable about charity. What Jesus is being asked is how he reads the law regarding one's neighbor. His response is that an authentic reading of the law is done by persons who have an open heart, and who have come to the aid of their neighbor.

This reference to Jesus' polemical parables is not intended as a proof that my wager is correct and complete for an understanding of the gospel. It is intended only as a way into the hermeneutic circle, a way of breaking into this closed circle and becoming convinced that the gospel itself, before giving us a response to our human problems, the problems of poverty, and so on, demands a preattitude, a preunderstanding—and that it only opens itself (as the very letter of the Gospel has it) to those who have this attitude. I wager on the attitude called the "option for the poor."

WHAT IS THE OPTION FOR THE POOR IN THE CONCRETE?

I do not believe that there is any other way of expressing the option for the poor concretely than to say that it is God's compassion for the most afflicted. When I say "for the most afflicted," I should not wish this to be understood as meaning some very sophisticated or subtle kind of suffering. The gospel is very clear, even materialistic, in its indications of the priorities of suffering. I know very well that a wealthy person can suffer deeply and profoundly. But if I see a poor person drowning and I am speaking with the rich about their suffering, I would immediately go to the aid of the person drowning and would leave the suffering of the rich for some later time. The option for the poor is an option for those in whom the lack of humanness appears before us as the clearest priority to be addressed.

I have indicated on other occasions that, in this option for the poor, there are various nuances, different conceptions, different mediations. At the risk of a caricature, I should say that there is a way of understanding this option for the poor that consists in a plain and simple interpretation of the Beatitudes: it consists in rescuing the poor from their poverty. The Beatitudes call the poor lucky not because they have any special, very valuable qualities in God's sight, but because they suffer more. And they say—and this is the good news—that they are no longer going to be poor. If there seems to be any doubt about this, one need only glance at the other Beatitudes as they appear in the source common to Matthew and Luke: the hungry are not lucky because being hungry prepares a person in a special way for the eschaton, but simply because they will be satisfied, because they will cease to be hungry. When those who weep are proclaimed blessed, the gospel also says why: because they are going to laugh—they are going to stop crying.

And yet—again at the risk of caricature—there is another conception of the option for the poor to the effect that the poor are closer to God, and that we must in some way become like them. It is not that we are to draw them out of their poverty; we are to become like them, because it is with them that God is in sympathy. They have qualities that God values. Surely this aspect of the Beatitudes, as well, has its foundation in the gospel, at least in what the gospel says about the rich by way of antithesis. Let us put it this way. The former conception would favor placing everything at the service of the poor—including the intellectual opportunities of a middle-class person—placing everything at the service of the poor and their liberation, without precisely valuing the poor more in themselves. The second consists in placing everything, even the intellectual function itself, in the most direct service of the poor in their very poverty, in the very situation of the poor. These two conceptions can be disputed. The only thing I am doing here is presenting them as different mediations of the option for the poor in liberation theology.

In conclusion: The option for the poor is the human attitude that we adopt, on our own responsibility and at our own risk, toward the Word of God, before the reading of that Word. We believe — it is an article of faith — that this preconception, this preattitude, will open its meaning to us. We wager our faith — and God grant us sincerely to wager our lives as well — that this is the truth.

Question. Someone might ask me the following question about my method. Does not your emphasis on the importance of a *previous option*, and of making that option, excessively neutralize the gospel text? Is the gospel in itself a dead letter? Does the gospel kill just as the law did? Then why did you accept the gospel and cite and analyze it?

You give the impression that your option for the poor is not as preevangelical as you say. It is evangelical, as well. This is why it is of interest to believers. But in that case you would have done well to analyze, in greater detail than you have, who the poor are in terms of the gospel — and not simply assume without further ado that they are the same as those for whom you have said you make your preevangelical option.

Answer. I think that this is a very important question. Let me give my answer in three parts. First, I think that there is a circle here. I am not very sure where this circle has begun. I do not know how far, by dint of reading the gospel, I have accounted for the gospel's saying something.

The second thing is that, when I speak of a preunderstanding, I am not saying that the text is neutral. I am saying that the text is open — that, while it has a certain force in itself, this force is insufficient to shake a false attitude, toward either the gospel or the law, in approaching the gospel. Just as the Pharisees approached the Old Testament without understanding the word of God, so also one can approach the gospel without understanding what it says. I see the proof of this in Latin America, which has read the gospel for five centuries without understanding it in the same way as I understand it now. That is, either I am mistaken, or the gospel, which has force in itself, has not succeeded in overcoming certain attitudes with which it has been approached.

The third thing is that, once we have entered into the hermeneutic circle with the preunderstanding of which we have spoken, obviously we shall become convinced that the gospel says this.

If I have used the gospel only negatively here, it is because I do not wish to begin where all the difficulties arise. My purpose is to show, especially, that the gospel says that before reading it, one must do something else. I have used the gospel not to say that the necessary preunderstanding is the option for the poor; I have used it to prove that the gospel itself says: do not read me without a preunderstanding, without a preattitude. This, in a way, breaks the circle; and although I have entered it from the other side, I am very concerned to accept what the gospel says about this preunderstanding.

CHAPTER 9

Revelation, Faith, Signs of the Times

The unusual theological approach to the topics of revelation, faith, and the signs of the times has been (1) God's revelation, (2) the human response of faith, and (3) the concrete problems of history or "the signs of the times." Segundo believes, however, that the more effective and liberative approach is just the opposite. We should begin with the signs of the times or the challenges of history, then move on to faith seen as good news, and finally arrive at a much deeper understanding of revelation, one that is liberating, not lethal.

Source: "Revelación, fe, signos de los tiempos," *Revista Latinoamericana de Teología* 5 (1988): 123–44.

The reader could think at first sight that the terms in the title of this article were three vaguely related items grouped together for an economical use of space. The very arrangement of the three items could suggest the arrangement of elements, in descending order, to be found in the customary theoretical treatment of the fundamental concepts of theology in any theological dictionary.[1] Indeed, it would have been strange if "revelation" had not been one of these concepts. How could there be a theology that did not treat of what God has revealed? Or still more basically, of what is meant by God's "revealing" something? And one might likewise suppose that, if a particular theology has some specific characteristic, it will have to reflect on the manner in which divine revelation is approached, studied, and used; and therefore that, after having treated of "revelation," it should have to treat of the "faith" with which human beings must respond to this revelatory message when they discover that it actually comes from God, from infinite truth. Finally, a theology like liberation theology, which, as we know, is characterized by, among other things, an attachment (even in its initial moment) to the practice of faith, cannot, in its work of "understanding" that faith, prescind from the signs that the history of that practice and its crisis throw up to it as so many interrogations: "the signs of the times," as Jesus calls them in Matthew's Gospel (16:3).

This amounts to detecting an order—all but necessary, apparently—proceeding from the "word of God" to faith to the most significant concrete problems presented by history, that these problems may be "illuminated, guided . . . and interpreted in the light of the Gospel"[2]—that is, submitted to the criterion of the revealed word of God.

This order, while doubtless logical, is not, I should think, the order in which the three elements are presented in the human being's existence and concrete history. It surely represents a "theological" order. Nor does this mean that its use will be restricted to scholarship. Reflection on the most ordinary pastoral activity will show that Christians follow this path routinely. It is not, however, the only possible order. What would happen, for example, if the order of these three concepts were reversed? Unless I am mistaken, this reversed order would be an "anthropological" or "existential" one. That is to say, we should now have the order in which the three factors appear (although in a different way, and at least as a problem) to believers and nonbelievers alike.

Let it not be thought that this hypothesis—which we shall examine here—indicates the need for an option for either of the two orders as being the "correct" order. Each, in its own domain, has its explanation and raison d'être. They are not mutually exclusive, then, and it would be imprudent and naive to regard one of them as constituting the only correct way of relating the three terms in the list.

Nevertheless, I hold that the second orientation or sequence, in that it represents a more general process transpiring among human beings, has pedagogical advantages, as I trust will become clear in the course of this article. I propose, then, to devote the three parts of this article to showing how each of the three items in the title conditions God's communication to human beings, and how, in this respect, the one last on the list is actually the first of these conditions.

I

When we proclaim that God has determined to "reveal" to human beings truths that they could by no means, or only with excessive difficulty, find by themselves (Denzinger 1785–86), we correctly indicate the bountiful, gratuitous origin, in the divine plan, of that intervention of God in human history. God has determined to communicate certain truths concerning God and the human being. And always *both at once*.

Anyone claiming this "communication" to be possible is constrained to admit from the outset that the message communicated must fall into the category of what is understandable and important for the human being. It would be vain to pretend to conceive a "word of God" addressed to human beings but not expressed in the language of human beings, or failing to call their attention to some value to be derived from knowing it.

Here, then, are two logical conditions, converging on the same activity: that of communicating. And in terms of the simplest definition, one who communicates conveys to the interlocutor "a difference that makes a difference."[3] If there is no understanding of the message, the (presumed) *difference* is not verified. Something whose identity is unknown is not added to what is already known. But secondly, if this transmitted difference does not *make a difference* in the existence of the one receiving the message, neither is anything communicated. And since knowledge, despite the old saw, really does "take up space" in the mind, our psychology rapidly strives (by forgetting) to regain the space taken up by supposed differences, which, while transmitted, change the receiver in no way.

Of these two preconditions for God's being *able* to "reveal" something to us (since any revelation is either accommodated to our human manner of communication or it simply does not exist), theology has by and large accepted the first, although not without certain strings attached out of respect for the divine initiative and the divine object of that special communication.

Obviously the Infinite Being cannot speak to us in a language of its own, which would have the characteristics of that limitless being. For example, it cannot speak in an atemporal manner to a being whose (transcendent) imagination is structured by time. To put it another way, the human being cannot understand an "eternal" language, because the one destined to be and permitted to be the receiver of the transmitter's self-communication varies with time and circumstances.

Even before becoming personally incarnate in the Son, God, having willed to become revealer, had to speak to human beings by "enfleshing" the divine word in a human language, which uses signs limited in their being and their power of signifying. Hence in that act of communication, what is understood is only an infinitesimal particle, as it were, of a truth that always reaches us only "to the extent that we can understand it" (Denzinger 1796; see Mark 4:33).[4]

The greatest risk of deviation, however, lies in neglect of the second precondition. It is not a mere matter of perceiving something (for which it is necessary that our knowledge receive a "different" content from the one it had before). The "difference" must also "*make* a difference." Otherwise the message, however well received and, so to speak, well "deposited" in the receiver, would not yet signify anything. And the mental mechanisms would soon take account of this "nonsignifying" difference and respond by forgetting it. The difference transmitted commences to signify when the receiver perceives what it should affect or change in his or her actual existence or behavior—that is, when the perceived difference is related to another, correlative difference that ought to take place in the existence of the receiver.

Let us have an analogy from the material order. When the air temperature becomes "different" from the limits established on the thermostat, it does not yet strictly "communicate" anything until the thermostat "understands" that what has been transmitted regarding the different temperature ought to "differentiate" its current state, so that it will now turn on the furnace that will heat the ambient once more to the desired temperature. Only then is there a true "communication": when there is a difference that makes or produces a difference.

This is a law of all communication. It is therefore valid for any self-revelation that God might wish to make to human beings. St. Augustine explains it in less scientific, but very expressive, language. Commenting on a passage from the Gospel of John (5:25), where Jesus is presented as promising a kind of "resurrection" of the spirit or mind, to take place *before* the universal resurrection of the flesh, Augustine declares that this resurrection must be understood realistically, but spiritually. Is it not the (spiritual) recovery of life, he asks, to pass "from unjust to just, from impious to pious, from foolish to wise?" Augustine indicates that the promise of these "resurrections" is a common thing. Every founder of a religion or sect has claimed to have a "divine revelation" vis-à-vis those transformations that may well be called resurrections, or radical changes of life.

And this is precisely what I mean here. "For, no one has denied this spiritual resurrection, lest he be told: If the spirit does not resurrect, then *why are you speaking to me?* . . . If you are not making me better than I was, then *why are you speaking to me?*"[5] Augustine's repetition of the question "Why are you speaking to me?" is intended to emphasize that, for the structure of the human mind, a communication, even a divine communication, that indicates (or signifies) no "difference" (direct or indirect, for the short or long term) has no meaning or raison d'être. It "signifies nothing."

On this precise point, Vatican II complemented, and in a certain sense corrected, a potential misunderstanding of the texts of Vatican I that suggested and asserted that, in order to speak to human beings, God could only "enflesh" the divine word in the limited language of human beings. It must follow that, if God wished to speak to us of the divine mystery itself, this could be done only in a limited, obscure way that our finite capacity for understanding would, as it were, place at the divine disposal. Thus, that God is at once one and three remains "mysterious" even after being "revealed" or communicated by God (see Denzinger 1796). Thus, it seems as if God had communicated something for the sole purpose of our knowing it, or better, had repeated it without its meaning any "difference" in our way of existing. Its relevance for us might seem to have proceeded not from our understanding our life more and living it better, but from a kind of power intrinsic to that message, which would be salvific before the judgment seat of God although having in no way modified the existence of the human being, like a magical safe-conduct, an "Open, Sesame!"

Vatican Council II, speaking of divine revelation, agrees with Vatican I that "God spoke by means of human beings *in a human manner*" (*Dei*

Verbum, no. 12). But at Vatican II the accent was no longer on the limitation that this "human manner" imposed on divine revelation, and thus on the mystery that the revelation allows to subsist. At Vatican II the emphasis was on the fact that all of God's messages to us are authentic, integral "communication": a difference in the conception of God intended to become a difference in the way in which we understand and live our creative, communitarian destiny.

Indeed, the most complete, total, and personal revelation of God is, indivisibly, also a revelation of ourselves and our destiny: "The *same* revelation of the Father and of his love [in Christ] *fully* manifests the human being to the human being himself, and discovers to him the sublimity of his destiny" (*Gaudium et Spes*, no. 22). The council, then, does not regard revelation as something that, without transforming our historical life — without "making us better," to use Augustine's expression — constitutes a "truth": that is, something that can be possessed, be deposited, and have value in God's sight (see Matt. 25:24 and parallels) by performing its salvific activity in a magical manner (see *Gaudium et Spes*, nos. 7, 43).

Thus, according to the council, the intent of God's revelation is not that we *know* (something that otherwise would be impossible or difficult for us to know), but that we *be* different, and act better.

When this conception of divine revelation is analyzed more in depth, it becomes possible to understand the dogmatic reorientation that a council that meant to be pastoral saw itself obliged to undertake in order that the "difference" entailed in its most novel orientations might be understood. Indeed, the council is teaching that faith in God's self-revelation, far from turning the mind from the temporal and ephemeral toward the necessary and eternal, "directs the mind toward fully human solutions" of historical problems (ibid., no. 11). Thus, Christians do not possess, not even by understanding it, the truth that God communicates to them until they succeed in transforming it into a humanizing "difference" within history. Until orthopraxis[6] becomes reality, no matter how ephemeral and contingent that reality, Christians do not yet know the truth. On the contrary, in virtue of an imperative of their moral conscience, they must "join the rest of human beings [Christians and others] in the *quest* for the truth" (ibid., no. 16).

But this places us precisely before the problem of the priority of revelation to faith or vice versa. We had thought that faith came second, as a response to God's revelation of divine truth. Now we perceive that, in order for us to receive this truth, it must find us somehow engaged in a common quest of human liberation. This of itself implies a kind of "faith" — and what is more, a kind of "Abrahamic faith" — that is, a faith occurring antecedently to any religious classification. And indeed, this is how Paul presents Abraham (Rom. 4): as someone who, before being "religiously classifiable" in a particular category, already believes in a kind of promise that the history of human liberation and humanization seems to address to those who struggle for it. Abraham believed in "the God who gives life to the dead and calls to being what is not" (Rom. 4:17; see 4:21, 2:6–7).

What is this "faith" that precedes "revelation," and which, as we have seen, makes revelation possible as the necessary precondition for the revealed "difference" to effect the essential praxic "difference" without which there could be no authentic communication between God and ourselves?

One of our essential dimensions as human beings is what we might call the quest for the meaning of our existence. Absorbed as we may be in the urgencies of day-to-day survival, and little as we may perceive that we have a freedom that opens to us a certain spectrum of opportunities or routes to various values or satisfactions, all the same we realize that our free existence is a kind of wager. Why a "wager"? Because we have only one existence, and cannot "test out" in advance what we are going to choose. We are not granted to traverse a course to the end, observe whether it is has been a satisfactory one, and then, in all assurance and (empirical) cognizance of cause, return to our starting point—and then make our option knowing beforehand what awaits us at the end of the road. When you fall in love, you have no way of knowing what your beloved will be like fifty years from now. When you choose an ideal, and spend long years in preparation for it (for example, a professional career), you can as yet have no experience of what awaits you at the end of the road of your professional practice. When you start a revolution, you do not yet know what historical price it will demand of you, or what will remain of your project even after you have paid the price. And so on.

History is exciting. It is like an open promise. But there is no antecedent verification of anything, at least no direct one. This does not mean that the wager of our entire freedom, and often our life (in one way or another) is blind and irrational. Human society provides each of its members with a kind of collective memory, within which the option under consideration becomes a reasonable one. But it is still a wager. The human species with its different cultures, the nation, the clan, the family, provide each individual with "witnesses" or "testimonials" of meaningful lives. The option of freedom is based on that memory, makes it its own, tests it, uses it, modifies it, and makes an option among the opportunities it offers. But at bottom, when all is said and done, it places its "faith" in one or more of the testimonials that the memory presents.

This faith—which we shall call an "anthropological faith," because it is a human dimension, and both religious and nonreligious persons possess it—is different in each human being. The proof of this is that there is no one who, in the course of their life, does not pay a high price for things that they have not experienced in advance, even when they are feasible or satisfying, regardless of whether they lead to felicity or frustration. Indeed, meaning is so important for human beings that they are able to give all of the being that they have at their disposal, including their very lives, that these lives may have meaning and thus redeem their value. In Latin America we know only too well that this is not the privilege or peculiarity of Christians. But the gospel does not mean to proclaim something meaningless when Jesus says: "Who seeks to save his life will lose it; but who loses his life for me and the gospel will find it" (Mark 8:35, Matt. 16:25, and par.).

In summary: human beings, as free beings, structure the world out of what for them bids fair to have meaning and value, relying on other existences that are testimonials to how a satisfying human existence can be lived. Everyone makes one or more of the choices that present themselves within this collective testimonial. This structuring option, while arising in connection with one or more testimonials, is complex — as complex as an existence that must confront ever different situations and select, in each of them, the most consistent option available in light of whatever value is esteemed most highly and which is always present and active in the mind (usually translated in terms rather of images than of abstractions). Thus we have a value, or constellation of values, dominated by one that faith has enthroned as *absolute*. Indeed, independently of whether an Absolute Being exists or not, and antecedently to that question, all human beings establish — by their "anthropological" faith — each of them, their *own* absolute: what each one seeks not as a means to something else, but for its own sake. Persons true to themselves will not negotiate it. They will not sell it for any price, even that of their lives. Its loss would be the death of meaning.

II

What does this have to do with our subject, which is God's "revelation"? A great deal. Why? Because the usual order in which the problem is presented is a theological order. And rightly so, in scholarly theology. But in the process of a human existence, the order is different — reversed, in fact. We are tempted to think: God reveals, and we, faced with this revelation (perceived and accepted as such), make an option to accept it or reject it (in unbelief or idolatry). But what we have just seen obliges us to modify this routine conceptualization. We are forced back on Augustine's radical question: If you do not make me better than I was, why are you talking to me at all? Augustine is not being impertinent. Human beings *understand only what affects them*, only what makes them better or worse. This means that, in God's revealing, faith does not come after something has been revealed. Faith is an *active*, indispensable part of revelation itself.

But there is more. True, the quest for the meaning needed to establish communication between God and human beings is not the same in everyone. But it is always "faith." God addresses the divine word to an (anthropological) faith that is always there, and that in each human being is the fruit of an option (antecedent to hearing).

To put it another way: the role of freedom is more active or decisive. It is part of the very process of "revelation." Orthopraxis is not an ultimate "application" of revelation to practice: it is a necessary condition of the sheer possibility that revelation actually reveal something.[7]

But so far we have taken only the first step. We have shown that, in its very definition, there is no such thing as divine revelation (although there is such a thing as the "word of God" in the Bible) unless there is a human quest that converges with this word, a quest for which the word of God signifies a liberation of human potential and human values: the making of human beings "better than they were." This is the game God agrees to play in the divine self-communication to the human being.[8]

And yet, there is a great deal more. What God communicates to this human being is not a pure, simple, ready-made answer, valid once and for all and for all questions, regardless of context or the problem before which we find ourselves. And this despite the fact that the church sometimes seems to utilize the Bible—the deposit of God's "revelation"—as a repertory of stock, universally valid answers.

In the first place, if we examine this "deposit" of revelation constituted, for us Christians, by the Old and New Testaments, it is possible, and even fitting, that we should be struck and overwhelmed by the multitude of images, words, testimonials, and episodes that we find there. God has supposedly made use of these to reveal something. Indeed, it is very possible that we should be equally surprised that such a process of communication between God and human beings is supposed to have terminated on a certain vaguely specified date, as if that revelation had exhausted its content, or as if we now needed no more of God's words in order to be delivered from all that prevents us from being collectively and individually human.

There are certain questions that Christians must ask themselves, regardless of their particular degree of perspicacity. One, perhaps the most obvious one, is the following. Now that God has revealed both God and the human being in the only-begotten Son, and now that, in that Son (and in the witnesses of his life and message), the deposit of revelation has been closed for good and all—why should we continue to regard the previous words, images, and personages as a revelation that continues to call for our faith (see Denzinger 783, 1787)?

Another question, a related one, arises from the fact that, as we have said, very frequently in all this "deposit" of revealed truth, stock answers are sought to the questions of the human being of today. For example: What about marriage? To this question the church generally responds with the words that Jesus is regarded as having said about marriage (see Matt. 19:1–9), forbidding the separation of the spouses ("what God has joined together")—the repudiation of the female partner ("except in case of fornication," which no one is quite sure how to interpret) and the contracting of another marriage on the part of the husband (or the wife—see Mark 10:12).

If faith obliges us to accept, on faith, this response for all cases today, then is that polygamy licit today that the patriarchs once practiced with

God's approval, as well as the repudiation of the wife approved of by the law of Moses (Deut. 24:1ff.)? If the answer to this question, which is only one in a thousand that we might ask, is yes, then it is in direct contradiction with what Jesus says. And if we answer no, then what meaning can there be in the claim that the entire Old Testament is the "word of God," just as the New? Thus, there would not seem to be any logical response to this question the disciples put to Jesus, as long as we keep thinking of the "revelation" or "word" of God as a repertory of questions and answers valid in some atemporal fashion, after the manner of "information," ever true, since it proceeds from truth itself.

And the solution is not that this occurs only with regard to moral usages and questions. Almost to the end of Old Testament times, we find that the authors and personages of that collection of writings do not believe in a life after death. In what sense, then, can Christians say they believe in God's "revelation" in the Old Testament in the same fashion and for the same reason that they believe in it in the New?

In fact, even with regard to God there are important variations among the various Old Testament authors. The most eloquent case is that of the Book of Job, where, on the basis of the misfortunes afflicting this legendary personage, the book presents a dispute between two theologies. According to the one, represented by Job's friends and by Elihu—as also by most of the books of the Old Testament—the evils that befall a person are in strict proportion to that person's sinful actions. Job, examining his own experience, and even taking his admitted sinfulness into consideration, denies such an equation, and thus opposes traditional theology. And God decides the question in favor of Job's position, despite Job's imprudence in demanding of God an account of his misfortunes. The "suffering just," who can even die without Yahweh's accommodating their fate to their moral behavior, thus become a theological crisis (see Ps. 73:44, Eccl. 3:16–22, etc.), to which Israel will give different solutions. After all, how indeed can the faithfulness of Yahweh—an essential divine quality—be reconciled with an entire human life in which justice does not have the last word?

Vatican Council II, precisely in its constitution *Dei Verbum*—that is, the document that treats of the "word of God" and the divine "revelation"—indicates the most deep-reaching and complete solution to these comprehensive problems. There we read that, although the books of the Old Testament "contain certain imperfect and transitory things, they nevertheless demonstrate the *true divine pedagogy*."

This declaration is worthy of consideration on a number of counts. The *first* is that "imperfect and transitory things" are said to be part of "true" divine revelation. Obviously, in speaking of "transitory things," the allusion is to things that have ceased to be true (or at least completely and perfectly true), although they have been true in times past. It would appear that the concept of "truth" is relativized. Jesus indicated the same thing in referring to the validity or truth of his conception of marriage (see Matt. 19:8), or, to recall only one celebrated instance, in the matter of knowing what obligations God has imposed with regard to human activities on the Sabbath day (see Mark 2:27). Once again, God seems concerned not that the divine "revelation" be true in itself—be eternal truth, unchangeable truth—but that it "become" true in the humanization of the human being. In other words, God speaks only to those who seek, and gives them no recipes, but rather guides them in their searching.

And this brings us to the *second* thing we must consider in the passage we have cited from *Dei Verbum*. "Divine revelation" is not a deposit of true information, but a *true pedagogy*. The divine revelation of God and the human being does not consist in amassing correct information in their regard. That revelation is a "process," and in that process we do not learn "things." We learn to learn—just as in any pedagogy, in which children are "guided" (the etymology of "ped-*agogue*") to learn to seek after truth through trial and error. In any process of education, then—even in the most *true*, indeed, infallible, educational process of all—there are "imperfect and transitory" things. Thus, it is enormously important to know where the "truth" is located in these kinds of educational processes. It is not irrelevant that the council uses the adjective "true" to characterize not the first level, but the second. Pedagogy is a process of *apprenticeship in the second degree*. And its truth lies not in some timeless truth on the first level, where information is accumulated, but on the second level, that of an apprenticeship, where the factors for seeking and finding truth are multiple.

Thus, to return to the example already given, if an author or reader of most of the books of the Old Testament is asked whether there is a life after death or not, we should have, on the first level, an erroneous (negative) response. To be sure, only rarely was this response explicit, since the question of life after death was not a problem that usually arose in an Old Testament context. But there is not the slightest doubt what answer we should have received had we actually asked about life after death (see Ps. 30:10, 88:11, 115:17; Eccl. 3:19–21; etc.). The answer would have been: there is no such thing. However, a pedagogy as correct and true as the God who conducts it is faithful and true, will one day lead to a resolution of the equation between a God who is justice, and the fact that a good, just person must live and die in pain. Thus, the day will come when human beings, guided in this fashion, will think that the justice practiced during life must survive death (see Wisdom 1:15). That moment, that of the *true* state of the question, will swell the liberative courage of the solution found, and a new, eschatological dimension will be added to the historical (limited to the earth and this life), factoring its meaning.

But—to continue with the same example—would "truth" have been gained if this same information about life after death had been imparted much earlier—for example, in the age of the exile, or of the great prophets? I realize, of course, that it is rarely either easy or useful to manage hypotheses not actually verified in history. Nevertheless, I think I can say that the educational processes that I know lead to the conclusion that "leaking" information—that is, giving it without waiting for the proper moment in the pedagogical process—would have obliterated a series of important truths whereby Yahweh was bestowing a self-revelation in Israel in the many critical experiences of fully historical quests. Premature information as to the reality of an afterlife would have plunged Israel into a misguided search for Yahweh outside history. And thus, while materially true—orthodox—this information would have generated deeper errors, difficult to correct in the future. This is the problem facing the pastoral ministry today.

Hence the necessity of conceiving "revelation" not as a mere providing of correct information about God and human beings, but as a "true pedagogy," a divine pedagogy. We must seriously modify our conception of the relationship between revelation and truth. However—and here we come to a *third* observation—*Dei Verbum* speaks of the imperfect and transitory only with regard to the Old Testament. It says nothing like this with regard to the New. This is food for thought. Will God have changed methods of "revealing" since the coming of Christ? Will God have begun to provide us with perfect and invariable, or perhaps merely explanatory, information? Indeed, in the presence of divine, eternal truth itself, now revealed, will God perhaps have terminated this process of search, demonstrated in the Old Testament?

Vatican II's attribution of the imperfect and transitory specifically to the Old Testament, as well as certain explicit declarations of the ordinary church magisterium (e.g., Denzinger 2012), might seem to suggest this. But there are serious reasons for thinking that, even after God's revelation in Jesus Christ, the only-begotten divine Son, the revelatory function of the Spirit of Jesus continues to accompany the process of the humanization of all human beings.

For one thing, the New Testament itself states this. According to the Johannine theology, the very physical disappearance of Jesus Christ, his transitus from this earth to his glorious invisibility, is "fitting." St. Augustine expressed it very simply, and with unmatched eloquence: "The Lord himself, as he deigned to be our Way, did not seek to detain us, but rather moved on."[9] Jesus himself says this, in different words, in his farewell discourse, according to the fourth Gospel (which, while not synonymous with historical fidelity, does belong to God's "revelation" or "word"). And he explains the reason for this strange fittingness: "If I do not go away, the Paraclete will not come to you. I should be able to tell you many other things, as well, but you could not manage them now. When the Spirit of Truth comes, he will guide you to the whole truth" (John 16:7, 12–13).

At once we find the concern of every process of apprenticeship in the second degree—the concern in any process of teaching a person to think—with not "leaking" information on the pretext of its being true. The "truth" at issue in this process is situated on another level, and that level demands that one problem lead to others, and that information be framed within the problematic of the real. But furthermore we find, as in any "pedagogy," that the need for (mere) information diminishes with increasing maturity. At some point, learning to learn postulates the absence of a teacher—or better, the replacement of the physical teacher to whom one can go in case of doubt, by the "spirit" of the teacher, which, through what has already been learned, and new historical challenges, will continue to carry the process forward.

Paul makes this maturity the very core of the Christian message. The "pedagogue"—in this case a revelation "deposited in writing"—has fulfilled its function. It must now make way for the Spirit, who will lead the community of Jesus to learn, by "creating" in history, daughters and sons that we are of our creative Parent (see Gal. 3–5; 1 Cor. 1:10–16, 3:1–9, 21–23; Rom. 8:14–21). God's progressive, gradual, "pedagogical" communication to us of the divine truth, which is our truth as well, the truth that sets us free in the history in which we become siblings to one another (see 1 Cor. 3:9; 10:23–24), cannot cease with Jesus. The teacher who speaks to us from a "Scripture" is no longer with us, but something more important, effective, and mature is: the Spirit of Jesus, who suggests to us that which Jesus, were he present, would have wished to say to us regarding the problems of today.[10] A question to which Vatican II points, although it seems to have been forgotten today, is whether the church believes, really and truly believes, in that Spirit that leads the community to all truth.

With what we have said up to this point, we have taken a second step in our consideration of the relationship between revelation, faith, and the signs of the times. At first it had appeared to us that the divine revelation was already complete from God's side, and that all that remained, from our side, was to receive it in faith, hold it in reverence, and apply it in praxis. With this second step, we see, revelation presupposes not only a search and an antecedent faith, but also the constitution of a people that will *hand on* a wisdom from generation to generation.[11] Through things ever imperfect and transitory, handed down by the very existence of the community, that "people" becomes "tradition."[12] This means that memory and collective pedagogy have a decisive function in the very process of revelation; thanks to these, each new generation is exempt from starting its (second degree) apprenticeship "from scratch." Through a process of remembering and readopting, in a vital fashion peculiar to its own identity, the past experiences of another process in which the search, solutions, and challenges of history converge, each generation is thrust toward a more perfect maturity, and toward a new, deeper, and richer truth.

In order to be part of this community-in-process-toward-the-truth, under the guidance of God, we must have "faith" in it. It is not in God directly that we place this "faith," because it is not God directly who speaks to us. God speaks through witnesses, and these divine witnesses are not isolated individuals: they constitute a community, a people, whom God, with a "true pedagogy," ever dispatches toward the liberative truth of all the creative potential of the human being.[13] The Israelite people, the Christian people, perform a function of interpretation and transmission without which we could not recognize where and how the "word of God" sounds today. Without Israel, or the church, in the world we know, and in Christian tradition, there is no revelation of God.

Thus, this second step that we have taken, from "revelation" to "faith," shows us that the very fact of God's revealing something with meaning supposes not only an individual in search of truth, but a community, a people committed to this intent to "learn to learn," as it searches for the truth. Only then does God communicate something. Faith is not the mere consequence of a passive, individual acceptance in faith of a word addressed to us by God. Thus, the faith community does not follow the fait accompli of a revelation wrought by God. It is an integral part of it.

But we must now take a further step, and discover to what extent, and in what way, the faith community is part of that revelation *in a creative manner.*

III

Indeed, from what has now been said, an important question still remains to be solved. How may we distinguish "God's" word from other, "merely human," words? The language used is the same, and the options posed by that language are ranged along a spectrum of more or less equivalent possibilities. We have also seen that it is not required that divine revelation even deal with or explicitly cite the divinity. We must not forget that, even in Israel, not to mention other religions, two prophets—for example Jeremiah and Hananiah—can appeal to the same God to justify contrary orientations on the part of the same "divine pedagogy" (see Jer. 28). What entitles us to include in the collection of "words of God" the prophecies of Jeremiah, and not those of Hananiah (especially since neither of the two prophetic messages was confirmed by subsequent events)? The Bible itself informs us that, for centuries, contradictory opinions—and biblical ones, espoused by different sacred authors—prevailed in Israel as to whether the institution of the monarchy represented the will of God, or Israel's sinful rejection of Yahweh as king (see 1 Sam. 8–10).

What is more, there is no radical change in this state of affairs when we come to the New Testament. It is not as easy to perceive this in the New Testament, since all the works it contains were redacted over the course of a period lasting surely no longer than half a century, while the redaction of the Old Testament extends over a millennium. But even in this reduced time span we notice serious unresolved divergencies between Paul and the author of the Letter of James (see Rom. 3:21–30 and James 2:14–26), or again between Paul and James the "brother of the Lord" (or at least his followers—Gal. 2:12). Here and there the question seems to have been resolved by the simple recourse of including only one of these opinions in the New Testament. In other instances, it is left to the Christian community of the future to solve the problem.

Although it constitutes an important datum for this particular question, we shall not treat here of the options the church will have to make regarding the "interpretation" of what had been consigned in that "deposit of revelation" that is the Bible. Our sole interest here is in this mystery constituted by the very existence of the Bible: How is the "word of God" recognized and distinguished from what seems to be that word but is not?

At the level of theoretical theology, the answer is simple, and almost tautological:

> When God reveals, we are obliged to offer him full obedience in faith ... This faith ... is a supernatural virtue by which ... we believe to be true what has been revealed by Him not by the intrinsic truth of things ... but on the authority of God himself revealing. [Vatican Council I – Denzinger 1789]

The whole difficulty for the ordinary person is in distinguishing "when God reveals" from very similar occasions that might wrongly be taken as God's revelation. To be sure, the ordinary person identifies this special "when" that is deserving of our faith with the redaction of the Bible that we hold in our hands today. But then it will doubtless occur to us to ask: How did the church make this collection that separates what God has revealed from what God has not revealed? Here again, the theological solution is easy, and once more is furnished by Vatican I:

> The church holds [the books of the Bible] as sacred and canonical not because they were composed by human industry alone and then approved by her; nor only because [they] contain revelation without error; but because, written under the *inspiration* of the Holy Spirit, they have God as their author. [Denzinger 1788]

As I have said, this answer is almost a redundancy. Obviously, if we claim that God has used something of human language to communicate to us, and if such writings nevertheless have a human author, then this author must be "inspired" by God in order for what is written to be regarded as "divine revelation." But we speak of redundancy because *historically speaking* the problem of a criterion is still unresolved. However, instead of claiming to know when God reveals (in order to be able to have faith in what is revealed), we must ask how we know when God "inspires" an author's writing.

The theology of liberation is especially sensitive to this question – a perfectly logical one, but one that is absent from the concerns of most current theology – because the recognition today of what would be, for "our" reality, the "word that God would speak," is a task that we must undertake a thousand and one times in the communities that form the base of the church and inquire into the enriching, liberative content of their faith. If God continues the work of divine revelation by the Spirit, how to recognize the divine "word" today becomes a crucial ecclesial criterion.

Actually, there are two answers to the question. One is Jesus' (paradigmatic and) absolute refusal to help his hearers identify the presence of God in God's deeds and messages by means of "signs from heaven." The other is constituted by the data furnished by the formation of the canon (or list of the books regarded as inspired by God) of the Old as well as of the New Testament. This history, while not completely known, is sufficiently well understood to support a judgment.

According to Luke, Jesus' refusal to call down signs from heaven as a criterion of whether or not his hearers are in the presence of God and a divine revelation, has a very precise context. Jesus has just restored the faculty of speech to a person who had somehow lost his faculty of speech. The bystanders now wonder whether they are in the presence of an event evincing the power and hence the presence of God, or whether there could be some other explanation—even, for example, the power of Satan (who was supposed to have deprived the victim of his speech in the first place) transferred to Jesus.

According to Mark, Jesus' refusal is absolute. This generation will be given no sign from heaven. But there is something else. As to the possibility that Jesus has delivered the victim of Satan's affliction by the power of Satan, Mark now indicates the argument that all three synoptics will use: even hypothetically, the objection has no meaning. After all, whether it be God or Satan who humanizes a person, that humanization, in and of itself, is a sign that "Satan's reign has come to an end" (Mark 3:26). Then the reign of God must be beginning, Luke explicitly concludes (Luke 11:20).

God's self-communication to us is bestowed by way of actions or ideas. In both cases, this communication will be understood only by one who is attuned to the priorities of the heart of this God. And for such a one, the historical sign of the liberation of a person is the sign of the presence and revelation of God—just as one who reads a book does not understand what God wishes of the Sabbath, however divine the book, or however many thunderclaps or bolts of lightning may have accompanied its publication. Knowledge of God as "revealing" something to us occurs when we are discovered to have a historical sensitivity that converges with God's own intentions.

Hence, in Matthew and Luke (in dependence upon Q), Jesus gives two examples of persons who, without knowing "biblical revelation," have understood what God wishes to communicate to them, and have perceived God's revelatory presence in history: the inhabitants of Nineveh, and the "queen of the south" (see Matt. 12:38–42). According to Luke, these pagans "have themselves judged what is just" (Luke 12:57)—that is, they have recognized a sign that is in history, or as Matthew says, a "sign of the times" (Matt. 16:3).

In other words, the identification of God's presence or "revelation," first in the history of Israel, and then in the deeds and words of Jesus, does not fall from heaven packaged and labeled. God has entrusted us with the responsibility of searching them out, of verifying them in the best way possible, with the eyes and priorities of God (which are also those of the reign of God). Only from a point of departure in this commitment, which is the fruit of a certain sensitivity, has it been defined "when" God has revealed what today comprises the Bible. Thus, it is true today, as well, that, in the task of interpreting when we are in the presence of God, the documents of Medellín define the task of a liberative theology:

> Just as another Israel, the first people, experienced the salvific presence of God when God delivered them from the oppression of Egypt . . . so also we, the new people of God, cannot escape the experience of the divine passage that saves whenever there is . . . a passage, for each and all, from less humane conditions of life to more humane conditions. [Medellín Final Document, Introduction, no. 6]

These "signs" are already sufficiently clear and experiential for us to "believe" that "all growth in humanity moves us closer to reproducing the image of the Son, that he may be the firstborn of many siblings" (ibid., "Education," no. 9).

I have said that, besides the evangelical paradigm concerning the basic importance of the "signs of the times," I have sufficient historical data to construct what might be called a paradigm of the "theological fact" of the formation of the canon. With these data in mind, let us construct an example of how that paradigm functions. Let us take the case of Moses in the exodus. For simplicity's sake, let us say that we are not interested, in the establishment of this paradigm, in knowing who wrote the actual account. Tradition attributes it to Moses himself, but I think that its redaction is actually that of one or more chroniclers writing in the time of David or Solomon. As I have said, the fact is that the account was written. Neither, for the purposes of this study, are we interested in the "historiographical" status of the account at the moment of its redaction—whether it was taken as actual history or as a mythical event. In either case—and this is what interests me—it came to form part of the Yahwist "faith."

One of the theologians who, to my knowledge, has taken most seriously the *theology* implied in the construction of a canon, or list of writings containing "divine revelation," is A. Torres Queiruga, in his *La revelación de Dios en la realización del hombre.*[14] Here is how this author summarizes the interaction of God and human beings in the creation of the word of God concerning the exodus—or, if you will, how "divine revelation" is recognized *in* the liberation of the Jewish people from their oppression in Egypt:

From his religious experience, Moses *discovered* the living presence of God in the longing of the Jews to be delivered from their oppression. The "experience of contrast" between the actual situation of his people and what he felt to be the salvific will of God, who seeks the human being's liberation, gave him the intuition that the Lord was present in that longing, and supported the people. As he gradually succeeded in instilling this certitude of his in others, helping them, as well, to *discover* this presence, he awakened history, promoted religiousness, and ultimately created Yahwism.[15]

Let us begin with this text, and make a series of observations on what it tells us, explicitly, and especially implicitly. And the reader should note that I use it for my own intent, and not to determine the thinking of the author.

First: Torres speaks of a personage who has what he calls an "experience of contrast." It is unimportant for the moment what the name of this personage is. The biblical account calls him Moses, and presents him as the protagonist of the exodus narrative. But it is evident that, whatever the historical value of his account, the author *of the account*, at any rate, must have had this actual, historical experience, since this author judges it relevant to recount it and set it in relief as basic for Israel's faith in its God. It is this author who "discovers," in the facts of the past that others transmit, a revelatory presence of God, and separates these facts from the rest.

The first thing we observe about this author is that this "experience of contrast," as it is designated here, *presupposes* an already existing (anthropological) "faith" — that is, a determinate structure of values that sensitizes the author to this situation of oppression and instills the notion that God cannot wish it, when others think that this was the normal situation, or the lesser evil (see Exod. 4:1–9, 6:12, Num. 11:5, etc.). Here is the source of the author's interest, which makes of a mere event or situation a "sign" of something to be done. And it is this that converts the action of the author, the narrative, into a transforming "onthusiasm" that then infects others.

Second: Why do we say that this "faith" of "Moses" (whether of Moses, the Yahwist, or the author of Deuteronomy) was "anthropological" — that is, something seemingly contradistinguished from "religious" faith in Yahweh? By this we mean that this Moses has no Bible. He cannot have recourse, as we customarily do, to the "word of God" in order to know what values to strive for, and in what order to strive for them. Nor, therefore, did he have access, among the manifold voices of historical reality, to an unequivocal "sign" that would enable him to make a divinely guaranteed "discovery" of the revelatory presence of God. To this purpose, he had to do what, according to the gospel, the Ninevites, or the queen of the south did, who worshiped gods who were not Yahweh.

True, in the account, narrated when Moses had already been accepted as Yahweh's witness, it is recounted that Yahweh gave Moses "signs from heaven" — that is, magical signs that his mission, his duty, actually came from God. But let us notice, first of all, that other persons in the account claim, on the basis of similar magical arguments, that this is not the will of God (see Exod. 11:22, etc.). Furthermore, other books of what today is the Bible have been acknowledged as "the word of God" without the mediation of any divine apparition to their author, indeed without so much as a single mention of God by that author (as the Song of Songs), in a work that could have been written, for example, by an atheist. "Moses," here, by definition, is — under pain of having to appeal to an infinite chain — the person without a Bible, without a deposited "word of God." Moses must place a wager on what God "must" wish. And those who follow Moses must believe in the same way.[16]

Third: Our text speaks of an "experience of contrast" — an experience of something that becomes a "sign" of what God does *not* wish, and therefore a sign of the divine will to "liberate" human beings from it, in this case the Israelites. However, there are other signs of the times that appeal to the same faith (to the same structure of value or of being), from other experiences than those of contrast: for example, the experience of the celebration of value attained (as in many of the Psalms), the experience of the covenant in the search for some of these same values (as in the preaching of various prophets), or the experience of the promise of a future or impending realization of such values (as in the Beatitudes).

Common to all these experiences is the presence in history of events or qualities in which the very meaning of existence is at stake. Whether or not these events or qualities will be noticed as signs — which is what happens in the case of Moses — rather than their being allowed to slip by as irrelevant, will depend on the strength with which this faith, which is antecedent to revelation (of which these peak moments are the vehicle), becomes sensitive to the vicissitudes of these values rather than others on our human earth.

Fourth: Let us move from the *facts* of the Book of Exodus to the *readers* of that book. And once more, we are not concerned with the difference between those who were with Moses in his deed and those who now, centuries later, excitedly, read of this same deed. In both, this accompaniment indicates the "contagion of an enthusiasm" and commitment. In consequence of the preceding, Moses' Israelite contemporaries regarded him as "inspired by God" — exactly as those who now read, with reverence, and as addressed to their lives, the Book of Exodus hold the writer as "inspired." (We, too, for simplicity's sake, shall call him "Moses" here, but he was the Yahwist, the Elohist, the Deuteronomist, and so on.)

Moses' contemporaries made an option between following him and following leaders who proposed other alternatives as the will of God. Later readers make an option among *books*, among various possible or real accounts of these events. There were works in which these same events either are not narrated, or are narrated in a different light, or finally, are not regarded as "signs" of the active presence of God. And all of this occurred also before a Bible existed. In fact, it is the Bible that arises from this selection among books (guided by the same witnesses and criteria as the events recounted there).

Fifth: The passage from Torres upon which we are commenting tells us that, by contagion of the enthusiasm aroused by the discovery of signs of a divine liberating presence, Moses—and hence the author or authors who recount his deed—"aroused history." This means that they gave rise to a historical process. And they did so by creating a community, a people, whose fundamental identity lay in the tradition (in the original sense of "transmission") that opted for the same values and for the same historical signs.

We say that it is a "process" that is created in this way, because that discovery of the presence of God is not static. For example, that discovery is different in Exodus (with its Yahwist or Elohist background) and in Deuteronomy. There are various "Moses." But their plurality lies along a growth line, in the face of various historical challenges. Moses does not teach a package of "truth." He teaches how to learn to learn—how to "discover" more signs in the history of the same revelatory, liberative presence of God.

Sixth: Torres has the colossal audacity to say that this Moses—multiple and progressive—who awakened history, "created Yahwism." But was it not "divine revelation," which inspired Moses, that created it? Of course. But the data we have on what we today call the Old Testament were compiled in Israel—that is, the written deposit of revelation—tell of the crucial participation in this historical creation, beginning with the exile, of the people of Israel themselves.

The restriction of divine worship to the one temple of Jerusalem under Josiah, the impossibility of that divine worship during the captivity, and its later limitations, along with a swelling diaspora, had the result that the doubly "lay" institution of the *synagogue*, centered on "reading" and interpretation, gradually displaced worship and thus became, "more than any other factor, responsible for the survival of Judaism [Yahwism] as a religion and of the Jews as a distinct people."[17] God speaks a human language, surely; but the divine revelatory word becomes such only when it is recognized, among so many other words, in the experience of the foundational liberation (in "Moses") and in the continuity of that liberation, which sustains Israel.

Seventh: Finally, there is no reason to suppose that what is said here, with complete historical foundation, of the creation of "Yahwism" would not hold as well for that of "Christianity." And I am not speaking of some parallel that imitates a previous event. From the historical viewpoint, it is the continuation of the process of that "Moses" whose discovery founded a people, a tradition, an apprenticeship in the second degree. The initial "being attuned" that is required for one word out of a thousand to be recognized as a sign that God is speaking is later criticized by this same word in the face of new challenges. The hermeneutics is circular, or, as some would have it, a spiral.

Jesus and Paul have a new liberative experience: that of leaving the servitude of a situation of privilege and trying to be on the watch for signs of the times that come from where human beings suffer, are poor, oppressed, limited in their human opportunities. Thus, as Paul sees it, new branches are grafted onto the old tree. The old people learns, or better, keeps on learning to learn. It does not cease to seek the truth, because truth is only truth when it is transformed into real humanization.

IV

Thus, too briefly, and with too little development, I have shown, or attempted to show, that the relationship of these three terms — revelation, faith, and signs of the times — can, like christology, be read in two directions, and that this is what must be done in order to seize their wealth.

The "theological" order is not erroneous: it draws from the dogma of revelation the logical consequence that, if God uses human beings and human language for that revelation, then the authors who, by divine inspiration, have consigned this "word" to writing are witnesses worthy of "faith" in the strictest and most theological sense of the word.

This is the sense in which Saint Thomas asserts:

> In faith, the *ratio formalis* is the first truth, that is, that we adhere to the truths of faith *only because they have been revealed by God*, and in the measure that they have been revealed by God.[18]

And in the same manner, we may conclude that this first truth must perform its function of interpretation and discernment of all human aspirations, which, like the aspiration for liberation, arise in history as signs of the times.[19]

Nevertheless, just as with christologies "from above," from God to us, we may be in danger of forgetting the order in which, in the process of our cognitive and practical history, truth proceeds from the less perfect to the more perfect. Following this route, which the gospel records and the history of redaction and of the canon of the Bible shows, the opposite order, as well, has its truth, and its great liberative meaning. It is the signs of the times, read with an open, sensitive heart, that prevent the "letter" by which the whole of revelation is bound to human language from becoming lethal (2 Cor. 3:6) — even the letter of the gospel — and lead us astray instead of leading us to an encounter with the heart of God. These signs show us a path that, in being shared, fashions a people, and history. They are as indications of the fact that history has meaning, and that it is reasonable to wager on that meaning. And from the wealth of this liberative experience, shared in community, springs a reasonable faith, not a fideism or a magical instrument. When that faith, become tradition, leads us to the truth that humanizes our sisters and brothers, and commits us definitively, then we know that God is present in it, guiding us—revealing to us the truth of the human being that should be.

CHAPTER 10

Ignatius Loyola: Trial or Project?

This article illustrates Segundo's lifelong concern with a liberating spiritu-
ality as an essential component of theological reflection. To achieve this,
he returns to the spiritual origins of his order, the Society of Jesus, to
illustrate the difference between a medieval spirituality that puts ultimate
value in avoiding sin in order to reach heaven (a trial), and the spirituality
of Vatican II, which saw human activity in history as essential to advancing
the kingdom of God (a project). He finds the trial approach in the Spiritual
Exercises of St. Ignatius (which he believes should be revised), while the
project approach is evident in the later writings of Ignatius, especially in
his letters while he was general superior of the Society of Jesus.

Source: "Ignace de Loyola, ¿prueba o proyecto?," *Recherches*
de Sciences Religieuse epreuve ou projet? (1991) vol. 79, no. 4:
507-33.

HUMAN EXISTENCE AS A TRIAL

When I read the Bible, as an adult, following the history of its redaction
as best I could, I came to a place where I experienced something like a
decisive watershed. The reader will doubtless suppose I mean the breach
between the two Testaments. But—strangely—this is not where it was.

The first time I read, as a Christian, a priest, and a Jesuit, the first five
chapters of the Book of Wisdom, I felt at home. Despite the fact that I am
a person of the New Testament—at least, I think I am—I felt at home in
these passages. I prescind, of course, from the fact that the Book of Wisdom
is classified as apocryphal (by Jews and Protestants), or deuterocanonical
(by Catholics), or intertestamentary (by scientific criticism).

I had never denied, of course, that the other Old Testament books were
also inspired. But the problems debated in them, and especially the presuppositions of these problems, were no longer mine. I could read many
passages of the Book of Job with emotion; but I knew that the suffering of
the innocent—especially on the basis of the case of Jesus—had received a

149

different response in the New Testament. The latter had dealt from the outset with a problematic based on the reality of a life after death, or, if you prefer, a resurrection, in which human beings would be judged and would pass to one of two eternal destinies.

It is likewise true, of course, that other intertestamentary books, like First Maccabees and Daniel, admitted the existence of a life beyond this earthly one, but they had not yet developed an anthropology, or, if you like, a spirituality, in conformity with this new, transcendent datum.

When I say that, on arriving at this point in my reading of the Bible I felt at home in these five chapters, I am not claiming that the New Testament, the writings of the fathers, the theoretical and practical medieval systematizations, and finally Ignatius Loyola's *Spiritual Exercises* themselves, had taught me nothing new. What I do claim is that all these later works fit quite nicely into the schema of the free human creature deciding before God his or her otherworldly destiny. That is, they all fit quite neatly into the basic schema presented by these five first chapters of the Book of Wisdom. Paul may have creaked a bit on the way into these pigeonholes, but at that time I had made no attempt to decipher his message — a rather particular and atypical one in the New Testament.

In a word — and I would ask the reader to retain this for an understanding of what follows — these five sapiential chapters presented me for the first time with the *four* "last things," within whose framework, from that time forward, spirituality moved, through the message of Jesus to the contemplations of the *Exercises*, and from there to today: *death, judgment, hell, and glory.* On the other hand, until a date almost as late as the redaction of the Book of Wisdom (which many reliable exegetes place around 170 B.C.), the final reality — the *novissimum*, the "last thing" — of the Israelite who wrote or read the Bible was death and death alone, along with the sheol that was almost its synonym: the place of all the dead, where the shades did not even have the breath to praise God (Ps. 6:6, 30:10).

I did not find it particularly difficult — to cite two examples (which any reader no longer very young will recognize) to situate the parable of the last judgment in the framework of the Book of Wisdom. In Wisdom, standing before the great unknown that is death, human beings with their freedom find themselves faced with two logical alternatives: either death does away with all human existence, or else there are human values that death is obliged to respect and therefore to allow to breach the frontier of the beyond, along with the persons who have made them their own. The only reasonable thing to do, in the face of this basic uncertainty, is to make a wager, to gamble, selecting one of the alternatives and its logical ethical consequences (Wis. 1:4–2:6ff., 3:5).

The second alternative, that death would permit a person to pass to another life without being destroyed, can be nothing else than a matter of what Wisdom calls *justice*, or the execution of the will of God. At all events, Christians, who read the parable of the Last Judgment in Matthew (25:31), will identify that justice with the love that goes in quest of one's neighbor hungering, thirsting, naked, weeping, imprisoned, sick, and so on; or, according to Matthew again (Matt. 5:17–20), with the fulfillment, to the last jot and tittle, of the law of Moses as purified and completed by Christ; or with the content of the single, new commandment placed by John on the lips of Jesus (John 13:34, 15:17).

What is one to think, then, of the successes and failures of human projects over the course of this corruptible life? What value do they have? Obviously they will have an *absolute* value for those who do not look for another existence than the one that ends completely with the human being in time. "Come ... let us enjoy the good things that are real ... for this our portion is, and this our lot" (Wis. 2:6,9). Success in amassing satisfaction will be absolutized, while justice as a norm of life will be relativized: "Let our strength be our norm of justice" (Wis. 2:11).

The logic of the just—that is, of those who look for "a recompense of holiness" (Wis. 2:22) beyond death—is precisely the contrary. Temporal success is not only ambiguous, it appears as dangerous. History, with its demigods, and the enthusiasm it arouses for plans and projects to be realized in time, makes a person forget that the important thing is what is reserved for eternity. The Book of Wisdom even says that it is a gift of God to be snatched from this life in the bloom of youth (Wis. 4:7–14). The first two *novissima* together—death and judgment—help a person get the norm of living clear in the face of decisions to be made. A human being will remember, keeping ever in mind these two "last things," the most essential element of this schema: that human beings are on this earth to be "tried," to be subjected to trial (Wis. 3:5).

Thus, the possible satisfactions that this world provides are not our property, however powerful an attraction they may exert upon us. The fact that we are reserved for the beyond makes our place in history that of strangers, foreigners, who may only enjoy the "licit" satisfactions that may come our way—those not prohibited in terms of the trial to which we are subjected. What awaits us beyond this world may be very beautiful, but the overwhelming sensation here, for those who seek to survive this trial, unlike those who set themselves no moral limits in their pursuit of pleasure, is the sensation of treading on foreign, dangerous ground. The Book of Wisdom refers to those who undergo this trial as (seemingly) "punished" (Wis. 3:4), and their lives as "sacrificial offerings" (Wis. 3:6).

But I have said that I shall present *two* examples of how elements familiar to Christians for centuries fit quite well in the schema outlined by the first five chapters of Wisdom. I owe the reader a second demonstration of the accuracy of this statement. Since at least as long ago as the midpoint of the Middle Ages, Christian children have learned, among the first prayers they are taught, the Salve Regina: the "Hail, Holy Queen." Here again, from my childhood until after my theological studies and priestly ordination,

I recited this prayer thousands upon thousands of times without feeling the least shock or discomfort.

And yet, in the center of this prayer, there is something that ought to give a Christian food for thought. Let us skip over the Marian praises it contains, and observe how the human being is pictured who places himself or herself under our Lady's "eyes of mercy." Let us observe that, in the semantic flash of the "figures of language" that describe human existence, we are referred to the same mental structure that presides over those five chapters written a thousand years earlier. We find ourselves once more in the schema of the Book of Wisdom—a schema of *trial*.

What manner of persons are we, who invoke Mary here? We are "poor *banished* children of Eve . . . mourning and weeping in this valley of tears," and we beg her: "after this our *exile*, show unto us the blessed fruit of thy womb, Jesus." I shall not belabor an analysis of this famous prayer or of the anthropology that it implies. I shall only pause for a moment on the word "exile," before bringing this already lengthy introduction to a close. The present life, with the history inherent in it, is regarded as an exile, precisely inasmuch as human freedom is endowed with a capacity to choose our eternal (positive) destiny not from *within* history, but only from without. The insurmountable walls of our valley prevent us from making that option in history.

In the second place, not only is history relativized, but freedom amid the relative can have only a transitory meaning, that of our having to elect what does not belong to this earth. Indifference to the latter is forced upon us: nothing can possibly keep us here, and the value of what we decide will be manifested only in our *final* "destiny" (Wis. 2:16c). In other words, as we must decide in favor of what we do not see, we are obliged to embrace an indifference toward what we do see. But the attraction exerted by the visible makes this earthly sojourn of ours a place of tears, like any exile, in which what is loved is far away.

Thus it is altogether clear, it seems to me, that in medieval spirituality, or at least in a very significant part of it, Jesus himself, who could have been exempt from the schema of *trial*, enters within it. He is the Just one par excellence, who passes through this earthly existence accepting his suffering in order to be an example for our freedom. This is redemption. God could have endowed us with glory despite our sins. God did not do so. God wished to try us, as Christ was tried. Thus, freedom acquires an enormous power of decision; but it is not required for any divine plan. God has simply willed that it bridge the gap between our creation and our salvation, and that it do so in a world in which sin has a greater power of attraction than virtue.

And so, since the Salve Regina fits into this theologico-anthropological schema of trial, it causes no shock to those who recite it from the depths of themselves—just as neither do the *Spiritual Exercises* of St. Ignatius Loyola shock us, and, unless I am mistaken, for exactly the same reason.

I want to bring this introduction to a close, then, with a quotation, because in it the reader will be able to see something that did shock me, and profoundly. It is another prayer—or, if you will, a declaration to God on the part of the human being. But this time, I felt for the first time that the schema of trial was not the only possible one. Perhaps this was because it was not a Christian prayer—if by "Christian" you meant what corresponded to the maturity of the message of Christ. It is a passage from Pierre Teilhard de Chardin. Let the reader be the judge:

> The more I examine myself, the more I discover this psychological truth: that no one lifts his little finger to do the smallest task unless moved, however obscurely, by the conviction that he is contributing infinitesimally (at least indirectly) to the construction of some absolute. . . . It is a fundamental law of . . . action. It requires no less than the attraction of what is called the Absolute, no less than You Yourself, to set in motion the frail liberty with which You have endowed us. And that being so, everything which diminishes my explicit faith in the heavenly value of the *results* of my endeavour, lowers irremediably my power to act.[1]

And to heighten the sense of shock, let us read, once more from Teilhard's pen, this summary of the previous statements: "What does it matter to us to become 'blest' in heaven, if, when all is said and done, we have added *nothing absolute*, with our lives, to the Totality of Being?"[2]

As for myself, when I read these pages I felt a sense of something verging on blasphemy—or else I was going to have to reinvestigate an important part of Christian anthropology (or, if one prefer, of the eschatology underlying the latter) and replace the absolute of trial with the absolute of a project in which I myself would be a decisive collaborator in a *plan* common to God and myself. I felt that these pages called into question many of my earlier certitudes, and among them, central points in the *Spiritual Exercises* of Ignatius Loyola.

It is to this last point that I now turn. Of course I might begin by examining the biblical foundation of the conviction with which Teilhard writes these formidable sentences—so foreign to my former spirituality—and decide whether they have sufficient biblical foundation for me to have to abandon my accustomed theological coordinates of "trial." In other words, perhaps this was the moment to investigate whether the passage from the concept of trial to that of project might not be precisely the Pauline passage to the gospel of Christian maturity (Gal. 4:3–7).

Nevertheless, I prefer to begin by examining, however briefly and summarily, how far the (christological) anthropology of the *Exercises* fits into the classification of *trial* or *project*—in order thereupon to see, in case it is the former member that is verified, whether this leaves some christological void that Ignatius Loyola may have attempted to fill in some other way in his later life.

TRIAL, THE KEY TO THE EXERCISES

The dimensions of this essay preclude an extensive or in-depth search through all the material that might be of help in an understanding of the theology of the *Exercises*. Readers themselves must fill in the lacunae that I shall be obliged to leave. Let it suffice to indicate the "symptoms" of a theology of trial that I observe in the key loci of the *Exercises*; and by this I mean the passages that constitute, to my understanding as well as that of many who are better versed in the matter than I, the very cornerstone of the edifice of the spirituality of the *Exercises*.

I propose to examine briefly the following points: the "First Principle and Foundation," and indifference; the "First Week," concerning Sin (i.e., the basic relation between God and the free creature); the "Summons of the Eternal King" (i.e., the vocation of the human being and especially of the knight); the "Three Modes of Humility" (i.e., the criterion for the taking of any Christian ethical decision); and finally, the "Contemplation [of God the Creator] for Obtaining Love." Quotations will be referenced by the paragraph numbers used in practically all modern editions of the *Exercises*.

It may be of interest to point out a certain singularity of these five, as it were, columns of the spirituality of the *Spiritual Exercises*, namely, that the first and the last make no mention of Christ, but only develop the relationship between God and the human creature in its consequences for life. This absence of a christology in such key loci might indicate that these two passages belong to the period that Ignatius devoted to studies in Paris. The other three, not merely by reason of their references to Jesus Christ, but because they are intrinsically bound up with the process of the "election" of life in which the exercitant is engaged, would date from the period of the creation of the *Exercises* — that is, from Manresa. In making this suggestion I am not emphasizing any possible incompatibility between the two series of passages. When Ignatius adds to the first redaction of the *Exercises* what he learns later, he maintains the basic unity of the original. For example, the First Principle and Foundation, in what we might call its "literary genre" differs from the rest of the work. It intervenes, explicitly or implicitly, throughout the whole.

1. The so-called "First Principle and Foundation" is not a contemplation. We can see this from its more theological style. To boot, it appears in the *Exercises* in a place of its own, coming before the first contemplation. The *Directory* calls it a "consideration," and doubtless its object is to establish the exercitant within the set of coordinates that should frame any fundamental decision that a human being seeks to make in his or her life.

There is a clear, obvious division in this initial page. The *first part* deals with the question, "For whom [or "for what"] is man created?" And the answer to this basic question is: "Man is created to praise, reverence, and serve God our Lord and by this means to save his soul" (no. 23). Rather than enter into a reflection on the four verbs or verb phrases bearing on this ultimate finality of human existence, it will be more in order, I believe, to make a (hypothetical) observation without which it would be difficult to understand the finality here being presented.

To judge merely from the construction of this assertion of Ignatius, it would look as if he were going to answer the question of the final cause that God had in creating the human being. If this were the case, he would be dealing with the insoluble problem of "the one and the many" of Greek philosophy (a problem altogether evaded in biblical thinking). My understanding is that, enemy that he is of abstract theologies, Ignatius is asking about something far more concrete. In a context of his free choice, the exercitant is interrogating himself about what God expects this faculty to choose.

Christians making the *Exercises* for the first time (not those who repeat them year after year, something the *Exercises* were not intended for) is not practicing or choosing an "ongoing" spirituality, if we may put it that way. The exercitant is in a state of suspension, as it were (see no. 20, the Twentieth Annotation), and is expected to break out of it and "seek and find the divine will" (no. 1) when the occasion arises to wonder about the latter. Nor is Ignatius troubled by this heteronomy. This is simply the context in which it begins to be defined what God wishes *in general* of human beings: that they be saved, and to this end, that they praise, reverence, and serve God. It is not to be wondered at, then, that the first part of the "First Principle and Foundation" reappears at the moment of the election (see nos. 169, 177, 179—just as it will reappear in the third part, vis-à-vis indifference, which is its logical consequence, as will be seen: see nos. 179, 187).

The situation of the exercitants here is that of Ignatius himself. They are not calling upon the Creator to give an account of the finality of creation; rather they are drawing the conclusion, precisely from their condition as creatures, that they ought to praise, reverence, and serve God—because, besides being appropriate to their creaturely condition, this is the route chosen by God for the absolute end willed by that God for creatures: that they save their souls eternally.

It is here that we begin to discern what, for me, is a christological vacuum. In other words, the Creator-creature relationship does not seem to have been modified by the life and message of Jesus the incarnate Son of God. No possible third alternative (the possibility of a free gift of heaven) is visualized in response to the problem posed by the dilemma of the soul's salvation or perdition. The divine will is to subject this gift to the conditions of a *trial*—the trial alluded to by the three verbs indicating the necessary "mediation" to this ultimate end.

And one final observation, this time on a matter that will call for more ample study. The last of these three "verbs of mediation"—"to serve"—is subject to an amphibology on which Ignatius' entire later life depends and will depend. Will it not mean, perhaps, that God is associating human beings to a project that God seeks to accomplish and for which God wishes to have as a collaborator — a necessary and gratuitous collaborator — each human being? Do not the central passages of the synoptics suggest this? And even more, Paul's concept of "Christian freedom"? Perhaps the maintenance of this amphibology is one of the merits, and no small one, of the Ignatian thinking. But at the level of the the *Exercises*, the "imitation" of Jesus, as I shall presently attempt to show, precludes the possibility of there being any *sunergoi*, any "co-workers" (1 Cor. 3:9), in a divine construction, plan, or project. (*The Imitation of Christ* is the only book expressly permitted the exercitant before the end of the First Week, according to the *Directory*, 3, 2.) On what do I base my assertion? *For the moment*, only on the decisive fact that this "service" is regarded as a *means* to the salvation of the soul. That is, it is regarded as a constitutive part of a trial, of which salvation or condemnation will be the outcome.

The *second part* of the First Principle and Foundation establishes that "all other things on the face of the earth are created to assist him in the prosecution of the end for which he was created" (no. 23).

In its full objectivity and abstraction, the statement is unobjectionable, and as it were, neutral. All theology, whatever its anthropological penchant, beginning with the biblical account itself, will be found to be in agreement with it. God creates the human being, and creates things to help the human being. But now we are in for a surprise. The entire *Exercises*, with their realism, give the lie to this logic!

In the first place, among these "created things" standing between the exercitant who is to save his soul and the Creator, are found "nonthings" — that is, persons, who make their appearance along the course of this trial that "man" — the exercitant — is to undergo.

In the second place, even without taking special account of the attraction or repulsion that persons necessarily exert on the human being — *independently* of whether they help or hinder the salvation of his or her soul — are thing things." By this I mean that the whole of creation does not present itself to the human being for what it is: a means. Instead, even things, to say nothing of persons, present themselves as already endowed with a positive or negative attraction for the human being's affectivity.

Ignatius' very definition of "spiritual exercises" suggests this clearly enough. He says that they are calculated "to *remove* from [the exercitant] *all disordered affections*" (no. 1). And if we have a question as to the origin of these affections, before the First Principle and Foundation has attempted to direct and order them, the answer is that "things" (things and persons) have the power to attract or repel the affectivity *before* reason can have directed them toward the absolute end, the salvation of the soul. This is the living portrait of human beings as they are. And the magic of the *Exercises* is that they procure the exercitant the opportunity (and psychic strength) to bracket this already imposed affectivity, in order to "dispose of his life for the salvation of his soul" (ibid.).

To pass over other reflections that might arise at this point, let us observe that this difficulty in ordering the already disordered — an affectivity imposed before reason establishes ends and means — is the peculiarity of a *trial*. Trial means difficulty, and only that one will be found to have stood the test who will have withstood the element of difficulty. From here the First Principle and Foundation moves on to show on what bases that parenthesis is constructed, that state of suspended affectivity that will permit an ordered "election" conformable to the end of the soul's salvation — despite created things and their manifold attraction.

The *third part* of the First Principle and Foundation is presented as a conclusion from the first two. But it is this only if we understand the second part in the way that we have — that is, in all mistrust of the alleged "assistance" of created things, and through the imposition upon them of a rational order: "Wherefore it is necessary to *become indifferent* to all created things wherever it is granted to the liberty of our free choice and is not prohibited . . . *desiring* and choosing only what is most conducive to the end for which we have been created" (no. 23).

This mistrust, if we may continue so to call it, proceeds from the fact that created things, in most cases, fail to help the human being. The independence with which they arouse the affections, whether or not the latter happen to be conducive to the salvation of the soul, appears altogether clearly in the course of the *Exercises*. The same may well be said, and is commonly said, of "becoming indifferent." It is not a matter of "being," but, as we repeatedly hear, of "becoming" such, by making an effort that (as we know) cannot be indefinitely maintained — but that may succeed, in a best case scenario, to introduce reason and its evaluation of means and ends into the election of a manner or structure of life. If these latter coincide with what God supposedly wills for the exercitant, grace will help him, despite the attraction of creatures, to save his soul.

The fact that, of themselves, creatures rather hinder than help, clearly appears in the last Annotation. The exercitant will more surely profit from the *Exercises* if he removes himself from all creatures, including here, as I have said, in the category of dangerous "things" or creatures, persons (no. 20). And as it is impossible to withdraw from them all, Ignatius counsels that, insofar as possible, he surround himself with "new" creatures — creatures that have not as yet had the necessary time to exert their powerful attraction on him. Hence he might well even change lodgings (ibid.).[3]

These summary reflections on the First Principle and Foundation will suffice, I trust, at least to have the working hypothesis that I have formulated here accepted as reasonable: that Ignatius' anthropological conception in the *Exercises* — as a logical continuation of this First Principle and Foundation — does not go beyond the schema of a *trial* (very similar to the one set forth by the Book of Wisdom). If, on the other hand, we should come to the conclusion that the New Testament does transcend that schema, even in the historical Jesus, and still more explicitly in the anthropology of Paul, and replaces it with that of a *project*, then Ignatius' later life would perhaps represent a more interesting theological font than his theology at the stage of the *Exercises*.

2. After this temporary sojourn in a kind of parenthesis of indifference, of course, the exercitant will be called upon to adopt more concrete attitudes in the orientation of his election. And the first sign of this concretion will appear in the contemplation of the eternal King.

Before arriving at this point, however, the exercitant will have passed *an entire week, the first* of the month of the *Exercises*. It will be necessary to say a word about that week, even though, in its broad lines, which bear on the reality of *sin*, it is governed by the First Principle and Foundation, which we have already examined. The consideration of sin is calculated to effectuate a general uprooting of the exercitant from his past life, and more in particular, from disordered affections for creatures—affections that have led him so far as to expose himself to the loss of his soul, and therewith, of the end for which he has been created (cf. no. 63).

Throughout the entire First Week, the contemplations continue to bear on relations between the Creator and the creature. Christ and his message are absent. The revelation arising from the person and message of Christ seem not to affect the subject under consideration. It will be said, of course, that the last three weeks are devoted precisely to the life of Christ, from his incarnation to his resurrection. And it will perhaps be added that what precedes the incarnation in time is sin, the original sin of Adam as well as the personal sin of the human multitude (see no. 102). Let it suffice to observe, however, that it is through this incarnate God and message that the essence of sin, and its gravity, as it partially frustrates the divine plan itself, is discovered. This is only another indication that christology is being subordinated to the theological schema of trial, and not vice versa.

It will doubtless be said that it is not true that the thought of Christ is absent from the matter being contemplated here, since the very first exercise concludes with a colloquy in which I am to "imagine Christ our Lord before me on the cross" (no. 53). Here, although this does not constitute the "matter" of the contemplation, it is said that this suffering and death before me, indeed the very incarnation, have all been due to "my sins." And I am counseled to ask myself what I have done for someone who has done so much for me. I recognize this fact, to be sure. But I do not believe that it should be forgotten that, while its importance for a sense of repentance is surely great, its theology is still very general and abstract—just as the grace of the redemption is abstract, since its effect on me will depend on whether death finds me in "actual mortal sin" (Denziger 693). Thus, in the colloquy that Ignatius directs the exercitant to make with Christ after the fifth exercise of this first week (the meditation on hell), I am specifically counseled to give thanks "because he has not allowed me to fall into any of these [classifications of condemned] by *putting an end to my life*" (no. 71).

After all, for Ignatius' theology, as for that of his whole age, humanity's redemption by Christ would be of scant avail, concretely, for any individual human being, were God to decide to end his or her life at the moment when, after having committed some grave sin, that individual had not yet had the time or occasion to make an act of perfect contrition or to receive the sacrament of penance. The case of a person who, "for a single mortal sin, has gone to hell" (no. 52) is a theological datum of the first importance for an understanding of the scope and foundation of a theology of *trial*. In the context of a trial, it seems that, under pain of divesting mortal sin of its gravity, God cannot unite in one quality the variety of a person's good and evil actions, and decide what destiny to assign that person on a basis of the combination. Only a (historical) project would allow for that. In not being able to decide which good or wicked actions hold the primacy over others—in the withdrawal to the conception of human existence as a trial, to which the moral education of the barbarian peoples had led the church[4]—it is decided that God will assign human beings one of either contrary eternal destinies on the basis of each one's last state or attitude. The injustice of this conceptualization lies in the fact that it allows one seriously evil attitude to overbalance the no less serious good attitudes, no matter how many they may have been, of an entire lifetime.

None of this is set right, to my way of thinking, by the celebrated stages of the spiritual life, commencing with the purgative way (First Week of the *Exercises*), continuing with the illuminative (Second and Third Weeks), and concluding with the unitive (Fourth Week or Contemplation for Obtaining Love). I recognize that this progression is not original with the *Exercises*, but is, as we should say of a pseudo prophecy *ex eventu*, one uttered after the fact, except that this is even worse, *de rigeur*. Ignatius begins with sin, because sin was the reality of his life before his conversion, and because God had preserved him from ending the decisive trial in perdition, leading him to repentance.

3. Be this as it may, it seems beyond any doubt that the Second Week of the *Exercises* explicitly introduces, into the Creator-creature relationship, the figure that will be central in the material of the contemplations from now until the end of the *Exercises*: that of Christ our Lord. Does this indicate that some christology will be found to modify, in any significant way, the human being's constitutive relationship—that of a trial—between the Creator and the creature?

Even before contemplating the incarnation of the Son of God, Ignatius proposes to the exercitant a solemn initial contemplation resembling the First Principle and Foundation, which is likewise of his own creative invention: "The summons of a temporal king helps in the contemplation of the *life of the Eternal King*" (no. 91). The contemplation of the eternal King has the same hermeneutic function as the First Principle and Foundation, which indicated how the material that followed it, up until the Second Week, was to be read and interpreted. Everything that follows the contemplation of the eternal King concerning Christ will have been condensed in the "summons" of the eternal King, who, in this case, is not God the Father, but Jesus Christ (see no. 95).

Even apart from all this, the "summons" in question would seem to annul the parenthesis created in the exercitant by his having "become indifferent." Indifference was the logical attitude before knowing to what I am called. But once I hear the voice that calls me, my affect ought to incline toward it, precisely in the degree that it gradually manifests itself. And thus the key question reappears: Shall we thereby be moving from the theology of trial to a theology of project?

Two things — intimately connected, it seems to me — strike the theologian in this contemplation. The first is the relationship between the "temporal king" taken as an *example* (no. 95) and the "eternal King" identified by Ignatius with Christ our Lord. And the second is a certain difficulty in assigning a content, let us say a material content, to the summons of the one king as of the other.

With regard to the *first point*, we have here a well-developed comparison or similitude. From the theological viewpoint, however, it is arresting that the known term, which bestows cognition on the other, is the temporal king. Translated into classic rhetorical terms, the temporal king is the "prime analogate" — that is, the (known) jumping-off point that sheds light on the second, less clear, term.

One explanation for this, surely an unquestionable and important one, but not a complete one, is that, in the sixteenth century, for a knight of the intermediate nobility like Ignatius, the European literature and culture that generally maintained some of the spiritual traits of the world of medieval chivalry was capable of bestowing a special luster on the concept of a trial by which a king would select his best knights for his military enterprises — in other words, that mentality endowed the atmosphere of trial of which we have been speaking with the character of noble competition. A Spanish knight was not content with the minimum demanded in the trial. It is this spirit of generosity, accentuated by the spirit of intimacy, with which the temporal king set before the eyes of the exercitant's imagination — a king "so liberal and so humane" (no. 93) — places himself at the head of his knightly friends, but not above them, that echoes in Ignatius' celebrated *magis* (going further, doing more). And it is this *magis* that characterizes the way in which Ignatius submits to the trial to which every human being is de facto subjected (as we find it prefigured in the Book of Wisdom).

The rest of the explanation will have to be sought, I think, in the vagueness that had been acquired by the figure of Christ in the exegesis of the time. We have an example in Thomas à Kempis's celebrated *Imitation of Christ*, in which there is practically nothing to recall the Jesus of the Gospels — apart, obviously, from his passion and death, which themselves are understood not as they appear in the synoptics, as the consequence of Jesus' message and activity (see Matt. 21:33–46), but as part of a quasi-liturgical plan in which God, from heaven, guides the footsteps of his Son to the sacrificial death that will permit God's reconciliation with a humanity become an enemy of the divinity by original sin.

I have already had occasion to indicate, in another work, that, in the christologies "from above" that dominated theology from the Middle Ages onward, the "divine and human natures" were intermingled in such a way as to make Jesus a kind of demigod.[5] While divinizing and absolutizing everything Jesus said and did, this removed those same words and deeds from any historical causality, and hence from any normativity for the human being who must act in the temporal.

Whatever be the merit of this explanation of why the eternal King, identified by Ignatius with Jesus Christ, seems strange, we shall now move on to our *second point*, which is simply a continuation of the first.

Having arrived at this contemplation, and hearing of a "summons of the eternal King," we shall surely think that Ignatius is about to withdraw us from a perspective of trial and introduce us into that of a *project*. That is, we should expect to be introduced to a "will" (no. 95), for which the King will require "toil" or "service" (nos. 96, 97) — the cooperation or aid of his knights. But Ignatius surprises us, where this royal "project" is concerned, with two elements, one positive and the other negative.

The positive element: to be sure, the eternal King defines his project altogether concisely. "My will is to conquer the whole world and all enemies." One might even say that the King is himself on trial, since he appends, to his definition of his project: " . . . and *thus* enter into the glory of my Father" (no. 95), a phrase reminicent of the ". . . and by this means to save his soul" of the First Principle and Foundation. It will perhaps be said that this universal conquest is an allusion to the conversion or salvation of the entire universe (see no. 102). But if we logically attend to the concluding words of the King's declaration, we see a "field of activity" rather than an actual, viable project. After all, this "will" has already been frustrated, before the coming of Christ, inasmuch as the incarnation takes place, according to Ignatius, when God perceives that, before its occurrence, "all were going down to hell" (nos. 102, 106, 107).

The negative element consists in the absence of any allusion to *historical* means that this project would require, and that would serve to measure the skill, ability, or degree of commitment on the part of each knight. More generally, there is no indication to what end or in what affairs the cooperation of each of them is necessary. It would appear that the project is no more than a pretext to test the extent of each one's valor: "That following me in *hardship*, he may also follow me in glory" (no. 95). It is a matter, then, of a competition not to further a divine project, but "to be content to eat as I, and so drink and dress, and so on . . . *in order that* afterward he may have part with me in the victory as he has had in the *labors*" (no.

93). Labor and hardship—synonyms—provide the field in which the knight can make "*offerings* [sacrifices] of *greater* worth and *greater* moment" (no. 97). Again we have the *magis* that characterizes the author of the *Spiritual Exercises*.

Having arrived at this point, I believe that it is necessary to analyze, very briefly, what is occurring, to judge from his first appearance on the scene as a subject of contemplation, with the central figure of Christ our Lord. The reader will recall that we have found the theme of trial, in its anthropological extension, in a reading of the first five chapters of the Book of Wisdom. Is anything added, or substantially modified, by the fact that God, the judge of this decisive trial, has become a human being and has lived and preached among us?

A priori, it would seem obvious that this should occur. Nevertheless— and here our general hypothesis returns—up to and including this moment of the contemplation of the eternal King—which is the hermeneutic key of the entire treatment of the illuminative way in the *Exercises*—the conception of a trial abides intact. True, the Book of Wisdom does not explicitly state that the *law* (of Moses) is the only possible criterion of the judgment to be rendered upon a person's life. The strict universality of this probation is implicit there, however, since even the patriarchs, like Abraham, Lot, or Jacob, are tried and declared "just" (see Wis. 10:5–6:10). And still more universally: holy Wisdom "understands what is pleasing in [Yahweh's] eyes and what is conformable with [his] commands" (Wis. 9:9: see 9:17). Those called "just" there, then, are simply those who have complied with the law.

What, then, is the anthropological function of Christ in a theology of trial? The contemplation of the eternal King—and of his prime analogate, the temporal king—show Christ as the supreme *example* of the justice (the wisdom) that God prizes—of what is "pleasing in his eyes." Jesus certainly does not deliver human beings from the law, as Paul's "gospel" claims he does (Gal. 3:13,24–25, 4:4–5,21, 5:1–4). On the contrary, Jesus embraces the law: he fulfills it "in all that is granted [by the law] and is not forbidden him" (no. 23; see 165, 167). In other words, we have the conception of the perfect "accomplishment" of the law that Matthew identifies as the mission of Jesus, the new Moses (see Matt. 5:17–19). We are dealing with the law brought to the perfection evinced in the words, and especially in the actions, of the Son of God, the "exemplar cause" of the success of the trial.

Ignatius adopts *one* New Testament christology, and pays the price of ignoring others that may be richer or more mature. And significantly, this christology is the one most consonant with an anthropology of trial. Ignatius does not have at his disposal, in the face of the variety of gospel material concerning Jesus—as neither did his age—the elements of literary criticism that would have enabled him to organize that material in a rational "historical project" in which Jesus would be calling for the collaboration of his disciples of yesterday and today. We have a further indication of this in the fact that the "mysteries of the life of Christ our Lord" proposed for contemplation from the Second Week of the *Exercises* to their conclusion (see nos. 261ff.) are drawn from a kind of concordance of the four Gospels (which resembles, in its theological conclusions as well as in the preeminence accorded to Matthew, the old *Diatessaron* of Tatian).

4. Thus the exercitant arrives at midpoint of the Second Week—the crucial moment at which he is expected to make an *option* ("election"), so that, according to the very definition of the *Exercises*, he may find "the divine will in the disposition of his life for the salvation of [his] soul" (no. 1).

This, then, to my view, is the culmination of the end the *Exercises* propose to achieve. Thus, the *Exercises* cannot be expected to produce a kind of "ongoing spirituality." Nor, therefore, can it be maintained that their underlying theology is that determined by the three classic stages of the mystical journey: the purgative, illuminative, and unitive ways.

On the contrary, in the *Exercises*, the "trial" by which the soul will be saved or lost enters a critical moment at which it is important to determine a certain structure or permanent "state" (no. 135). And I say a certain "structure" because Ignatius himself seems clearly to intend the *Exercises*, in principle, for use by a person for whom the question is pending of whether to embrace the secular or the religious life (see no. 15), or whether to accept or decline charges and (especially) ecclesiastical benefices, with the corresponding offices and perquisites (see no. 16).

That this moment is critical for the trial that has governed the entire development of the *Exercises* thus far seems to be indicated by two "meditations": those on the "Two Standards" and on the "Three Classes of Men" (see nos. 136ff.). I believe that these two considerations, using a discursive rather than an affective approach (as indicated by the term "meditation"), are intended to reinforce the principles already established.

The consideration on the three classes of men is calculated to warn the exercitant, by means of three examples, that indifference (that of the First Principle and Foundation) is not easily acquired, while it is easy to fall into the trap of the affections already possessed, and that thus it is frequently "of profit, in order to extinguish this disordered affect, to beg in the colloquies" that it be the will of the Lord to choose to despoil him of that to which he is attached (no. 157). We note that Ignatius does not say that, in dealing with a disordered affection for a thing, it is always better to abandon that thing. According to Ignatius, this will depend on the "service and praise of [the] divine goodness." Thus, if it were to be the will of God that a person continue in possession of that to which he is attached, what he would have to "elect" is a change in the "motives" for which he prizes and esteems the way or state in which he lives. This supposes that God has one path in mind, not so much for the salvation or perdition of each person, as for favoring with his grace, in the trial, the one who will have conformed with the "divine will."[6]

The consideration on the two standards repeats, in the face of the summons of Lucifer, the summons of the eternal King. This is consonant with our position that the contemplation of this second summons is not indicative of a change of perspective from trial to project. We are still dealing with a spirituality of trial. with all its conditions and criteria. The only essential difference is that, here, what had been an image of discipleship is translated into a hierarchy of virtues, seen as ascending rungs in the competitive imitation that the King proposes in contrast with the descending rungs of Lucifer's call: "the first, poverty rather than wealth; the second, opprobrium or contempt rather than worldly honor; the third, humility rather than pride ... " (no. 146). This is the difficult challenge that the King proposes to the knight "in order that, following me in *hardship*, he may also follow me in glory" (no. 95).

Thus the exercitant arrives at the central moment of the election, which, in a certain measure, will determine his existential response to the *trial*. Freed from his disorderly affections, he is now ready, at this decisive moment, by way of exercises to be performed at various intervals over the course of an entire day, to "attach himself (*se afecte*) to the true teaching of Christ" (no. 164). The "affection" to be created or accentuated here constitutes a definitive breach with the antecedent (and provisional) attitude of indifference, and generates an attraction—in a summary of what has intervened since the summons of the eternal King—for the "example" of Christ and of his specific "humility."

To attain "humility" is to open the door "to all the other virtues" (no. 146), as the exercitant has already learned in the meditation on the two standards. Why precisely "humility"? Because I cannot pass the test without subjecting myself to what someone else—before whom I must "abase and lower myself"—desires of me. There is no question, then, of making use of my own freedom in order to carry forward some project that that freedom may initiate. What is at issue, in this third step of the "standard of Christ," is a more precise definition of what I must observe in order to pass the test by which God wills that I save my soul.

After all, what God wishes of me in the first two degrees of humility does not extend beyond the observance of the law. Hence, in these first two degrees, as far as other things are concerned—that is, in matters in which my comportment is not dictated by commandments of grave (the first degree) or light (the second degree) obligation—indifference to creatures continues to be counseled as the proper attitude to have (see nos. 165–66).

But God desires *more* from the knight who seeks to "distinguish himself." The third degree of humility, the degree that renders humility *most perfect*, consists in the observance of a second criterion, one that goes beyond the observance of the law: where neither is any obligation imposed, nor any penalty or reward is at stake. That supreme criterion is christological. It is a matter of the imitation of a divine exemplar: Jesus as seen through the eyes of Ignatian theology. This has already been indicated, in altogether general terms, in the contemplation of the eternal King. But now Ignatius minces no words. He indicates what it means to imitate this King:

> I choose poverty with Christ poor, rather than riches, derision with Christ heaped with the same rather than honors, and to desire rather to be taken for foolish and insane for Christ who was first held for such, than for wise or prudent in this world. [no. 167]

I believe that we (today) are faced with a theological problem of the first magnitude here. The three traits of Christ set in relief in the Ignatian text commit a very serious distortion of what the Gospels (principally the synoptics) present as the Christian memory of Jesus' public life. They reduce it to the "cross"—to suffering, although this suffering is expressed in the terms to which a knight of Ignatius' time would be most sensitive.

To my understanding, two questions arise here. The first is how Ignatius, in his reading of the gospel, could have arrived at such a reduction. And the second is what value this suffering could have that could make of it, and it alone, what we have rightly called the "exemplary cause" of someone's passing the test of the salvation of his or her soul.

To be sure, Ignatius has not invented this reduction of God's will for Jesus, his Christ, to suffering. Ignatius has received the christology of his age. Elsewhere I have attempted to show that, despite its express prohibition of "mixing" Jesus' two natures, Chalcedon did not succeed in preventing christologies "from above" from replacing the historical causes of Jesus' death with others seemingly more worthy of a divine plan: the Father sends his Son to earth to die for the forgiveness of human sins. To put it another way, the suffering of Christ is still real, but its historical cause (and consequently the way in which the *human* Jesus lived) disappears, giving way to the satisfaction owed God by humanity for its sins.[7] In this "redemption," only suffering counts.

But Ignatius, as the reader will recall, incorporates, into the theology of his age, the spirit of chivalry, which seeks to "distinguish itself" in what is most difficult in the following of Jesus: "in order that, following me in *hardship*, he may also follow me in glory" (no. 95). The reader may recall that, at the time of his conversion, as he himself recounts, in reading the lives of the saints as if they had been knights, the question Ignatius asked himself was: If they, why not I? It is not strange that the question asked should concern what, in all logic, appears as the most difficult thing in the following of the "supreme and true captain, Christ our Lord" (no. 143).

But it is in the second question that a theological problem arises that, even today, is central in christology: What is the *value of pain* in the life of Jesus? Or to put it another way: Whence does it come to occupy practically the totality of Jesus' exemplarity? Here we touch on the very nerve of the two hypotheses with which we are working. If we select the hypothesis of trial, then God wills pain because, when all is said and done, this is what is at stake in a trial. God wills the trial in order to learn what quantity of pain a person is willing to suffer in order to emerge victorious. On the other hand, in the hypothesis of a *project*, pain is the price to be paid for the realization of a historical value even when the latter is not realized—which is tantamount to saying that the value of pain is measured not by the quantity of suffering borne, but by the enthusiasm with which someone maintains to the end the historical causality tending to the realization of the goal of the project. The historical Jesus suffered not in order to give us an example, but because the values maintained by the entire establishment of Israel, contrary as they were to those of the reign of God, could not but make it terribly dangerous for Jesus to preach the priorities of the reign that God was to establish upon earth in order that his will be done in history—on earth (Matt. 6:10 and parallels) as it is already done in heaven. Here there is no value in suffering as such, least of all as a route to the soul's salvation. One suffers because one must pay the price of the humanization of the human being in a conflict-ridden history where human beings' most immediate, and often most powerful interests (Matt. 10:34–36) are opposed to the change that delivers other human beings (the poor, the marginalized, those despised as sinners) *and even God* (Matt. 25:31–46) from their suffering.

When Jesus' suffering is removed from the context of a project that God has not yet realized and that is in the hands of Jesus and his fellow human beings, and when this project is lost among the postpaschal interpretations of the glorious Jesus, we begin to wonder why and whether Jesus' cross should continue to be normative. This is my personal impression from a reading of perhaps the most erudite and comprehensive Catholic study of Jesus in this century, Edward Schillebeeckx's *Jesús: La historia de un viviente.*[8]

5. In conclusion, let us entertain a brief but important consideration on the last contemplation of the *Spiritual Exercises*: the "Contemplation for Obtaining Love."

Throughout the remainder of the Second Week, and during the next two weeks, the election that has been made on the basis of the criterion of as "ordered" an affection as possible is confirmed, above all through a contemplation of the death and resurrection of Christ our Lord.

It comes as something of a surprise, then, that, in terms of the title of the last contemplation, "love" should be regarded as not yet having been "obtained" or reached—or, more likely, that a complementary or superior reason by which this love might be attained is lacking—even as the exercitant is preparing to take leave of the *Exercises*.

Another surprise is that, after all the contemplations on Christ of the last three weeks, the mind of the exercitant must now return, from the mysteries of the life, death, and resurrection of Christ, to the Creator-creature relationship that dominates this final contemplation. Here as in the First Principle and Foundation, we have a certain undeniable "christological vacuum."

Be this as it may, I should only like to indicate here that, according to Ignatius, the reality of creation ought to produce in the exercitant a powerful sensation of the loving presence of God, and thereby arouse a love for the Creator.

What should not be surprising, for it is such a logical consequence of the theology of trial, is that the created universe, despite all its injustices, sufferings, and unfulfilled promises, appears in this contemplation as perfect, in its presentation as a motive for love. Once more St. Paul is ignored, with his claim in Romans 8:20–21 that "creation was made subject to futility," and that it can only be extricated from this situation by the creative freedom that is the source of the *projects* of the children and heirs of God: human beings. The notion of trial implies that God has no need of human beings' success in this examination to which their moral fiber is subjected. It is the human being who disappoints; the created universe abides in its perfection. In a theology of *project*, God is passionately interested in what human freedom can create in terms of love, justice, and solidarity in a world under construction, where God has willed to have need of the creative liberty of the daughters and sons of their divine parent. In other words, in a theology of project, the finality of the created universe is the implementation of human creativity. And Sartre's response, in his drama *The Flies*, to a Jupiter who had presented, in language worthy of Thomas Aquinas, a perfect order to which Orestes was to return—"I am a man, Jupiter, and every man must invent his way" (Act 3, scene 2)—had become Christian teaching long before, in the daring thought of Paul.

IGNATIUS AS SUPERIOR GENERAL: A SECOND CHARISM?

Ignatius Loyola felt that, in founding his Company—not alone, of course, but surrounded by his nine companions—he was "inventing a way" in the history of the religious life.

I am not unfamiliar with the conventional notion, so convenient for solving certain organizational problems of the Society of Jesus, that that society was a kind of socialization of the Manresa experience. In other words, it is taken for granted that the theology underlying the *Spiritual Exercises* is the "charism" of the group of persons who gathered about Ignatius and became the religious order of which Ignatius was superior general until his death. For my part, I doubt that the succession of events was quite so rectilinear. To my understanding, we can discern a theological quantum leap here, although not necessarily one that was reflexively articulated by those making it.

Thus far, this article has been an attempt to demonstrate that the *Spiritual Exercises*, while surely a genuine "creation" of Ignatius as a system for the intense living of a Christian spirituality at the moment at which one must make an important life decision, rest upon a theology of *trial*, common to the religious and spiritual life of Ignatius's time. This is not to deny that Ignatius' spirit of chivalry, without departing from this basic characteristic, added to it a "more" that characterized a knightly competition in the imitation of the "supreme captain of the good," Jesus Christ.

From this point forward, however, my working hypothesis in the rapid sketch to follow will be: in addressing himself to the task of creating a religious order that would differ from those already in existence at the time, and in solving, as its superior general, problems related to the history of his time, Ignatius moved to a different kind of spirituality—one based far more on a theology of *project*, and hence on a theology on whose basis decisions, too, were made differently. No longer would such decisions be made so much in function of an "imitation" of the supreme captain—"eating, drinking, dressing as he, working as he by day and watching by night" (no. 93)—as with a view to a historical efficacity, orientated wholesale to the "greater service of God," which familiar concept will now have been extricated from its old semantic context of merit and transferred to a certain understanding of the unity and extension of the church—in particular, of a church that was emerging from the Middle Ages and confronting a different world.

In this already overlengthy article, the *hypothesis* to which I have just referred cannot be "verified" or "falsified" in the way that the *thesis* of the foregoing section has been shown or demonstrated—for reasons that may be of interest to the reader, as well as excuse the author from a task for an article already long in terms of maintaining the reader's attention (and hopelessly short in terms of the material it ought to treat).

Of course, the "theology of trial" to which I have referred is not explicit as such in the *Spiritual Exercises* of Ignatius Loyola. We had to verify our thesis in terms of the internal logic or consistency of the little *system* of spirituality that the *Exercises* are. The hypothesis of a "theology of project," on the other hand, must be examined in the light of material that not only is not explicit, but, besides being merely implicit, is to be found only scattered throughout the heterogeneous experiences of Ignatius' fifteen remaining years, those of his tenure as superior general until his death in 1556. My hypothesis is that, throughout this entire period, especially in his conduct as superior general of the Society of Jesus and in the criteria to which he had recourse in order to determine that conduct, Ignatius, perhaps without realizing it, functioned on the basis of a theology that gradually departed from the one that had underlain the *Spiritual Exercises*.

In order to support this hypothesis, I must examine, at least by way of a bird's-eye view, Ignatius's mentality subsequent to his election as superior general of the nascent Jesuits. I believe that it is safe to say that, for this period, the most pertinent documentation will be found in the letters—more than seven thousand of them—that he either wrote himself or directed his secretary, Polanco, to write in his name. Obviously it will not be out of place to include certain data from his *Autobiography*, his *Spiritual Diary*, the *Constitutions of the Society of Jesus*, and even his first printed biography, the one written by his near contemporary (despite their age difference) and disciple of predilection, Pedro de Rivadeneira.

The corpus of the Ignatian letters (published in twelve volumes of the *Monumenta Ignatiana*) is, in principle, of all the more interest to the theologian for the fact that, in most cases, they are apparently lacking in theology. When theology is present, here and there, appearing incidentally in the course of some argumentation or other, it is not systematized, as it is in the *Exercises*. On the other hand, it is surely unfortunate that I must confine myself in this article to a few letters, from this immense corpus, that the reader will be able to find (with one exception, which I shall indicate) in the collection by Fathers Ignacio Iparraguirre and Cándido Dalmases in *Obras Completas de Ignacio de Loyola* (which I shall cite by the number assigned the particular letter in that collection).[9] Furthermore, as I am not a historian, I hope that the reader will not be too impatient with me for selecting my citations on the basis of the theological criterion of what I have called my *hypothesis*.

1. Before examining the material from the letters, I ask the reader to permit me to make a very brief comment on an Ignatian anecdote that would seem to have made quite a deep impression on someone who was present on the occasion in question. I refer to a dialogue between Ignatius and Diego Laínez, one of Ignatius's first companions, presently to take his place among the theologians of the Council of Trent. Rivadeneira reports that the conversation occurred on "a day in the month of July of the year one thousand five hundred forty-one," four years before the first session of Trent, "Father Master Laínez, with our Father Ignatius ... and I being present." And Rivadeneira continues:

> There came a moment when our Blessed Father said to Father Laínez, "Tell me, Master Laínez—what does it seem to you that you would do were God our Lord to propose to you this case, and say: 'If you are willing to die on the spot, I shall withdraw you from the prison of this body and grant you eternal glory. But if you wish to continue to live, I give you no surety of what will become of you, but leave you to your fate: if you live and persevere in virtue, I shall award you the recompense; if you fall away from good, as I find you so shall I judge you.' If our Lord were to tell you this—and you were to understand that, by remaining in this life for some time you could render some great and notable service to the divine Majesty—what would you choose? What would you reply?"

I think it will be worthwhile to pause a moment before hearing Laínez's (and Ignatius's) reply. If this question were to be asked in a context of the underlying theology of the *Exercises*, one would surely expect the response to be that of the first alternative. First of all, it corresponds exactly to the human being's end and purpose as defined in the First Principle and Foundation. But there are more subtle, theological reasons, as well. When Ignatius asks, at the moment of the election, that we make a well-founded judgment, and not one based on mere caprice and subjectivism, he speaks of the day of our death and the day of judgment as paradigms (nos. 186, 187). What should we wish to have chosen at that moment, when, we see, there would no longer be any history to seduce us and perhaps confuse or entrap us?

Not for nothing, then, does Father Laínez, perhaps more attentive, as a theologian, to consistency with the *Spiritual Exercises* than is Ignatius himself, answer, according to Rivadeneira:

> Father, I confess to Your Reverence that I should choose to depart at once to enjoy the vision of God, and thus assure my salvation and deliver myself from dangers in a matter of such importance.

Let us notice something interesting and suggestive here: that the matter in question can be of "importance" only to the human being. It does not seem to occur to a person, in a conception of life and its decisive choices as a *trial*, that, in the free disposition of divine providence, God might have an actual *need* of the freedom of human beings in the implementation of some divine plan. The human being is on earth as an exile, only to be judged. Freedom is decisive, yes, but only for that human being—not to "invent a way" for the divine plans.

We are surprised, then, at Rivadeneira's report of what comes next. In fact, Rivadeneira must have been mightily impressed himself, as he carefully noted the date of Ignatius's response:

> Then our Father said: "Now, I certainly should not have done so. Rather, had I judged that, remaining in this life, I could have rendered some singular service to Our Lord, I should have besought him to leave me in it until I should have performed that service. And I should place my eyes on it and not on myself—having no regard for my danger or security."[10]

Ignatius relegates to second place the outcome of the trial that issues in salvation or condemnation. But it may not be quite so clear to Rivadeneira's reader with what he replaces it. Ignatius's response to Laínez's changes the subject, as it were: suddenly he is discussing how to conjure away any fear of the danger in which the second alternative proposed by God could seem to leave the person making the choice. That is, he goes on to say that that person need not fear for his salvation, since just as any "temporal" king would surely not forget the gratitude that a knight would deserve who would abandon his own safety in behalf of his lord, so neither would God neglect the salvation of a person electing the more generous, the second, of the alternatives proposed. Should we wish to learn the *intrinsic* value of what is preferred to his security, however, we must attend to the Spanish expression that, according to Rivadeneira, Ignatius twice employs.

Ignatius prefers the opportunity of using the remaing time of life (without security) to perform what he calls once a "singular service," and again, a "notable service".[11] In Spanish, as in other Romance languages, there is an important conceptual difference between "serving notably or singularly well," and rendering or performing a "notable or singular service" for someone. The former merely denotes the special quality of the service being performed for that person. The second, however, indicates a *specific mutual situation* that renders the service notable or singular. This fact of language, applied to theology, transports us from the situation of trial to that of project. There can be no "notable or singular service" without extreme need or desire on the part of the person *to whom the service in question is rendered*. The service must be a solution to that person's urgent need or desire.

Here, if I mistake not, is something that suggests a change, and surely a profound change, vis-à-vis the latter two "modes of humility" (nos. 165–66). In the *Exercises*, the criterion of the "imitation" of Jesus Christ "poor, dishonored, esteemed as foolish and insane" is supposed to resolve any equilibrium a person may have acquired. And this equilibrium supposes "equal service of God and salvation of my soul" (that is, equal "praise and glory of the divine majesty"). The reason why the order of preeminence can now be inverted is that the service in question is something on which the general plan or reign of God depends.

We have come to the parable of the Last Judgment (in Matthew), or that of the talents or coins (in Matthew and Luke), in which God is defined as someone who suffers in our brothers and sisters, and the human being as someone presented with the exhilarating opportunity of enabling this God to reap without having sown and gathering without having scattered.[12] Or else God will be deprived of this harvest—if human freedom loses its creativity. That is, we have an anthropological situation like that portrayed by Paul in his most characteristic letters.[13]

2. The principal *theological* difference between an orientation to trial and one to project is that, in the latter, something definitive, something of "supernatural" interest to God, is at stake in the element of contingency in human history—not only the salvation of the individual soul, then, but a "creation," in which God cooperates with human beings of good will.

The notion may appear rather too abstract. I hope that the characteristics that I shall now identify in this definition will demonstrate its concreteness, just as has occurred with the theological notion of "trial."

In a letter written in Italian to fathers setting out for various apostolic ministries, Ignatius expresses himself as follows:

As for the neighbor, regard first the persons with whom you deal, who ought to be those from whom greater fruit is hoped (as you cannot deal with all): those most in need, and persons of great authority, learning, temporal goods, and other persons suitable to be apostles, and generally those who, once they have been assisted, will then be able to assist others, for the glory of God. [Letter 79][14]

Here we glimpse, along with the novelty of Ignatius's order, a characteristic that the society will maintain at least up until its suppression: a *tension* between the two poles of the divine project being realized in the midst of human history. How are we to reconcile, in one and the same historical orientation, "assistance" to "those most in need," on the one hand, and the cultivation, in the service of this assistance, of what we might call "power," which requires "authority, learning, temporal goods," and "apostolic suitability"?

I am not suggesting that Ignatius had any very clear notion of how to reconcile these two elements. But he is altogether clear with respect to the extremities of the antinomy. On the one hand, as the letter (Letter 39) to the Jesuits of Padua shows, "those most in need" are not, for Ignatius, the wealthy and powerful, wrapped up in their psychological conflicts: "Jesus Christ was sent to earth now: 'For the oppression of the destitute and the poor now,' saith the Lord, 'I must arise . . .' "

As he writes to the abbot of Salas, the poor are the de jure proprietors even of ecclesiastical goods not strictly necessary for the maintenance of the one upon whom the benefice in question has been conferred:

I do not speak [in this case] of injustices in the external forum; rather [I am saying] that any goods of the church not necessary for the maintenance of your mercy according to your state, belong to the poor, and that only with great injustice are they deprived of them, according to the holy doctors; and it is not enough that the Rota bestow upon your mercy possession and usufruct, or papal parchments, for you to be able to mount an adequate defense before the tribunal of Christ our Lord. [Letter 153]

On the other hand, Ignatius does not claim to be able to escape this antinomy by the facile route of the society's insertion among the poor, proclaimed by a certain theology of the religious life today in a context of liberation theology in Latin America. We know that he counsels the society to seek out those who possess temporal goods (see Letters 79, 127, etc.), approach persons of power (Letter 50), and wherever possible, become confessors to princes (see Letters 52, 69, etc.).

From the viewpoint of a possible comparison between the underlying theology here and the one founding the most radical options of the *Exer-*

cises, it is interesting to see what Ignatius writes concerning the selection of means for assisting the neighbor:

> It will be the part of discretion to know which [pious works] to embrace, inasmuch as not all can be [thus embraced], keeping one's gaze ever fixed on the service of God, the common good, and the good reputation of the Society. [Letter 69; see Letter 52]

But the better to imitate Jesus, the exercitant is encouraged to say, "I seek and choose rather poverty with Christ poor than riches, rather opprobrium with Christ heaped with the same than honor, and to desire rather to be esteemed as foolish and insane for Christ ... than wise or prudent in this world." But in his encounter with the complex reality of the history of his company, Ignatius has discovered something more profound: that the power to do good requires the "good reputation of the Society"—that is, that nothing can come of being held for foolish and insane, however much one could thereby resemble Christ.

3. Finally, from the contempt for the world that, in the cave at Manresa, he learned in his "Gersoncito"—Thomas à Kempis's *The Imitation of Christ and Contempt for the World*, at that time attributed to Gerson—Ignatius passes to a mystical spirituality in which not only the thematic alternative between God and creatures goes by the board, but "profane" history, if one may so call it, comes to be of interest to the glory and service of God. This occasions many relative novelties in the first constitutions of the company, such as freedom from choir for the sake of availability for occupations in which union with God would continue without ceasing to be action, or such as permitting the professed of the society to limit the time they gave to mental prayer, in such wise that there might be a creative synthesis between prayer and action.

This synthesis, so rich in its historical implications, had at times to be emphasized by Ignatius in the face of a customary distinction between the natural and the supernatural that alienated persons from the historical in favor of a preeminence accorded the contemplation of divine things. Thus, he responds to the complaints of Father Godinho that the temporal affairs with which the latter was charged prevented his union with God:

> As for the burden of temporal matters, while they could appear to be, and could actually be, somehow distracting, I have no doubt that your holy intention and direction of everything with which you deal to the divine glory renders it spiritual, in conformity with his divine will, interpreted by obedience, so that [such temporal affairs] may be not only equivalent to the union and recollection of assiduous contemplation, but actually more acceptable, as proceeding from a more violent and powerful charity. [Letter 72]

From a similar viewpoint, it will be in order to observe how Ignatius goes about presenting the position of the Society of Jesus with regard to the proposed establishment of the Inquisition in Germany, for the purpose of attacking the infant Reformation there. He has recourse neither to a theological evaluation nor to any of the (individual?) criteria set forth in the *Exercises* for making an election. He bows to what we should today call the "signs of the times," observing that the imposition of sanctions like exile or death, or, for that matter, the very institution of the Inquisition, "seems more than Germany in its present state might be able to bear" (Letter 127).

But the synthesis goes much further. From his place as superior general of the society, Ignatius is not content, for example, to bless and support the military campaigns of Charles V against the Turks, although the matter was now more political than ecclesiastical. His secretary, Polanco, writes of an "impression which [Ignatius] seems to have these days":

> It appears that, seeing these Turkish armadas coming to Christian waters year after year, and doing such damage ... he has come to feel very strongly in our Lord that the Emperor ought to assemble a very powerful armada, and dominate the sea himself. And not only does he feel moved to this by zeal for souls and charity, but also by the light of reason, which shows this to be a very necessary thing, and one that would require a smaller expenditure on the Emperor's part than he is now required to make ... And so convinced of this is our Father that, as he has said, if he thought that he could thus please his Majesty, or if he were to receive some considerable sign to this effect from the divine will, he would gladly spend the rest of his years in such efforts himself. [Letter 75]

We may well think that Ignatius betrays, in some of these profane historical options, a certain spirit of oversimplification, or, if you will, a latent Manichaeism, with the emperor and the will of God on one side and the Grand Turk and Satan on the other (to say nothing of the ambiguous, subtle French policy vis-à-vis both). This may be. But I am not examining Ignatius's systematized theology of history. I am examining his passion for what happens in history, and his conviction that all of it bears profoundly on the service of God that is the duty of human freedom.

And that we may see how deep is his passion for what is at stake in history and for the governance of the threads that weave that history, we could scarcely do better than to cite a strange letter which, probably for fear of shocking his readers, Father Iparraguirre did not choose to include in his *Obras completas de Ignacio de Loyola*. It is a "minute letter," a kind of letter-telegram, to be sent to the Jesuits of Ingolstadt, February 14, 1550, to inform them of the election of the new pope (to whom the whole society would be bound by a special fourth vow of obedience): "First. The Pope is

[del] Monte, who gave them their doctorates. Second. The cardinals who can do the most with him are Burgos, Carpi, Teatino, Santa Cruz, and Mafeo, in that order" (*Monumenta Ignatiana*, series 1, vol. 3, Letter 1061). I think that, had we no data to certify Ignatius as an authentic mystic, this communication of a scale of ecclesiastical *power*—obviously, to be *used*—would shock, as I confess it shocked me the first time I saw it. But my hypothesis comes in here. What we see, of course, are all the signs of a historical project more founded on a human prudence or ambition, but which in Ignatius's spirituality simply reflects a different experience of God than that of Manresa, an experience that becomes more and more a part of his life: that of a God revealed in the historical challenges posed to human liberty, and in the realistic projects that arise from those challenges.

Ignatius could not yet have had (as neither have I been able to prove the corresponding hypothesis in this article) a theology of project, since the basic foundations of such a theology—the historical Jesus and, especially, the theology of Paul—had not yet been rescued by critical exegesis from the oblivion into which they had fallen during the Middle Ages—and for that matter, a great deal earlier, in the time of the New Testament itself. As I have indicated, I have concerned myself with this topic elsewhere. But as for Ignatius, I maintain that the foregoing suggests that, in large measure, Ignatius Loyola, as superior general of the new Society of Jesus, began in Rome to practice a spirituality different from that of the *Exercises*, one destined to have increasing influence on the church—first of all in the errors or successes of the society itself, which, thanks to Ignatius, was also introduced, often in very ambivalent fashion—but most effectively, as even those who disagreed with it had to admit, at least during the first period of its life—into the history of the modern world.

It will scarcely be necessary to add that, from the more particular perspective of a theology of liberation in Latin America, many of the points of Ignatius's spirituality while he was superior general might well be applied in terms of the development of a liberative theology—with all the dangers and opportunities that that theology may have in store.

CHAPTER 11

The Legacy of Columbus and the Hierarchy of Christian Truths

Here Segundo uses the phrase "hierarchy of truths" from the Second Vatican Council to characterize the evangelization needed for Latin America in the present and the future. He believes that the two previous evangelizations, that of the upper classes and that of the Indians and blacks, were unable to communicate the gospel as good news. He has, however, considerable hope for the evangelization of the next five hundred years, since liberation theology has provided the resources needed to proclaim the gospel as good news for both the upper classes and the poor.

Source: "Legado de Colón y la jerarquía de verdades cristianas," *Miscelánea Comillas* (l988): 107–27.

Not being a historian, not even in the field supposed to be mine—theology—I am able to conceive only after the fashion of a symbol the event whose fifth centenary is being celebrated. Indeed, does it not seem that fate itself has invited us to take this kind of approach? Consider the event's central personage, whose birth and burial are both lost in the mists of history, as if to lend him an even greater significance—just as with Melchisedech, whose material past and future are shrouded in darkness, thereby serving to set in still bolder relief the "symbolic" importance of the encounter of the father of Israel with the *Deus altissumus* whom he serves and represents.

When I say that I can think of that event only as symbolic, I am not suggesting that it ought to be stripped of its material reality. In some sort, plaited with numberless other variables, the concrete manner in which Europe collided with America by way of those caravels that landed on a Caribbean shore half a millennium ago is present in problems of the caliber and urgency of the Latin American foreign debt. It is only that that debt, which appears to me in the familiar faces I see around me every day, does not symbolize my precise Latin American, or Hispano-American if you like, identity.

What I am preparing to celebrate hits home still more forcefully. It is the symbol of an origin—a very precise origin, conditioning the very way I think, conditioning my place in the world. And precisely on that account I must say that the symbol I celebrate and on which I meditate is not the "discovery of America." I do understand that this is how it influenced life in Europe: the conquest of a new space, temporal and spiritual, for Europe. This new space, first available to Spain, then to Portugal, then to other European nations, was thereby largely to change and determine the lot of all of those nations of the "Old World."

But in Latin or Hispanic America, the symbolic event is not a discovery. It is rather the *mutual* encounter of two remarkably distinct, but equally "human," worlds. I am celebrating, then, not so much a discovery, but the "first communication" between a pair of human worlds destined, by this event, to live in symbiosis.

Obviously I shall make no attempt to describe, still less evaluate, this symbiosis or its results. The very fact that I think and write in the "new world" begun by Columbus places me in a particular, "interested," and perhaps guilty position. At all events, it surely renders me incapable of pronouncing an impartial word on the symbiosis in question.

I can only meditate on certain elements that have been part of that symbiosis, and that are present in the event whose first half-millennium we are commemorating—and write some brief annotations on one of the problems posed by the mutual communication that started up then. Columbus not only brought to America the European culture of his age. He also brought—or rather, brought as part of that culture—the *cross*, the sign of something that will henceforward form an integral, central part of the communication between these two human worlds: Christianity.

My approach to this encounter between the Christianity brought over by Columbus and the religions of the pre-Columbian world will prescind from a very critical point of historiography—something which, doubtless, will have considerable influence on whether the fifth centenary of that symbolic event of the arrival of Columbus in America will be observed in joy or in sorrow. I refer to what some call the "Black Legend." The Black Legend (together with its criticism of the Inquisition) is one of the logical fruits of the European Enlightenment. True or false—or better, correct or incorrect—the weight it is assigned constitutes the protest of human reason against the intent of civil society to impose a religion by force, by coercing the freedom of thought of the inhabitants of any territory.

I exclude this question from my approach, in full knowledge that I thereby depart somewhat from the more unambiguous direction taken by Latin American liberation theology itself. Indeed, it has been that theology's dominant concern, in looking to our continental past, not precisely to excuse Spain, and the missioners who accompanied its Conquistadors, but to demonstrate the remarkable dose of liberative content that the interests of the *conquista* were unable to stifle, and which cried out for the liberty and other human rights of the subjected peoples. This liberative Christian ferment is said to have continued to be active in the synthesis effected by the dominated peoples between Christianity and their own autochthonous religions. Although these religions were erased from history in appearance, their more humane elements, we are told, have survived, under the Christian names with which the oppressed have managed to maintain so many of the most profound elements of their own cultures. This, in the logic of liberation theology, is a criticism of the Enlightenment, which sees only oppression and loss of identity in the "Catholic" religion that we see professed, and to a certain extent practiced, by the vast majority of the Hispano-American peoples.

My approach does not imply any concern to ignore the questions accompanying the introduction of Christianity into America. I only mean to ask, in celebrating the fifth centenary of the "communication of cultures" occasioned by Columbus's landing, a question precisely more intimately connected with the event itself: What *kind of Christianity* do we find in this communication?

I

Lest I leave the reader "hanging" at this point, let me confess from the outset that my approach will consist in an anachronism. According to Vatican Council II, in matters of ecumenical dialogue, one must recall that "there exists an order or 'hierarchy' of truths, since they vary in their *relationship to the foundation of the Christian faith*" (*Unitatis Redintegratio*, no. 11).

The anachronism is plain as day, since it is scarcely logical to ask a personage of the past a question formulated nearly five hundred years after him and the event that made him famous. Indeed, the principle that lies at the basis of the question is posited apropos of *ecumenism*, and I believe that it would be an injustice to Columbus were we to inquire into how he accomplished a task that he certainly did not have *in mente*.

To play the devil's advocate against my own claim, I beg leave to broach my subject by holding a little discourse on the "novelty" of this theological principle set forth in the Vatican II decree on ecumenism, *Unitatis Redintegratio*.

Generally speaking, "novelty" nearly always sounds bad in theology. It has a "bad press." St. Augustine, it is recounted, addressed to certain heterodox theologians this briefest of arguments: *Mira dicitis; nova dicitis; ergo falsa dicitis* ("What you utter is remarkable — therefore new — therefore false").

However, I doubt that many theologians will be found to deny that the principle in question is "new"; although it will not be without utility to look for something similar in other documents of the extraordinary or ordinary magisterium of the church. Be this as it may, if they are not in agreement with it, theologians will probably prefer to say that Vatican II, being "pastoral" in its intention, "defined nothing," and that, accordingly, theological principles like the one just cited are intended "less for 'faith' and 'contemplation' than for doing better work"[1] on the terrain in question, which is ecumenical practice.

Pope Paul VI, however, would scarcely have smiled in approval. In his closing discourse at Vatican II, he speaks of the "doctrinal wealth" of the council. It will be difficult to reconcile the fact of this "wealth" with the mere repetition of the already known. The truth is that "the magisterium of the church, although it has not wished to make pronouncements with extraordinary dogmatic authority, has been prodigal in its bestowal of its authoritative teaching concerning a quantity of questions that today call for the human being's conscience and activity."[2] The allusion to "today" in connection with this appeal or call cannot only mean that certain truths, until now only obscurely present, begin, in virtue of their "new" clarity, to set Christians "new" tasks.

That this wealth is an enrichment, and therefore signifies a "novelty" — that is, presents aspects of the "faith" that were not perceived before the council, or at least not perceived with the same clarity as in the council — is evident, furthermore, in the frustrated attempt of Karl Rahner to apply this principle to the dialogue with separated Christians. In a book written in collaboration with Heinrich Fries, Rahner advocates an ecumenical dialogue simply based on the common fund of the Christian faith as accepted by the first ecumenical councils — that is, by the councils celebrated by a *united* Christian church, before the so-called Eastern Schism. This proposal provoked a very critical article from the pen of D. Ols in *L'Osservatore Romano*, February 25, 1985, after Rahner's death, in which the proposal of Rahner and Fries was declared to be "irreconcilable with the Catholic faith." According to Ols, his article had been written at the behest of Cardinal Ratzinger.[3]

This so-called novelty, however, is in reality nothing of the kind — at least not for a theology attentive to certain elements of great importance that we see in the past. Even Cardinal Ratzinger, who is so concerned to interpret Vatican II along the same lines as Trent and Vatican I, should be able to recall that the very explanation of the latter's definition of papal infallibility implicitly used the principle that I have cited in order to delimit the field of *ex cathedra* definitions.

In the debate on this matter provoked by Hans Küng, Harry J. McSorley criticizes Küng for simply supposing that papal infallibility practically has no limits in matters of faith and behavior. McSorley points out:

It is certain that, merely by studying the acts of Vatican I, especially Bishop Gasser's presentation, one can discern the intent of the Council to limit the infallibility to revelation, and matters necessary to explain and preserve revelation.[4]

In order to show that this constitutes a delimitation as meaningful as it is necessary, McSorley employs two arguments. In the first place, Bishop Gasser showed:

> That it was the intent of Vatican I that these "matters" (vaguely designated as faith and behavior) were *either revelation itself or truths intimately related to divine revelation.*

And Gasser went on to show this by means of a concrete example, explaining why Vatican I rejected proposition 45, which would have extended the field of infallibility to all moral principles. He said that it only extended to those moral truths "that *belong in every respect to the deposit of faith.*"[5]

Indeed, it appears obvious that this refusal must be taken seriously. And if it is so taken, and one asks what the council sought to avoid, it seems clear that it would be to declare as a truth of faith something that, however *true* it might be, does not pertain to the actual *substance of the Christian message.* In other words, Gasser was indicating the crucial importance of identifying a core of principles or truths that "belong in every respect to the deposit of faith, that is, something substantially identical with what the aforementioned principle on ecumenism called the foundation of the Christian faith" (which is nothing else, clearly, than God's revelation). On the contrary, one must also admit an area of moral truths indeed connected with faith, but in a *hierarchically* inferior way (to borrow the vocabulary of Vatican II).

McSorley's second argument, against the actual existence of the danger Küng fears of a potentially ubiquitous infallibility, does not reduce this infallibility to the plane of moral truths, but extends it to that of (theological) truths in general. The intent of Vatican I to *limit* the scope of infallibility to revelation and those matters necessary to explain and preserve revelation was *explicitated,* McSorley holds, in the text of Vatican II (*Lumen Gentium,* no. 25), in which it is said that "this infallibility that the Divine Redeemer wished his Church to have . . . is coextensive with the deposit of Divine Revelation." This limitation, this *tantum . . . quantum* (which does not appear in the Spanish translation of the Latin text), is important, because it was insisted upon by the *relatio* made before the vote precisely to specify and clarify its sense:

> The object of the infallibility of the Church, thus expounded, has precisely the same extension as the revealed deposit. Accordingly, it extends to all of those things and only to those things (*et ad ea tantum*) that *either directly touch on the revealed deposit or that are required for the religious and faithful preservation of the revealed deposit.*[6]

McSorley's argument seems to me to be extremely clear and solid. Vatican II reasserts, leaving no room for doubt, even more explicitly than does Bishop Gasser's *relatio* on the limits of infallibility at Vatican I, the intent to reduce the area of possible definitions *ex cathedra* to that which can have no other name than the "foundation of Christian faith"—that is, to that and only that which might constitute an article *stantis aut cadentis revelationis*—matters of life or death for the gospel. But this logically indicates that such a limitation, already present in Vatican I, presupposes an "order or 'hierarchy' " among the truths that, with the passing of time, have come to form part of the faith of a Christian—which is what the seemingly "new" principle of the Vatican II decree on ecumenism propounds.[7]

But if *returning* to the essential is especially important when Christianity dialogues with separated Christians on differences in certain points of Christian faith,[8] or with other religions—and the reader will perceive that, after this "theological" excursion, we are once more approaching the subject of Columbus's centenary—then the time has come to ask: How does one return to the foundation of the Christian faith? How is the essential of revelation rediscovered?

Indeed, the Christianity of Hispanic America today comes down to us in a direct line from the encounter symbolized by Columbus. On one side are the pre-Columbian religions, destined to perish (in their official, public form). On the other side is Christianity, destined to replace them. But once more: What Christianity do we mean, if the truths in which a Christian believes stand in varying degrees of proximity to the foundation of that Christian's faith?

II

I doubt that it is necessary to be a historian, or have any technical expertise, to answer this last question. Columbus brings Christian Spain to America at the close of the fifteenth century—a Spain that, this same year of the "discovery" of a new world, brings to its close the only crusade ever to have met with success, at least complete and stable success: in 1492, Granada, the last bastion of the Islamic empire established throughout almost the entire peninsula eight centuries before, falls into the power of Christian Spain.

It is a special Spain. It will have no past, as the other European peoples have their medieval past. This will give this Spain a kind of deep freshness in its Christianity, quite far removed from the crisis of "fatigue of the medieval" that, in the rest of Europe, leads to the Renaissance and the Reformation. For Spain, one might say, one crusade has ended and another is just beginning. Its cultural and religious thrust predestines it to lead the Counter-Reformation. Within a mere century, Spain will be at the head of Europe in the fullness of its "golden age."

In America, just a few years after Columbus, the first European-style university will appear, in Lima. On the heels of the *conquista*, with lightning rapidity, comes an ecclesiastical hierarchy. With both, arrives the theology of European Catholicism, from its popular devotions to its most academic forms. I doubt the utility of attempting to authenticate an only too familiar story with superfluous data.

What I am interested in showing is that, with all of this enormous baggage, brought "as is" from "civilized, Christian Europe," a dialogue with the new "barbarous people" of America (whether they actually were barbarous or not — they need only have seemed to be to the eyes of Columbus's companions) waiting across the sea becomes practically unavoidable.

To show something of this, in relationship with the foregoing section, will be my object here. The dialogue of which we here treat has a technical name: "evangelization." Vatican II did not specifically deal with this question in its documents. But if the theological principle of the variable relationship of the truths Christians believe in with the foundation of the Christian faith is valid for ecumenism, it should be even more valid for the initial dialogue with the nonbeliever — for evangelization, or the first proclamation of the Christian faith.

I doubt that I wrong Columbus if I say that the first communication between the two worlds — the old and the new — whose fifth centenary we are about to celebrate, is perhaps the symbol of a first awkward communication between two cultural worlds; indeed, that it is the symbol of what was generally done here — of that whose end result was the transformation of Latin America into a Christian continent. You can count on the fingers of both hands the cases in which this dialogue was integrally an "evangelization."

What is it to "evangelize"? André Seumois, consultor to the Sacred Congregation for the Propagation of the Faith and counselor of the Preparatory Missionary Commission of Vatican II, defines it, in synthesis, as follows: To evangelize is (1) to communicate the essential, nothing more; (2) to communicate it as good news; and (3) to move beyond that fundamental core (the good news) only at a rate that will maintain the essential as essential.[9]

It seems to me that it is on the first of these three "items," perhaps rather to the detriment of the other two, that the interest of European theology has focused. It has been perceived that the church cannot conduct a dialogue on its "dogma"without jettisoning items that have accrued over the centuries by way of the most diverse avenues of cognition, avenues along which the peripheral has frequently prevailed over the essential. It is in the reduction of dogma to the few truths that could have been understood by the natives of Latin America that the principle proposed today by Vatican II, of an "order or 'hierarchy' of truths," ought to have been tested. This is the prevailing interest, it seems to me, of the fine book by Heinrich Fries and Karl Rahner. I think that, instead, implicitly or explicitly, Ibero-American Christianity sets this first item in strict connection with the others, so that a single problem arises: that of a necessary, but difficult or impossible, new evangelization of the continent.

Obviously this is not the place to undertake a detailed historical demonstration of this necessity, and of the corresponding difficulty or impossibility. I shall here refer only to certain symbolic elements, which speak, surely with sufficient eloquence, of the historical prioritization of this first item in the case under consideration. And I do so with the understanding that the problem was posed from the moment of the first encounter of the two cultural worlds whose fifth centenary we celebrate.

Christian roots, tended for better or for worse over ten centuries in the medieval church, seem to exempt Christianity from the second constitutive "item" of evangelization (until recently; and in some regions or countries more than in others): to present the essential—and only the essential—of Christianity as "good news." That which has grown to be connatural frequently replaces the "only reason" to be a Christian: believing in the *good news* (*evangelium*). But the latter could not have prevailed in the first meeting of those two cultures—between, first, the pre-Columbian (the native), and then the African (the slave), on the one hand, and on the other the Christianity of the Conquistadors. The destruction of one's own culture is never an *evangelium*, a gospel.

It is scarcely to be wondered at, therefore, that the most original attempts at an intercultural, and to a certain extent interreligious, dialogue in Hispanic America should have been born, have lived, and have died *in isolation* from what Columbus was attempting to do: gather the Indies into the kingdom of the Catholic monarchs.

Actually, it cannot be denied that, in catechesis, there was indeed an attempt at simplification of dogma. But as I have said, this is not where the most original element lay; the most original element lay in the attempt to associate Christianity with a cultural "good news." Here the reductions, Franciscan and Jesuit, sought, insofar as possible, to begin at the beginning.

By way of a symbol, again, I recall an example I read in the accounts of the Franciscan missions in the north of Mexico or southwestern United States. To the question posed by "unreduced" Amerindians as to why these (native) Christian settlements existed, the missionary answered with this marvelously ad rem response: "This is what it is to be Christian." We shall be told that this was an appeal to human greed. To be sure. But there is no other way to begin to associate Christianity with good news. In Exodus, Moses speaks of the "promised land." Jesus proclaims the "reign" promised to be at hand to the poor, in full knowledge of the expectations associated with this ambiguous term.

Whether or not the anecdote is true, sociologically speaking it is evident that the good news that issued in the creation of native settlements and reductions in New Spain was an "ingathering," an invitation to live a fuller, more just, more humane social life, and to live it in association with the central message of Christianity. In other words, although we should have to ask history for a more detailed account of what these natives were taught of the Christian message, we can say that, at least at first, a certain rhythm was observed whereby the essential, as good news, continued to be the essential. We should have to investigate whether, in the reduction of the dogmatic truths of Christianity to those few that could be understood by the natives, the Vatican II modern principle of the "order or 'hierarchy' of truths" was being followed.

It was of enormous consequence for the future of Christianity in America that the price of this incipient evangelization was *separation*. This is what finally sealed the fate of the Paraguayan reductions. To have obtained the consent of the king to remove by force, and "reduce" (that is, "lead apart"), the Indians from the greed of the Spaniards who had settled in their area and from their fashion of living "Christianity," will later become the reason invoked for destroying this work, certainly an original one, of evangelization. If the church was to be, and continue to be, a church of the masses in Ibero-America, it was ultimately going to have to be *fashioned from the kind of Christianity brought and practiced by the European Conquistadors.*

The need of separation, at least for a sad, truncated commencement of evangelization in the case of the slaves, stands symbolized in the work of St. Peter Claver. The Africans, the future slaves, entered into contact with their owners and tasks only after a superficial introduction (for which they had been sequestered) to Christianity by the great missionary. Baptism followed, and that symbol of liberation was the signal for them to be carried off to the places where they were to begin their lives as slaves.

For the rest of the population, European Christianity was the norm. And those who were destined to prosper on the new continent (whites and mestizos) were obliged to acknowledge as their own the Christianity of a thousand-year-old culture that was foreign to America—a Christianity that had been constructed for other circumstances and needs. The poorest and most marginalized peoples (the natives, and some mestizos and mulattoes) were obliged to keep up the appearances of a Christian practice. But they generally contrived to continue their worship of the autochthonous gods, under Christian forms.

Here too, a fact can have the value of a symbol. I refer to the familiar fact that in practically all the more developed pre-Columbian cultures, worship was offered to the Pachamama (Mother Earth). The Virgin Mary would assume the religious function of Pachamama in all those places where the Indian's culture (or cultures) would fuse with that of the Spaniard. Let us limit ourselves to a single citation. Clodomiro L. Siller A. writes:

> In the transmission and application of the message of Guadalupe, *the old culture is adopted* [emphasis in the original]: what already existed in the Nahuatl world is complemented. Thus, we find that the Virgin of Guadalupe presents herself to Juan Diego as the Mother of the principal gods of the native theology. "Know and understand, thou

the least of my children, that I am the ever Virgin Holy Mary, mother of the true God (*inhuelnelli Téotl*) by whom is life (*inipalnemohuani*), the Creator (*inteyocoyani*), present to all things (*in Tloque Nahuaque*), Lord of sky and earth (*in Ilhuicahua in Tlalticpaque*)."[10]

It is not the object of this article to undertake a detailed analysis of these assertions. Here again, what we have observed must be taken as the symbol of a situation destined to stagnate. The events narrated in the *Nican Mopohua* took place less than forty years after Columbus's arrival in America. And five centuries later (in the presence of divergent, even contradictory, value judgments) these same data are still verified of the reality of the entire continent, as thousands of books, articles, and scientific investigations attest. Here again let us cite a single example. If we would know what happens to religion in regions of indigenous culture like that of the Aymaras in Bolivia, we can read the book written by a Canadian missioner who lived among them all his adult years: J. E. Monast, *On les croyait chrétiens* (Paris: Cerf, 1969) (And you thought they were Christians).

What I should like to leave with the reader before taking the next step along theological lines is that evangelization was soon paralyzed by a two-fold conservatism, paralleling the division of labor already present in Columbus's first encounter with the Indies. Four centuries before Marx, the first communication between the two cultures-in-encounter resulted in each of the two relying in some fashion on the "Christian" element in order to defend something it regarded as profoundly its own. Hence the creation of *two religious worlds*, each with its Christian label. One, supporting the dominant groups, was the Christianity imported wholesale from Spain, which by and large turned its back on the new "reality" of the American human being. The other, the world of the oppressed, had recourse to Christianity in order to preserve, concealed and secretly alive, the wellsprings of its threatened, oppressed culture.

As both kinds of religion were vaguely aware of defending something of supreme importance for the survival of the respective human groups they represented, it is scarcely to be wondered at that they both harbored a great deal of conservatism, and that, for centuries, no coexistence developed between them. There was no dialogue. The official church, blind to the division, and even to the separation, of these two religious worlds, regarded them both as Christian. How do we "get back" to the essentials? How can the essentials be presented *again*, when all concerned feel that their survival depends on the status quo?

III

We could pause on this point, a key one. And I think we might say that, until a few years ago, it was something to which theology, even Latin American theology, paid no attention. We need only read, for example, the acts of the plenary council of Latin America, held in Rome less than a century ago in 1899, to observe that the theology with which our continent was regarded was still completely European.[11]

I think that it is to the credit of the theology of liberation to have attended, seriously, and with its own theological structures, to this reality, whose symbol, once more, is in this first encounter of a European Christianity with the pre-Columbian American religions. Indeed, on other occasions, and by other routes, I have taken the opportunity to show that the series of problems we have just seen is so profound, and so far from being solved, that it has led to a certain division in liberation theology itself. Liberation theology, to my way of seeing, has been successively attracted, first, by the opportunities represented by a middle class descended from culturally European groups that have maintained their culture and their Christianity as it was in sixteenth-century Spain, and then by the liberative values manifested by an oppressed people in a religious syncretism whose Christian element is far from having been a mere disguise for idolatry or superstition.

But let me not tarry here. Once more, and again at the risk of misunderstanding, and the false accusation of elitism, I should like to propose, as a hypothesis, a view of what, in one way or another, has fettered "Christian" creativity in Latin America, and prevented, or considerably retarded, a reevangelization of this continent.

To this purpose, the reader will permit me another visit to my earlier theological excursus. That detour may have seemed a long one, but, actually, I broke it off halfway!

I shall attempt to show, then, by way of a theological argumentation, that both councils, Vatican I and Vatican II, when we examine their acts, and even their language *in speaking of the extent of papal infallibility*, hold the conviction that, in the common faith of Christians, many things are intermingled, having important qualitative differences vis-à-vis that which is fundamental—the deposit of Christian revelation and its necessary suppositions. And this is all the more significant in view of the fact that Vatican II states it explicitly, apropos of the dialogue that the Catholic Church ought to maintain with the churches that appeal to the same deposit of Christian revelation.

Karl Rahner, especially, has strongly emphasized that many merely human traditions have been mixed in, over the course of the centuries, with the one *divino-apostolic* tradition; and that the church, having no clear criterion of discernment, has allowed them to be included in the "obligatory" content of the Christian faith, teaching them in authoritarian, unanimous fashion through its ordinary magisterium.[12]

And thus, when Rahner urges a return to what the Catholic Church universally believed after the close of the first ecumenical councils, I believe that what he has in mind is a church that would be better off for purposes of dialogue after it had reduced its paraphernalia of "obligatory truths."

In our case we might say that we Christians today would have a better celebration of Columbus's arrival in America if that gentleman had brought with him a *more abbreviated list* of Christian truths—a list reduced to the essentials.

The reader will recall that this was the first of Seumois's requirements for an "evangelization." *But only the first*. If I may permit myself a slight criticism of a theologian of Rahner's stature, I think that he is still keeping within the limits of an academic theology that would like to simplify or reduce its content. That content, of course, must *inform* the Christian faithful. Seumois, perhaps because of his more *practical* interest in the missionary task, posited, in his two remaining requirements, the need for a *response* of a group or a people thought to be candidates for acceptance of the gospel—a response that divine revelation of itself can arouse only when it finds an echo and verification in human experience.[13]

Further: the reader will recall Harry McSorley's criticism of Hans Küng. McSorley appealed to Bishop Gasser's presentation of the dogma of papal infallibility at Vatican I, and to the *tantum quantum* by which that dogma is explicitly limited at Vatican II, in order to demonstrate the acknowledgment, on the part of these councils, of an order or hierarchy among the various "truths" in which the Christian faithful believe.

I have been saving up an argument developed by the theology of liberation—although not exclusively by that theology—in view of the particular circumstances in which it experiences the gospel. I refer to the fact that both Vatican I and Vatican II indicate a crucial element in the papal infallibility: that the latter is *not something additional* (as if it were a question of a particular infallibility) to the infallibility bestowed by the Lord on the entire church. I think that this is very revealing, and deserves further development. Vatican I says:

> The Roman Pontiff ... by the divine assistance promised to him in the person of blessed Peter, *enjoys that infallibility with which the divine Redeemer willed that his Church be provided* in the definition of teaching on faith and mores. [Denzinger 1830]

Vatican II, in its very syntax, provides us with an even better demonstration that the infallibility of the entire church and that of the supreme pontiff *non faciunt numerum*, as the scholastics used to say—"cannot be added up," are not distinct things:

> This infallibility that the divine Redeemer *wished his Church to have* when it defines the teaching of faith or morals *extends just so far as is embraced by the deposit of divine Revelation entrusted for safekeeping and exposition. This infallibility belongs to the Roman Pontiff*. [*Lumen Gentium*, no. 25]

There can be no doubt that, from the *formal* point of view, both formulas mean to say, and do say, the same thing. Not for nothing does the text of Vatican II, throughout this entire section, make four consecutive references to Bishop Gasser's explanation of infallibility before the vote taken in Vatican I. And well does J.-M. René Tillard write, carefully weighing his words:

> Like *Pastor Aeternus* [Vatican I], Vatican II relies in the last instance not only on the personal judgment of the Roman Pontiff, but on the active presence of the Spirit in the church. Here the *sensus fidelium* comes into play, as a *conspiratio* of faithful and bishops. This will have to be taken seriously, without interference from the old ultramontane mindset.[14]

I think, however, that "taking this seriously" means, to begin with, attending to two seemingly small differences in the texts of the two councils. Vatican I initiates its pronouncement with the papal infallibility. Vatican II begins with the infallibility granted to the church. Hence the former is led to conclude the dogmatic definition with these words: "Therefore the definitions of the Roman Pontiff are irreformable in themselves and not by the consent of the church" (Denzinger 1839). Vatican II, which has begun with the infallibility granted to the church as a whole, incorporates (citing Bishop Gasser), by way of conclusion, something very important:

> These definitions [of the Roman pontiff] can never fail of the assent of the church, *by virtue of the activity of the Holy Spirit, by whom the entire flock of Christ is preserved and makes progress in oneness of faith.* [*Lumen Gentium*, no. 25]

We may conclude that if, as Vatican I stipulates, the infallible definitions of the supreme pontiff need not evoke or invoke the consent of the church, this was not because they could be separated from that consent, but on the contrary, because the Holy Spirit, working to preserve and increase one and the same faith throughout the church, has made the supreme pontiff the interpreter (in extraordinary or critical circumstances[15]) of one, common faith.

It likewise follows that, in God's plans, an infallibility possessed by one person or group of persons would be completely pointless if, for lack of relevancy, or by reason of defects in the preparation and creativity of the church, it failed to correspond to the experience of the Christian life throughout the church community. The development of this experience, and its intimate and creative communication with what is basic in the gospel—the two remaining points in Seumois's explanation of what it is to "evangelize"—is a constitutive condition of the "infallibility" granted by God to the church in order to maintain and preserve intact the deposit of divine revelation. Hence we have both the need to make the essential of this deposit a piece of "good news," and the urgency of further developing it only at a rate that will permit the essential to remain the essential, and not be replaced by the more peripheral or less relevant.

I have said that sensitivity to this need was perceived or experienced more in Latin America—precisely by reason of the absence of its fulfillment. This is not the case, however, in the area of theology. From Europe—although from a Europe very sensitive to the inquietudes of Latin American theology—comes the wonderful book about "divine revelation" and its relationship with human realization written by A. Torres Queiruga.[16] In it, by way of logical continuation of a journey merely begun by the church with Vatican II, we read of the need of historical experience in order for the process of enlightenment and realization of the human being, initiated by God in the past, and culminating in Jesus Christ, may continue its route toward "all truth" (John 16:7,12–13), guided by the same Spirit of Jesus.

After all—still on the level of sweeping comparisons that may be useful, but that also may admit of many exceptions—we might say that the upshot of this encounter of peoples occasioned by the Columbus event is characterized by its theological paralysis at the level of the faithful, both those whose model of Christianity follows that imported from Spain, and the others, the people who are the most oppressed, and who preserve with might and main the remnant of their religion and worldview, concealing it from the heteronomous power of the invader and from an obligatory Christianity.

Here as well, only certain symbols can be sufficiently eloquent to nourish our reflection. The fact that, at least before the appearance of liberation theology on the scene, the Christianity of the relatively Europeanized middle classes of Latin America gave no signs of living, experientially, the crises that attack, but also enrich, European Christianity, evinces a kind of dull, tedious orthodoxy, in the sense of an orthodoxy that is not experienced in its crises and its reactions. This poverty of a Christianity just-barely-adopted may be symbolized in the fact that, five centuries after this "encounter," Latin America, the most "Christian" continent in the world (and the only one), nevertheless requires a continuous, tragic "blood" transfusion—priests, pastoral ministers, and enormous economic assistance—from a continent incomparably "less Christian," at least in appearances: Europe. How could people have read the same gospel without making the commitment to continental reality that it inculcates?

But perhaps another symbol can show how a Christianity that in any way shuns experience can be unanimously Christian and not reflect on what its faith represents. I find this symbol in the special issue of *Servir*, from which I have extracted a citation concerning how the peoples of oppressed culture on the continent have kept their beliefs intact under Christian labels. In a most interesting and provocative article, A. Zenteno presents various testimonials on the part of selected members of base church communities in Mexico who had been invited to reflect on the *Nican Mopohua*, or account of the apparitions of Our Lady of Guadalupe, for centuries the patron of the Mexican people.

Obviously, the article has two premises (explicit, by the way). First, liberation theology, and its hermeneutic key — the "option for the poor" is present, and everything turns upon it. Second, the account of the apparitions is utilized as an element of "evangelization" in the sense that I have explained the word here.

To synthesize these testimonials, which the reader may savor much better in the actual language in which they were expressed: these members of the oppressed people understand that the Blessed Mother's choice of Juan Diego to carry her message to none other than his excellency, the bishop himself (a Spaniard), constitutes a testimonial that our Lady is making the same option for the poor. One testimonial has it that the message requires his excellency to "build a temple to her, that her children [the poor] may be there with her, and [thus] find relief from their pains and sorrows." And it continues: "The most interesting thing is that our Lady appeared to a lowly one, and asked him to go tell the bishop [what to do] when it would have been so much easier just to appear to the bishop [so that] he would believe; but she *chose someone poor*, someone lowly, one of the 'least ones.' "[17]

There is a beginning here. And this beginning recalls another evangelization: the one that was to guide Israel all through its history, to the threshold of the definitive good news of the reign of God declared to be at hand in Jesus' preaching. But this similarity with the exodus (a similarity so exploited for purposes of a liberative praxis) does not stand up to a serious comparison. I do not enter, of course, into a discussion of the historicity of the account of the apparitions of the Virgin Mary to Juan Diego. But there are important elements of symbolism and reflection here for the viewpoint that concerns us.

The first, it seems to me, is that the figure who makes the option for the poor (the Indians) is not God, but the Virgin of Tepeyac. I prescind from the datum that the Virgin explicitly indicates her desire to be surnamed "of Guadalupe" — an adaptation to a Spanish religious nomenclature that, to my modest view of the matter, suggests a hurried integration of any protest content that might have attached to the other Marian appellation. Instead, let me focus on the fact that the option made for the Indian poor has its subject in a prototypically maternal figure. I do not adduce this fact, which is emphasized in the testimonials of the Christians of the base communities, in order to belittle the feminine element as such. If in the image itself there is a feminine element that indicates this "option," it is not destined to change the structures of society. It may be due simply to a tacit machismo on the part of those who composed the account. What is important is that the Virgin of Guadalupe, unlike the God of the exodus, does not sound the call for a historical deed. From the viewpoint concerning us so far, there is no doubt in my mind of the weakness implicit in an evangelization based on the periphery of Christian dogma. When it comes to be observed, as it will be, that this option does not structurally modify the situation of the poor, this observation does not seem to affect the idea held of God, of the projects of God, and of the priorities of God. The experience of the divine remains untouched.

Second, the commission is indeed entrusted to someone poor, to an Indian. But with what is it concerned? With the construction of a sanctuary. Here again, the secularized Western mentality, or even the secularization that is to some extent intrinsic to Jewish and Christian religion, can play us a cruel turn here. It can make us forget that, for so many religious peoples, a sanctuary is a kind of navel of the world, the place where one enters into communication with the divinity. But, once more, the future of evangelization is at stake here. In this sanctuary, one supposes, Mary will hear the laments and see the afflictions of her children—which means, first, that she does not call them to be the agents of any historical task. It also means that prayer, with the corresponding times of pilgrimage, is to be a compartmentalized area of social and individual life. Anything else, including the burden of a situation of oppression and marginality, remains untouched. And finally, the sanctuary is not to be a native sanctuary: it is to be constructed by a church of Spanish roots and power. It is not strange that one of the reflections perceives something of this: "And *now*, well, I don't know. At best, if [the Blessed Virgin] appeared to somebody, I think the first thing she'd say [is that] for now *there are already a lot of churches.* I think the first thing she'd say is how we have used the churches."

Third, in a beautiful sentence midway through the introduction of the Medellín documents, we read: "Thus, as in times past Israel, the first people, *experienced* [emphasis added] the salvific presence of God, who delivered them from the oppression of Egypt . . . and led them to the land of promise, so we, too, new people of God that we are, *cannot but feel* God's saving passage, whenever there is true development—which is the passage, for each and all, from less humane conditions of life to more humane conditions." But if that first people could not endure the forty years that separated promise from fulfillment without murmuring and turning against the divine representative, what will a people think for whom the Virgin Mary is supposed to have made an option and promised relief from their miseries, and then who have been waiting five centuries? And still nothing is happening. Experience does not count.

To be sure, there are criticisms, like those we have read, and others even stronger, even leveled by Christians of the people in their reflections and testimonials. But these criticisms only indicate the abuse. They indicate no critical experience of dogma itself. Reflection on dogma seems beyond their reach. And the road that begins with these hesitant criticisms is so full of pitfalls and dangers for the future that any hope that they might be extended to a point just short of the foundations of the Christian faith seems a vain one. Indeed, to the extent that these criticisms became sharper, they would most probably be rejected by the people themselves, not to mention the hierarchy.

In conclusion: I am led by all these examples to pose a problem whose original symbolization, it seems to me, is represented in an encounter of two worlds five centuries ago. I have limited myself to posing it in a form that, to my understanding, reaches more deeply, and could thereby suggest that the solution is still very far off, or more difficult than commonly believed. I do not possess, needless to say, the key to any solution—or at least any practical short-term solution. I do believe, however, that the road to a reevangelization of the Latin American continent must pass by way of the conditions here indicated.

Moreover, I believe that Latin America has already discovered this road. The theology of liberation, through trial and error, and no doubt with a great deal of improvisation, is shaking off the lethargy and paralysis that have afflicted the church in two areas that, I believe, are decisive. First, it has gained the conversion of an option for the poor among important sectors of a middle class that until now has limited itself to importing theology and spirituality from Europe. Next, we are beginning to see reflection, and critical reflection, on the part of the people themselves. If this route, with all its dangers and crises, continues, it may be that what has appeared to be a frustrating encounter (for Christianity) between two opposed worlds will be transformed into a new, more authentic, more profound way of living the essential of the Christian good news.

Notes

1. THEOLOGY AND THE SOCIAL SCIENCES

1. Buenos Aires, 1969.
2. Passages cited are from Verón, *Lenguaje y comunicación social.*

2. CAPITALISM-SOCIALISM

1. See Gustavo Gutiérrez, *A Theology of Liberation* (Maryknoll, N.Y.: Orbis Books, 1973), passim. This book, and that of Hugo Assmann, *Opresión-Liberación. Desafío a los cristianos* (Montevideo, 1971), are as far as I know the only two books of the theology of liberation that raise the debate to the level of a well-documented scientific dialogue with European theology.
2. See Juan L. Segundo, *De la sociedad a la teología* (Buenos Aires, 1970), III, pp. 127ff.
3. Thorsten Veblen, *Theory of the Leisure Class* (New York, 1899).
4. See Juan L. Segundo, *Pastoral latinoamericana. Sus motivos ocultos* (Buenos Aires, 1972), chap. 5.
5. J. B. Metz, *L'homme, anthropocentrique chrétienne* (Paris, 1971), p. 111.
6. Ibid., p. 136.
7. J. Moltmann, "Dieu dans la révolution," in *Discussion sur la théologie de la révolution* (Paris, 1972), p. 72.
8. See Gustavo Gutiérrez, *Theology of Liberation,* pp. 212ff. See also Hugo Assmann, *Opresión-Liberación,* pp. 154ff., and Conrado Eggers Lan, *Christianismo y nueva ideología* (Buenos Aires, 1968), pp. 46ff.
9. R. Weth, "La théologie de la révolution dans la perspective de la justification et du royaume" in *Discussion sur la théologie de la révolution,* p. 86.
10. M. Luther, *OEuvres* (Geneva, 1985), V. p. 120 (Quoted by Weth, "La théologie de la révolution").
11. H. de Lavalette, "Ambiguïtés de la théologie politique," *Recherches de Sciences Religieuses,* Oct.-Dec. 1071 (vol. 59, no. 4): 559.
12. See Gustavo Gutiérrez, *Theology of Liberation,* chap. 1.
13. Assmann, *Opresión-Liberación,* pp. 86ff.
14. See Gerhard Von Rad, *Old Testament Theology,* II (New York, 1965), passim.
15. Henri Cazelles, "Bible et politique," *Recherches de Sciences Religieuses,* Oct.-Dec. 1971, p. 512.
16. Martin Lotz, "le concept de révolution dans la discussion oecuménique" in *Discussion sur la théologie de libération,* p. 32. In the same sense, and although the word "left" is absent, the following remarks are relevant: "A solidarity of faith united Christians with the stranger who is always unknown ... Christians have

always had a privileged place for the prisoner, the refugee, the poor, and the foreigner"; see M. le Certeau, *L'Etranger ou l'union dans la différence* (Paris, 1969), pp. 12–13. It is plain enough who (between left and right) shows continuing signs of this feeling of solidarity.

5. THE SHIFT WITHIN LATIN AMERICAN THEOLOGY

1. Leonardo Boff, "Teologia à Escuta do Povo," *Revista Eclesiástica Brasileira* 41 (March 1981): 65.

2. Gustavo Gutiérrez, *A Theology of Liberation* (Maryknoll, N.Y.: Orbis Books, 1973). Original Spanish version: *Teología de la liberación: Perspectivas* (Lima: CEP, 1971).

3. See the first lectures given from the perspective of liberation theology, which were presented at a theological conference in Santiago, Chile, in 1967: *Salvación y construcción del mundo,* G. Gutiérrez, J. L. Segundo, J. Croatto, B. Catão, J. Comblin (Barcelona: Dilapsa—Nova Terra, 1968).

4. See Leonardo Boff, *Eclesiogénese* (Petrópolis: Vozes, 1977). English translation: *Ecclesiogenesis* (Maryknoll, N.Y.: Orbis Books, 1986).

5. Maryknoll, N.Y.: Orbis Books, 1983. Original version: *La fuerza histórica de los pobres: Selección de trabajos* (Lima: CEP, 1979).

6. Boff, *Eclesiogénese,* p. 55.

7. Maryknoll, N.Y.: Orbis Books, 1987. Original version: *Paixâo de Cristo— Paixâo do Mundo* (Petrópolis: Vozes, 1977).

8. Jon Sobrino, *Resurrección de la verdadera Iglesia: Los pobres, Lugar teológico de la eclesiología* (Santander: Sal Terrae, 1981), chapter 1, "El conocimiento teológico en la teología europea y latinoamericana," pp. 21–53. English translation: *The True Church and the Poor* (Maryknoll, N.Y.: Orbis Books, 1984), pp. 7-38.

9. Ibid., p. 34 (Spanish).

10. Ibid., p. 163 (Spanish).

11. See in the collection edited by the Instituto Fe y Secularidad entitled *Fe Cristiana y Cambio Social en América Latina* (Salamanca: Sígueme, 1973), E. Dussel, "Historia de la fe cristiana y cambio social en América Latina," especially pp. 91 and 97, as well as the explicit reference to Levinas, p. 69, note. See also citations of Levinas in the collection edited by R. Gibellini, *La Nueva Frontera de la Teología en América Latina* (Salamanca: Sígueme, 1977) by Dussel and Scannone: E. Dussel, "Supuestos histórico-filosóficos de la teología desde América Latina," p. 183, and J. C. Scannone, "Teología, cultura popular y discernimiento," p. 215. English translation: *Frontiers of Theology in Latin America* (Maryknoll, N.Y.: Orbis Books, 1979).

6. A NOTE ON IRONY AND SORROW

1. See Hugo Assmann, "Os ardís do amor em busca de sua eficácia: As reflexões de Juan Luis Segundo sobre 'O Homem de Hoje Diante de Jesus de Nazaré,'" *Perspectivas Teológicas* 15 (1983): 223–59, a review of Juan Luis Segundo, *El Hombre de Hoy ante Jesús de Nazaret*, 2 vols. in 3 (Madrid: Cristiandad, 1982).

2. The task indicated by Hugo, that of creating gospels "from bottom to top," in connection with the new types of organization and popular expression, always in particular contexts, obviously cannot be expected to be performed by a general work. On the other hand, the work under review altogether clearly emphasizes its

necessity. It is likewise obvious that not all discourse upon Christ can guarantee its fidelity to the Christian message simply and solely on the basis of proceeding from below. The reader may consult the new edition of our *Teología Abierta*, from Ediciones Cristiandad in Madrid, especially the third volume, *Reflexiones críticas*.

3. The Brazilian translation is being prepared by our former editor, Benno Brod, S. J. for Edições Paulinas.

4. Here the Spanish editor, thinking to correct one error, in the Spanish, has me fall into another, theological one. Surely it would be foolish to pretend that the expression "place oneself at the *service* of the poor" is simply rhetoric. What the original indicated as rhetoric was the expression, "place oneself in" (or accept) "the *discipleship* of the poor," used frequently by Enrique Dussel among others.

5. *Revista Eclesiástica Brasileira*, vol. 41, no. 161 (March 1981): 55.

6. I do not think that I explicitly criticize any other Latin American theologian, at least not among the better known. I recognize, of course, that any theologian feeling under attack by any of the arguments I use in support of my ideas will, altogether justifiably, see that argument as a criticism. Furthermore, it is very likely that Hugo can put names with opinions criticized in a general way in my work. But I do not think it would be fair to draw the conclusion that I am biting or ironical vis-à-vis John Doe or Richard Roe.

7. Barcelona: Dilapsa—Nova Terra, 1968. If I make no reference to the other addressees, it is not because these (with the possible exception of José Comblin's) take another tack, but because I am mainly interested in the case of Gustavo and his direction, which was such a decisive one for the theology of liberation.

8. See what Leonardo Boff emphasizes, fifteen years later, out of the same considerations of popular liberation, apropos of the concept of "redemption" in his article, "Teologia à escuta do povo" (as cited in n. 5, above).

9. Gustavo Gutiérrez, "Libertad religiosa y diálogo salvador," in *Salvación y Construcción del Mundo*, by various authors (Barcelona: Dilapsa—Nova Terra, 1968), p. 42.

10. Here the reader may profitably consult a very intelligent and beautiful book that couples literary criticism with liberation theology: Pedro Trigo, *Arguedas: mito, historia y religión* (Lima: CEP, 1982; with an afterword or conclusion by Gustavo Gutiérrez, "Entre las calandrias"). It is interesting to follow Trigo's systematic, critical analysis of the role played by ("mestizo," that is, containing imported Christian components, but with these components deeply inserted into other, native and pre-Columbian elements) religion in the heroes of Arguedas's novels. One of the critic's main concerns is to decide in each case whether this role is that of preserving a past or of humanizing the future, and he ultimately decides in favor of the latter hypothesis (see pp. 61, 74, 100, and passim). To be sure, it is a literary work that is being analyzed here, not reality directly, but it is clear that the author thinks that Arguedas's work reflects the profound reality of Peru.

7. ON ABSOLUTE MYSTERY

1. On Juan Luis Segundo, "Cristología," *Christus*, no. 577 (1984), pp. 57–61.

2. Madrid: Cristiandad, 1982. The criticism, discreetly framed as a question, probably refers to volume 2/2, entitled *Las cristologías en la espiritualidad*. More specifically, I daresay, the reference would be to part 3, chap. 1: "Jesus and God: Approach to the Council of Chalcedon." At all events, that chapter, upon which I

am commenting here, and to a certain extent reformulating, will surely be crucial for any attempt to respond to the criticism in question.

3. What follows in this section owes a great debt to Nikolai Berdyaev's profound observation that the key terms or concepts of philosophy were actually developed in the great theological controversies—for example, the concept of person, which owes its presence in philosophy and its central status in it today to the problematic of the Christian Trinity and christology. Let me indicate from the outset that a consequence of this impinges fully on the problematic posed by Jiménez Limón. The "mystery" of God is not found, at least not at its root, in the infinitude of the divine being. In essence, the mystery of God is the mystery of total freedom: only the self-revelation of this freedom as history, that beginning of love that consists in giving oneself "to be known," opens the authentic route to the personal. Every person, even the human person, contains that "mystery," that "I am what I am." The infinitude of the divine nature imposes insurmountable limits on our curiosity, but does not prevent the self-bestowal (even cognitive, always loving) of God. See Juan Luis Segundo, *Berdiaeff: Une réflexion chrétienne sur la personne* (Paris: Aubier, 1963), esp. part 1, chap. 3; part 2, chap. 4.

4. It is important to point out, in this text, that the criterion of God's "nearness," valid for the Jews as for other peoples, implies not that God's self-revelation is intellectually more "clear," but that, on the basis of this revelation, there is a growth in human wisdom, intelligence, and justice on the part of this particular people. Not having known Yahweh before, this people would have no basis on which to judge a divine self-revelation to be intellectually more "clear."

5. Here, to my view, is to be found one of the central points of the theology of liberation. And consequently, one of the points that, it seems to me, is most dubious in the theology employed by the Instruction of the Commission for the Doctrine of the Faith on "certain aspects" of liberation theology is its refusal to assert that "God becomes history" (*Instruction on Certain Aspects of the Theology of Liberation* [Rome, 1984], no. 9, par. 3). Will it then be incorrect to say that the Word became flesh? Does not "flesh," in biblical language, mean creaturely, contingent, historical existence, a nomad's "tent" that the Word, according to the Prologue of John, pitches among ours? Where is respect for Ephesus and Chalcedon here?

6. Henri de Lubac, *Por los caminos de Dios* (Buenos Aires: Carlos Lohlé, 1962), pp. 127, 133.

9. REVELATION, FAITH, SIGNS OF THE TIMES

1. I have been asked to write this article for inclusion in a collective work, *Mysterium Liberationis: Fundamental Concepts of Liberation Theology* (ed. Jon Sobrino, Ignacio Ellacuría, forthcoming from Orbis Books). It also appears, in more developed form, in my book *El Dogma que libera*. English translation: *The Liberation of Dogma* (Maryknoll, N.Y.: Orbis Books, 1992).

2. Congregation for the Doctrine of the Faith, "Instruction on Certain Aspects of the Theology of Liberation" (Vatican City, August 1984) part 2, no. 4.

3. Gregory Bateson, *Pasos hacia una ecología de la mente* (Buenos Aires: Carlos Lohlé, 1972) pp. 487ff.

4. It cannot be said that this first condition for a "revelation"—a communication between God and the human being—has been generally understood. Accepted, yes. But a current originating outside Christianity and biblical thought (and introduced

into them with Neoplatonism) has, throughout the centuries, placed its deepest hopes of approaching God in a certain "emptying" of the mind—as if it were by way of a denial or suspension of the limits of the linguistic, conceptual, and historical signs that one could arrive at a deeper, surer understanding of these signs. The mystics themselves, perhaps under the influence of this philosophy, in transmitting their experiences conceptually, have spoken of experiences of God bearing almost no resemblance to those of the Bible: alienation from or contempt of the created.

5. Augustine of Hippo, *In Ioannis Evangelium Tractatus*, XIX, 14.

6. Correct praxis is the final *truth*. Hence, for the Johannine theology, truth is not "had," but "done" (see John 3:21, 1 John 1:6). Truth is not something that can be "put down" in a book or a formula, or in the perfection of some knowledge. Truth is *done*—put into operation.

7. Readers wishing to see an example of this, propounded by the magisterium of the church itself, although the term "anthropological faith" does not occur, can find the equivalent of that term in the explanation proposed by *Gaudium et Spes* of the process leading the person of good will to atheism. Others, on the contrary, despite their repetition of the words of "divine revelation," may practice (and lead others to practice) a "faith" that is actually idolatry, since the values with which they confuse the "word of God" do not correspond to the true God: "Atheism results not rarely from . . . the absolute character with which certain human values are unduly invested, and which thereby already accords them the stature of God . . . Believers can have more than a little to do with the birth of atheism . . . To the extent that they . . . are deficient in their religious, moral, or social life, they must be said to conceal rather than reveal the authentic face of God" (*Gaudium et Spes*, no. 19).

8. "Behold, I stand at the gate and knock" (Rev. 3:20). Of course, this does not mean that God recognizes any obligation to "say" precisely what we are ready to hear. Along with confirming our most authentic expectations, the "word of God" also "judges" us. As we shall presently see more clearly, there is a circularity in this hermeneutic process. Hence the "word" invites us to "conversion," or to the "betterment" of something existing. But even in this case, in order to be understood in its human element, the word of God must be addressed at least to a kind of search or aspiration that we may have relegated to a second level, to a hypothesis that would be valid if reality were better, to something that "could be," and that therefore we favor even though it would mean the overturning and upsetting precisely of values (or antivalues) that we are applying.

9. *PL* 34:33. Cited by Henri de Lubac, *Catolicismo* (Barcelona: Estela, 1963), p. 52.

10. Indeed, in the first centuries, the writings of the fathers and dogmatic declarations of the first ecumenical councils were assimilated to the inspired "word of God," worthy of belief to the "last jot and tittle," even though they were not "deposited" in the Bible (see Denzinger 164–65, 270). The fact that Jesus does does not detain us, but *moves on*, as Augustine wrote, is the ultimate foundation of the great theological principle adopted by Vatican II in the matter of ecumenism, but which goes much farther still: from the Bible on down, there is "an order or 'hierarchy' in the truths of Catholic teaching, in view of the diversity of connections between such truths and the foundation of Christian faith" (*Unitatis Redintegratio*, no. 11). This is tantamount to saying that the final truth is the aim of a pedagogy, not a piece of information.

11. What Von Rad wrote of the "wisdom" whose most specific quest character-izes especially the last period of the Old Testament, is true here of the *entire* biblical process and "tradition": "One might almost say that knowledge of the good is acquired only in the common life, person to person and from situation to situation; however, an absolute beginning is not made each time, because there is always the base of an ancient knowledge, of a very rich experience" (Von Rad, *Israel et la Sagesse* [Geneva: Labor et Fides, 1970], p. 98). And he explains how this "base" of collective wisdom is laid: "No one would live a single day had he or she not suc-ceeded in being guided by a vast empirical cognition. This knowledge, drawn from experience, teaches one to understand what is occurring round about one, to foresee the reactions of one's neighbor, to employ one's strength at the opportune moment, to distinguish the exceptional from the ordinary event, and a great deal else. We are not particularly conscious of being guided in this way, as neither of having ourselves developed more than a small part of this experiential knowledge. This knowledge is imposed on us, we are steeped in it from our most tender age, and [we are aware of it] only if we ourselves somehow modify it . . . This experimental knowledge acquires its importance and character of obligation only when it comes to represent the common good of an entire people, or a great part of the popula-tion" (ibid., pp. 9–10).

12. This is what was called, and should continue to be called today, "tradition"—not the dubious and unverifiable notion that Jesus personally "revealed" to one or more of his apostles or disciples things that were not consigned to the New Tes-tament, and thus remained lost until they reappeared years or centuries later. This is how the existence of a font of revelation "other" than the biblical is understood. While Vatican II did not wish to settle the question of the single or double font, everything in *Dei Verbum*, as well as the best post–Vatican II theology, tends to understand by "tradition" not a separate, "other," font, but the fact that the process of transmission consists not in a book or a formula, but in a knowledge transmitted in the experience (institutional, to be sure) of a living community, the church.

13. While this faith is in continuity with what we have called "anthropological faith," it has special characteristics that make it "religious." Indeed, it is the adher-ence of a community that possesses a "truth" about God and about what this God means for all humanity.

14. The rigorously dogmatic problem posed by the formation of the canon (list) of the books containing "revelation"—the Bible—is conspicuously absent from works otherwise as perspicacious and profound as Karl Rahner's *Curso fundamental sobre la fe* (Barcelona: Herder, 1979). One of the most recent theological works to have attempted to remedy this lack, and to have gone most to the heart of the matter, is, to my knowledge, that of A. Torres Queiruga, *La revelación de Dios en la realización del hombre* (Madrid: Cristiandad, 1987). Note, in this work, the sim-ilarity between the application the author makes to the Bible of the Socratic "maieu-tic," and what we have here called "second-degree apprenticeship," or "learning to learn." Both methods presuppose that truth, even the truth of the mysteries of God, is not received from "without," as if it were mere information.

15. Torres, *Revelación de Dios*, p. 63. I do not want to make this author respon-sible for the conclusions and extensions that I add to the passage cited. I do permit myself, in the spirit of friendship, to *use* this passage from his work for my intent. However, I understand that this excerpt has not been penned hastily, but is pre-sented by way of conclusion of a lengthy discourse. The author repeats this sum-

mary, in the same or similar terms, in other places in the same book (see ibid., pp. 122, 125–26).

16. What I say of Moses here is paradigmatic, as I have indicated. Did Jesus not find himself in a similar situation? It will be said that Jesus did have the Bible, and thus could base his claims on the "word of God"—and that he never hesitated to use it. But would this be strictly the case? Hans Küng is correct (although he draws a conclusion different from ours): "Jesus' whole preaching and behavior are nothing but an interpretation of *God* . . . Anyone accepting Jesus with firm trust necessarily observed at the same time an unexpected, liberative transformation of what he had thus far understood by 'God' " (Hans Küng, *Ser cristiano* [Madrid: Cristiandad, 1977], p. 402). Thus, Jesus could not rely on the Bible alone, without indicating an attitude that would cause a different hermeneutics of that Bible. Hence his allusions to the signs of the times, and to this antecedent, hazardous criterion: "Why do you not judge *for yourselves* what is just?" (Luke 12:57)—and this in the presence of God and of the "word" of God present in the Bible.

17. John L. McKenzie, "Synagogue," in *Dictionary of the Bible* (New York: Bruce-Macmillan, 1965), p. 855. I call the synagogue "doubly" lay in the sense that not only was it an institution where the people (*laos*) assembled to feel themselves to be and maintain themselves as a people, with their own identity (among those who surrounded, governed, and oppressed them), but it was directed by laity (nonordained persons, elders). And the ordained, priests or scribes, when they visited the synagogue, were not essentially distinguished from the others, although they were treated with special courtesy (cf. ibid.).

18. Cited by A. Liège, in *Initiation Théologique*, by various authors (Paris: Cerf, 1952), 3:518.

19. Congregation for the Doctrine of the Faith, *Instruction on Certain Aspects of the "Theology of Liberation,"* I, 1–2; II, 1–4.

10. IGNATIUS LOYOLA

1. Pierre Teilhard de Chardin, *The Divine Milieu: An Essay on the Interior Life* (New York: Harper & Brothers, 1960), p. 24.

2. Idem, "Christianity and Evolution," unpublished manuscript of 1945, cited by E. Rideau, *La pensée du Père Teilhard de Chardin* (Paris: Seuil, 1965), p. 378.

3. Karl Rahner's great article, "Sobre el concepto de concupiscencia," *Escritos de Teología,* vol. 1, will be found useful on this point.

4. See Hans Urs von Balthasar, *Esperer pour tous* (Paris: Desclée, 1987), pp. 40–41.

5. Juan Luis Segundo, *Le Christianisme de Paul: L'histoire retrouvée* (Paris: Cerf, 1988), "Conclusion," II: "Signification anthropologique de la Divinite de Jésus," A: "La transcendance a-historique," pp. 322–29.

6. On this point, and on its impact on the election, see Roger Haight, "Foundational Issues in Jesuit Spirituality," *Studies in the Spirituality of the Jesuits,* no. 19/4, pp. 32–35.

7. See a solid critical work, B. Sesboüé, *Jésus-Christ l'unique médiateur: Essai sur la rédemption et le salut* (Paris: Desclée, 1988).

8. Edward Schillebeeckx, *Jesús: La historia de un viviente* (Madrid: Christiandad, 1981). English: *Jesus: An Experiment in Christology* (New York: Crossroad, 1981).

9. Fourth edition (Madrid: BAC, 1982).

10. Pedro de Rivadeneira, *Vida del Bienaventurado Padre Ignacio de Loyola* (Madrid: Apostolado de la Prensa, 1920), part 5, chap. 2, pp. 492–93.

11. Ibid.

12. See Schillebeeckx, *Jesús,* p. 148.

13. See Juan Luis Segundo, *Christianisme de Paul: L'histoire retrouvée* (Paris: Cerf, 1988).

14. Juan L. Moyano Walker, "San Ignacio: espiritualidad y política," *Boletín del CIAS* (Buenos Aires, 1985), n. 344, pp. 286–302), presents a collection of Ignatian letters of particular interest for secular, and especially political, history. Most of my citations here are from that article. [Note that almost all of the letters mentioned may be found in English and in accordance with the *date of writing* in William J. Young, S.J., ed., *Letters of St. Ignatius of Loyola* (Chicago: Loyola University Press, 1959).]

11. THE LEGACY OF COLUMBUS

1. So writes well-known theologian Hans Urs von Balthasar, in his *Puntos centrales de la fe* (Madrid: BAC, 1985), chap. 3, "The Council of the Holy Spirit," p. 85. In less technical terms, as might be expected in an interview, Cardinal J. Ratzinger speaks similarly (in J. Ratzinger and V. Messori, *Informe sobre la fe* [Madrid: BAC, 1985], pp. 34–35): "As for content, we must recall that Vatican II is in strict continuity with *the two preceding councils* [Vatican I and Trent; emphasis added] . . . It is impossible for a Catholic to take positions *in favor of* Vatican II and *against* Trent or Vatican I. Anyone who accepts Vatican II, with the clear expression of its letter and the clear intentionality of its spirit, asserts at the same time the uninterrupted tradition of the church, *especially in the two preceding councils* . . . The aftermath of the council seems cruelly contrary to everyone's hopes, beginning with those of Pope John XXIII, and then of Paul VI. Christians are once more a minority, more than at any other time since early antiquity." In this hermeneutic key for an interpretation of Vatican II, it is not easy to see why *tradition*, taken in its classic, strict theological sense, should oblige one to interpret "the letter and spirit" of Vatican II in such "strict continuity" with "especially" the two preceding councils. Rather it would seem either that *all* previous councils ought to be taken into account, and even more so the deposit of divine revelation itself, or else it ought to be taken into account that the contexts (that help to understand the spirit of a council) to which the various councils refer are separated, especially between Trent and Vatican I, by centuries of substantial changes in the human problematic; which is even the case for the century that separates Vatican II and Vatican I.

2. Allocution pronounced by his Holiness, Pope Paul VI, December 7, 1965, in St. Peter's Basilica in the Vatican, at the public session of closure of Vatican Council II (no. 12). A short while later the pope formulates this question: "With all of this, and all that we might add with respect to the human value of the council, has the mind of the church-in-council perhaps deviated in the anthropocentric direction taken by modern culture?" And he gives the answer: "Deviated, no; turned, yes" (ibid., no. 14). A "turn" this radical cannot be ignored if we hope to understand the change in "spirit" at Vatican II even vis-à-vis Vatican I, let alone Trent.

3. See G. Zitola, *La Restauración del Papa Wojtyla* (Madrid: Cristiandad, 1985), pp. 243-46.

4. Harry J. McSorley, in *The Infallibility Debate*, ed. John J. Kirvan (New York: Paulist, 1971), p. 85.

5. Ibid., p. 36.

6. *Schema Constitutionis de Ecclesia* (Vatican City, 1964), p. 97, cited by McSorley, *Infallibility Debate*, p. 86. It is beyond the scope of this article to show that, in reducing the extent of papal infallibility to those matters alone that either directly touch the *revealed deposit* or are required for its faithful preservation, what the fathers of the Second Vatican Council understand by "revealed deposit" is sacred scripture. As we know, a number of theologians have indicated, with good grounds, that the Constitution *Dei Verbum* had no intent of solving the question of a single or double font of divine revelation. It would be possible, however, to argue that, at least on the level reached by this constitution, the council is clearly inclined to admit a single font—sacred scripture—while ascribing due importance to its interpretation—to "tradition"—in the church community. I think that it is to belittle the "doctrinal wealth" of the council—in Pope Paul VI's words—to seek to show its neutrality on this question. And a refusal to admit an oral "tradition" that would be independent of scripture obviously has a great deal to do with the limits of the essential of the "deposit of faith."

7. For my part, I think that, of the four Marian dogmas (Mary's virginity *ante et post partum*, her divine motherhood, the Immaculate Conception, and her Assumption into heaven after her death), only one—her virginity *ante partum*—has at least explicit or apparent biblical support, provided, however, that we prescind from the (theological and christological) literary genre of the so-called infancy gospels. True, Cardinal Ratzinger disagrees, declaring to Messori in the report cited above that "the four Marian dogmas have their indispensable basis in scripture" (Ratzinger and Messori, *Informe sobre la fe*, pp. 116). Karl Rahner thinks that, on the contrary, at least with regard to Mary's Assumption, "a truth less perceptible, immediately and directly, in scripture than this one can scarcely be imagined." Keeping account of all three of these elements—explicit biblical basis, direct pertinency (required by Bishop Gasser's official explanation at Vatican I), and the principle of the hierarchy of truths proclaimed by Vatican II—the two Marian "dogmas" declared as such by the supreme pontiffs (the Immaculate Conception and the Assumption) need not be regarded as such. The reason for this is not any flaw in the papal infallibility, but the nonpertinence, direct or indirect, of these "dogmas" to the foundation of faith. The case of the Immaculate Conception is clearer, as it was not pronounced *ex cathedra*, but relied on the same formula as other documents where papable infallibility is not at stake, as in the bull (commonly regarded as being in error) *Unam Sanctam*: "We declare, state, define, and pronounce as being utterly necessary for salvation . . . " Neither is papal infallibility at stake, however much the supreme pontiff, Pius XII, may have erroneously believed that he was engaging it (explicitly stating that it was an *ex cathedra* definition), in the definition of Mary's Assumption, by reason of its nonpertinency (although we do not deny its truth) to the deposit of revelation such that the latter would fall should someone not believe this pontifical declaration. See a fortiori the arguments of Karl Rahner on the virginity *in partu* (*Theological Investigations*, vol. 4).

8. There are problems here that theology has yet to investigate, in all seriousness, with an eye to safeguarding both the function of the magisterium and consistency in Christian reflection. In the article just cited, Karl Rahner shows that "it cannot be said that *only* [what has been taught over a long time, de facto universally, and without discussion in the church] belongs to [*divino-apostolic* tradition], nor that *everything* [emphasis added] that has been taught over a long time, de facto

universally, and without discussion in [all] tradition, and everything held to be true, thereby possesses the guarantee of *traditio divino-apostolica*" (ibid.). For instance, when the bishop of Rome, patriarch of the West, and the (Greek Orthodox) patriarch of the East—without the latter's renouncing his dogmatic position against the Western *Credo*, which asserts that the Holy Spirit proceeds from the Father "and the Son" (*Filioque*)—embrace, and mutually lift the excommunications under which their predecessors have mutually placed them, ordinary Catholics no longer know how they can be in communion with someone who does not profess an article of the creed that they profess. Can it be that one of the truths in the creed—like the *Filioque*, obviously—does not belong to the deposit of faith or to those things necessary for the safeguarding of that deposit? But then how did that doctrine get into the creed in the first place?

9. See A. Seumois, O.M.I, *Apostolat: Structure Théologique* (Rome: Pontificia Università de Propaganda Fidei, 1961), pp. 88–89.

10. Clodomiro L. Siller A., "El método de la evangelización en el *Nican Mopuhua*," *Servir* (Jalapa, Mexico—a theological and pastoral review), year 17 (1981), nos. 93–94, pp. 257–93.

11. See *Acta et Decreta Concilii Plenarii Americae Latinae in Urbe Celebrati* (Rome, 1900), 2 vols. As a symbol of the almost completely European mindset of this Latin American regional council, it will be worthwhile to indicate that, among the "impediments and dangers to faith" in an ill-evangelized continent on which the vast majority of the Christian continent was, especially at the turn of the century, illiterate, are listed "the principal errors of our times" (materialism, pantheism, rationalism, naturalism, liberalism, etc.), and secondly, "evil books and periodicals" (see ibid., pp. 53–68).

12. See n. 7, above.

13. The treatises on "revelation" published since Vatican II themselves show the rising importance attributed in the revelatory process to the receipt of revelation by an "active," experiential acceptance on the part of the faithful. G. Moran, in his *Theology of Revelation* (New York: Herder & Herder, 1966), pp. 136, 139, writes: "There is no such thing as a pure word of God contaminated in some measure by human distortion. No, human reception, understanding, and interpretation are intrinsic to revelation itself . . . Exactly as Christ's human experience was necessary for the development of revelation in his earthly life, so also the experience of all peoples and all times is necessary for complete, perfect revelation in the church." But we need only read today of the striking relevance of these elements of active community reflection in a book as beautiful as it is serene and rich—A. Torres Queiruga, *La revelación de Dios en la realización del hombre* (Madrid: Cristiandad, 1987)—in order to appreciate the whole, lengthy route traversed from Vatican II up to today by the most serious and promising theology in this area.

14. J.-M. René Tillard, *El Obispo de Roma: Estudio sobre el papado* (Santander, Spain: Sal Terrae, 1986), p. 83. This balanced work contains a brief reflection, like the more extensive one by McSorley cited above, on the explanations given by Bishop Gasser, just before the conciliar definition of papal infallibility, in order to prevent what Tillard rightly appraises as a serious error and serious danger: making of the supreme pontiff "something more than a pope."

15. See ibid., chap. 3.

16. See n. 13, above, and in Torres Queiruga, *Revelación de Dios*, chap. 4, pp. 117–60.

17. A. Zenteno, "Experiencias," *Servir*, year 17 (1981), nos. 93–94, pp. 297–324. The quotations and testimonials that follow are all from that interesting and suggestive article.

Index